THE PASSION PROJECTS

The Passion Projects

MODERNIST WOMEN, INTIMATE ARCHIVES, UNFINISHED LIVES

Melanie Micir

PRINCETON UNIVERSITY PRESS
PRINCETON & OXFORD

Copyright © 2019 by Princeton University Press

Princeton University Press is committed to the protection of copyright and the intellectual property our authors entrust to us. Copyright promotes the progress and integrity of knowledge. Thank you for supporting free speech and the global exchange of ideas by purchasing an authorized edition of this book. If you wish to reproduce or distribute any part of it in any form, please obtain permission.

Published by Princeton University Press
41 William Street, Princeton, New Jersey 08540
99 Banbury Road, Oxford OX2 6JX

press.princeton.edu

All Rights Reserved

Library of Congress Control Number 2019931723
First paperback printing, 2024
Paperback ISBN 978-0-691-25926-0
Cloth ISBN 978-0-691-19311-3

British Library Cataloging-in-Publication Data is available

Editorial: Anne Savarese and Jenny Tan
Production Editorial: Jill Harris
Jacket/Cover Design: Pamela Schnitter
Production: Merli Guerra
Publicity: Alyssa Sanford and Keira Andrews

Jacket/Cover images: (Silhouette) Lucie Delarue-Mardrus. (Inside silhouette) Sylvia Townsend Warner

This book has been composed in Miller

For Anna and Maeve Anna

I felt like I was managing a huge building site, from which I was going to excavate a miniature model of modernity, reduced to its simplest, most complex form: a woman telling her story through that of another woman.
—NATHALIE LÉGER, *SUITE FOR BARBARA LODEN*

CONTENTS

Illustrations · xi
Acknowledgments · xiii

INTRODUCTION Modernism's Unfinished Lives   1

*The Unfinished Business of 1928: Modernism,
Feminism, and the Biographical Act*   4

Intimacy and the Archive   9

Passionate Commitments   13

Between Women, Between Generations   15

CHAPTER 1 Intimate Archives: The Preservation
of Partnership   18

Intimacy Issues   21

*Claiming Radclyffe Hall: An Almost
Archival Story*   24

Sylvia Townsend Warner's "Two Tenses"   32

T. H. White and the Idea of Queer Futurity   36

*The Tin Box: Intimacy, Memory,
and the Archive*   41

Archival Scenes: Intimacy across Generations   47

CHAPTER 2 Abandoned Lives: Impossible Projects
and Archival Remains   50

*Djuna Barnes and the "Disquiet Spirit"
of the Baroness*   52

*"The Cult of the Past": On the Late Refusal
of Hope Mirrlees*   60

*"More than a Daughter to Her": Tracing
Reputation, Resisting Identity*   62

	Unfinished Acts: Facing the Problem of "What to Say & What to Leave Out"	65
	Historic Preservation and Biographical Extravagance: The Case of A Fly in Amber	73
CHAPTER 3	Modernists Explain Things to Me: Collecting as Queer Feminist Response	77
	Modernism's Midwife: Sylvia Beach's Unfinished Jobs	82
	The Queer Disinheritance of Alice B. Toklas	88
	Beyond Biography: Margaret Anderson's "Collection"	95
CHAPTER 4	The Sense of Unending: Revisiting Virginia Woolf's *Orlando: A Biography*	110
	Queer/Late/Modernist Biography	113
	Love Letters and Passion Projects	123
	Vita Sackville-West's Queer Inheritance	127
	Toward an Unfinished Modernism	128
CODA	Biographical Criticism and the Passion Project Now	131

Abbreviations · 141
Notes · 143
Bibliography · 173
Index · 187

ILLUSTRATIONS

1.1. Final entry in Una Troubridge's day book, 1943. The Radclyffe Hall and Una Troubridge Papers. Harry Ransom Humanities Research Center, University of Texas at Austin. 32

2.1. Djuna Barnes, "Preface," draft. The Elsa von Freytag-Loringhoven Papers. Special Collections, University of Maryland Libraries. 56

3.1. Manuscript page from Margaret Anderson's unpublished "Collection," featuring photographs of Margaret Anderson and Jane Heap. The Elizabeth Jenks Clark Collection of Margeret Anderson. Yale Collection of American Literature, Beinecke Rare Book and Manuscript Library, Yale University. 104

3.2. Manuscript page from Margaret Anderson's unpublished "Collection," featuring a single photograph of Jane Heap and annotations (typed and handwritten) by Margaret Anderson. The Elizabeth Jenks Clark Collection of Margeret Anderson. Yale Collection of American Literature, Beinecke Rare Book and Manuscript Library, Yale University. 105

3.3. Manuscript page from Margaret Anderson's unpublished "Collection," featuring a hand-corrected typescript. The Elizabeth Jenks Clark Collection of Margeret Anderson. Yale Collection of American Literature, Beinecke Rare Book and Manuscript Library, Yale University. 107

ACKNOWLEDGMENTS

IT IS BOTH AN IRONY and a relief to have finally finished a book about unfinishedness. I could not have done so without the unrelenting support of both individuals and communities. My late grandfather, Slavo Micir, who worked in a steel mill for forty-five years, always told my dad that he wished he could have been a college professor. I grew up knowing this, but the idea that his dream could be a real possibility for me didn't even cross my mind until I received the steadfast encouragement of my undergraduate teachers at Columbia University, especially Julie Crawford, Jenny Davidson, Jean Howard, Bruce Robbins, and Joey Slaughter. Special thanks to Julie, whose irreverent pedagogy and patient (like, *really* patient) mentorship continue to provide me with the best possible model of who I want to be when I grow up; thanks, too, to Ann Douglas and the late Edward Said, for admitting me into grad seminars before I was ready, and to Gayatri Chakravorty Spivak, from whom I have never stopped learning.

At the University of Pennsylvania, I won the mentorship lottery again. Jim English was an ideal director: not only has he read and responded to everything I have ever sent him with almost superhuman speed, but his pointed questions helped me reframe the project at several crucial junctures, and his wry humor kept me sane. Paul Saint-Amour's brilliance is matched only by his compassion, generosity, and kindness; I will never stop trying to live up to the example he sets both in and out of the classroom. Heather Love gave this project time and attention during years when both were in short supply; it was only after spending a few years on the tenure track myself that I realized exactly how generous she had been to me. She never questioned why I would want to write a book about women, and her unabashed conversations about class in academia gave me a much-needed model for how to navigate the mysterious rituals and assumptions of our strange professional world. I continue to benefit from Jed Esty's almost uncanny ability to see the best possible version of a project at all times; his genuine delight in other people's ideas is both inspiring and fortifying. No matter how many times I rewrite them, the sentences in this paragraph are simply not enough; they cannot convey the depth of gratitude I feel for the utterly professional ways in which these four individuals shaped not only my scholarship and teaching but my ongoing, unfinished attempt to be a better person in the world.

In its early stages, this project benefited from the ongoing support and critical input of the supremely kickass members of my Philly writing group: Julia Bloch, Megan Cook, Sarah Dowling, Emily Hyde, Greta LaFleur, Jess Rosenberg, Poulomi Saha, and Emma Stapely. Special thanks to Julia, Sarah, and Emily for continuing to read pieces of the project as it evolved over the years. I am grateful for the collegial discussants of both the Mods and Gen/Sex working groups at Penn, especially Kate Aid, Cal Biruk, Julia Bloch, Beth Blum, Todd Carmody, John Connor, Shonni Enelow, Jonathan Fedors, Andy Gaedtke, Isabel Geathers, Laura Heffernan, Benjy Kahan, Grace Lavery, Cliff Mak, Jane Malcolm, Dan Morse, Amy Paeth, Katie Price, Mearah Quinn-Brauner, Kelly Rich, Josh Shuster, Greg Steirer, Lance Wahlert, Bronwyn Wallace, and Jason Zuzga. In true "it takes a village" spirit, I thank Rita Barnard, Nancy Bentley, Charles Bernstein, Warren Breckman, David Eng, Al Filreis, Tsitsi Jaji, Amy Kaplan, Suvir Kaul, David Kazanjian, Ania Loomba, Vicki Mahaffey, Jo Park, Bob Perelman, Val Ross, Melissa Sanchez, Emily Steiner, and Chi-ming Yang for rigorous coursework and challenging conversations. And, finally, thanks to Dalglish Chew, Stuart Curran, and Phyllis Rackin for endowing the prizes and funds that made it possible for me to undertake the early archival research underpinning this book.

I am grateful to my Behrend colleagues—Hilary Baker, John Champagne, Sara Luttfring, Janet Neigh, Dan Schank, Mara Taylor, Craig Warren, and Sara Whitney—for their intellectual and social support during my snowy year in Erie. Janet, in particular, read and commented on several iterations of this project and others; both her criticism and her example have proven invaluable to me over the years.

My colleagues at Washington University in St. Louis have been both welcoming and inspiring; I am lucky to work in a place where I count so many colleagues as friends. I am particularly grateful to Miriam Bailin, Cynthia Barounis, Guinn Batten, Kurt Beals, Maggie Gram, Musa Gurnis, Caroline Kita, Bill Maxwell, Paige McGinley, Amber Musser, Anca Parvulescu, Jessica Rosenfeld, Trevor Sangrey, Vince Sherry, and Rebecca Wanzo for reading and commenting upon my work with attentive generosity. I am grateful for the ongoing support of the Center for the Humanities at Washington University, where I spent a semester in residence as a First Book fellow in 2015. The incomparable Jean Allman and Rebecca Wanzo hosted a manuscript workshop for this book, and I am extraordinarily grateful to them and to participants Ellen Crowell, Ann Cvetkovich, Victoria Rosner, and Vince Sherry for crucial conversations that refocused the final stage of revisions to this book. I want to express my delighted relief at having landed in the same city as the brilliant and hilarious Rachel Greenwald Smith. And, finally, I thank my students at Washington University, particularly those in my Feminist Modernist Studies and Queer Historical Fiction seminars, for their enthusiasm and engagement. Special thanks to Katie Collins and Grace Lillard, who each provided outstanding research support as I was preparing this manuscript for publication.

I have benefited enormously from the knowledge shared by librarians, archivists, staff, and fellow researchers at the following institutions: the Beinecke Rare Book & Manuscript Library, the Dorset County Museum, the William Ready Division of Archives and Research Collections at McMaster University Library, the Newnham College Archives at the University of Cambridge, the Harry Ransom Center for Research in the Humanities, the Princeton University Library's Department of Rare Books and Special Collections, and the University of Maryland Libraries. I am particularly grateful for the support of the Dorot Foundation Postdoctoral Research Fellowship in Jewish Studies, which funded my Harry Ransom Research Fellowship in the Humanities in 2015–16. For conversations, invitations, suggestions, and general encouragement over the many years I worked on this project, I thank Dave Alff, Nadine Attewell, Rachel Banner, Erin Carlston, Erica Delsandro, Madelyn Detloff, Beth Freeman, Anita Helle, Brenda Helt, Allan Hepburn, Scott Herring, Janice Ho, Anna Ioanes, Lise Jaillant, the late Georgia Johnston, Peter Kalliney, Janet Lyon, Michelle Massé, Wendy Moffat, Christen Mucher, Cynthia Port, Megan Quigley, Eric Rettberg, Rochelle Rives, Claire Seiler, Scott Selisker, Chris Taylor, Aarthi Vadde, Rebecca Walkowitz, Sarah Wasserman, and Ian Whittington.

Princeton University Press has been a dream to work with from start to finish. I thank Anne Savarese and Thalia Leaf for their expert guidance throughout this process. Thanks, too, to Jennifer Backer's attentive copyediting for repeatedly saving me from myself. Two anonymous reviewers for the press delivered astute commentary on the manuscript; their rigorous suggestions were instrumental during the revision process, and the remaining shortcomings of this book are entirely my own. Parts of chapters 1 and 4 have been previously published in different forms: "'Living in Two Tenses': The Intimate Archives of Sylvia Townsend Warner," *JML: The Journal of Modern Literature* 36, no. 1 (Fall 2012): 119–31; and "The Queer Timing of Orlando," in *Queer Woolf*, ed. Madelyn Detloff and Brenda Helt, special issue of *Virginia Woolf Miscellany* 82 (Fall 2012): 11–13. Thanks to Indiana University Press and Southern Connecticut State University for permission to include portions of these articles here.

Published and unpublished material by Margaret Anderson is used by permission of Mathilda M. Hills. Published and unpublished material by Djuna Barnes is used with permission from the Authors League Fund and St. Bride's Church, co-executors of the Estate of Djuna Barnes. Quotations from published and unpublished writings by Vera Brittain are included by permission of Mark Bostridge and T. J. Brittain-Catlin, Literary Executors for the Estate of Vera Brittain 1970. Published and unpublished material by Alice B. Toklas is used by permission of Edward M. Burns. Quotations from published and unpublished writings by Sylvia Townsend Warner are included by permission of the Estate of Sylvia Townsend Warner. Quotations from unpublished material by Hope Mirrlees are included by permission of Newnham College.

In closing, I want to thank my family—biological, legal, chosen—for their love, support, and good humor over the years. Mom and Dad; Lauren and Ian; the Campbells and the Other Micirs; Barry and Sandy and the Pittsburgh Maciaks; Joanie, McNulty, and the late great Kezzie; and, finally, my two great loves, Phil and Maeve. I would never have finished this without you.

THE PASSION PROJECTS

INTRODUCTION

Modernism's Unfinished Lives

IN THE FIFTH CHAPTER of *A Room of One's Own*, Virginia Woolf's narrator randomly chooses a book from the shelves, pulls it down, and begins to read: "*Life's Adventure*, or some such title, by Mary Carmichael."¹ Skimming, at first, she runs her eye up and down the page, trying to determine whether the author "has a pen in her hand or a pickaxe."² She continues to narrate the process of reading, until, deploying the Woolfian ellipses that litter earlier chapters, she suddenly pauses to address her audience directly:

> I turned the page and read . . . I am sorry to break off so abruptly. Are there no men present? Do you promise me that behind that red curtain over there the figure of Sir Chartres Biron is not concealed? We are all women, you assure me? Then I may tell you that the very next words I read were these—"Chloe liked Olivia . . ." Do not start. Do not blush. Let us admit in the privacy of our own society that these things sometimes happen. Sometimes women do like women.³

When I teach *A Room of One's Own*, I tend to read this last line to my class in a mocking whisper—a hand flung dramatically across my brow, eyes darting from side to side with exaggerated suspicion. The story of Chloe and Olivia is now canonical, a "founding revolutionary moment" in feminist modernist studies.⁴ And while I dutifully explain Woolf's reference to Sir Chartres Biron, the judge who had presided over the previous year's obscenity trial of Radclyffe Hall's *The Well of Loneliness*, and we discuss the significance of Chloe liking Olivia "perhaps for the first time in literature,"⁵ it is that final line—"Sometimes women do like women"—that sparks the shock of recognition in so many of my students. They are impressively adept in the application of the so-called Bechdel Test across genre, media, and historical period; they are all too aware of the cultural failures it demonstrates. And so, even when temporarily befuddled by Woolf's historical references, they immediately understand and sympathize with her desire for more complicated representations of relationships between women.

Yet the question of what Woolf means by "like" remains murky. Does Chloe like Olivia *like that*, they want to know? Or are Chloe and Olivia *just friends*? In other words, is this a story about lesbian or queer history, or is this a story about feminist history? Should they agree with Lillian Faderman, who argues that Woolf "meant to indicate an emotion far more intense than mere 'liking,'" or, especially given Chloe and Olivia's shared laboratory, should they be swayed by Nancy K. Miller's attention to the way in which this "liking between women" becomes positively and dynamically transformed "when combined with work"?[6] In their frustration with the ambiguity inherent in the spectrum of possible relationships that might be indicated by "like," my students unknowingly concur with Sharon Marcus's assertion that since poor Chloe and Olivia are "overworked," we now "need more than two proper names and a verb to do justice to the variety and complexity of women's social alliances."[7] As a call to action, this is apt. But using Chloe and Olivia as shorthand, as we so often do, obscures the significance of the other name Woolf has already offered to us in the same passage: Mary Carmichael. The author.

For it is not enough for Chloe to like Olivia, no matter what we decide that may mean. Chloe and Olivia are fictional characters. Several pages after they were first introduced, Woolf again pulls away from the plot—away from the description of Chloe and Olivia's relationship—in order to draw our attention to the writer's role in her historic hypothetical. "For if Chloe likes Olivia *and Mary Carmichael knows how to express it*," she continues, "she will light a torch in that vast chamber . . . [of] half lights and profound shadows . . . where nobody has yet been."[8] To find more than two proper names and a verb, we also need to find our Mary Carmichaels—and her colleagues at work in genres other than the novel. Chloe and Olivia don't exist at all without the woman writer who will set down their stories. And Woolf's recognition and restoration of the missing Mary Carmichaels of literary history is a project continued throughout the twentieth century in both academic scholarship and independent publishing.[9] While indebted to this work, this book ultimately departs from the perennially necessary search for Mary Carmichaels (and Judith Shakespeares, for that matter) in order to turn attention to the historical counterparts of Chloe and Olivia. That is, rather than continue the rich tradition of recovering women novelists writing the stories of fictional Chloe and Olivias, I write about women writers who are themselves embroiled in the story of Chloe and Olivia—women who *are* Chloe and Olivia.[10] How has the torch been lit, I ask, when it is Chloe herself who must write the history of liking—and sharing a laboratory with—Olivia? What happens when Chloe is both the author and the subject of *Life's Adventure*?

The Passion Projects: Modernist Women, Intimate Archives, Unfinished Lives locates our writerly Chloes in the years after the height of Anglo-American literary modernism, when women began to feel themselves being marginalized and excluded from emergent accounts of the period. I trace the ways that queer women, in particular, wrote themselves and their Olivias into a literary and cultural history that refused to accommodate them. These life stories were frequently "sanitized," their subjects rendered "apparitional," as in Terry Castle's study, or they were rendered clearly and unapologetically before being censored, suppressed, or destroyed.[11] In each case, *Life's Adventure* turns out to be a biography—or, at least, it is a biographical act, a project driven by an impulse toward life writing, collecting, and other forms of documenting the personal, intimate, and private. This study thus begins with the assumption that the stories we tell about our most intimate lives, and the structures—the torches in vast chambers—in which we preserve them, are of singular importance. This is a bigger, more complicated claim than it may at first seem: it is both formal and material, both literary and historical. What is important here is not only the historical content of the recovered life story—the exact meaning of "Chloe liked Olivia"—but the methods employed by our writerly Chloes, our ancestors both biological and chosen, to write these life stories. To the extent that this is itself a kind of recovery project, it recovers not an identity but a genre: the biographical "passion project."

This book thus reassesses the importance of biography, broadly conceived, for modernist, midcentury, and contemporary women writers and scholars. By drawing together a diverse archive of biographical acts—published and unpublished books, drafts, outlines, fragments, letters, annotations, collections, objects, and ephemera—I read biography as an activist genre undertaken in late career by queer feminist writers determined to resist the marginalization and exclusion of their friends, colleagues, lovers, companions, and wives from dominant narratives of literary history. Some of these biographical acts were published immediately, some were published only after a substantial delay, and some remain unpublished today. In the experimental life writing of canonical mainstays like Virginia Woolf, the intimate archives of Radclyffe Hall and Sylvia Townsend Warner, the abandoned projects of Djuna Barnes and Hope

Mirrlees, the midcentury memoirs and literary collections of Margaret Anderson, Sylvia Beach, and Alice B. Toklas, and the more contemporary recovery projects of Lisa Cohen, Jenny Diski, Monique Truong, and Kate Zambreno, the biographical impulse signals a shared ethical drive to develop a counternarrative of literary history grounded in women's lives. By tracking this interest in preservation across biographical novels, histories, and archives, this book uncovers the modernist prehistory of the contemporary queer feminist recovery project.

The Unfinished Business of 1928: Modernism, Feminism, and the Biographical Act

The history of Anglo-American literary modernism is full of declarations about the decisive significance of individual years. Think of Virginia Woolf's assertion that human character changed "on or about December 1910"; think of Wyndham Lewis's crowning of the "Men of 1914"; think of Willa Cather's observation that the world "broke in two in 1922 or thereabouts," and Ezra Pound's habit of dating letters "*p s U*" after the publication of James Joyce's *Ulysses* in the same year.[12] Generations later, feminist and queer scholars turned our attention to the impact of 1928, the year in which English women gained full suffrage and the year in which Radclyffe Hall's now classic novel of lesbianism, *The Well of Loneliness*, was published and put on trial for obscenity.[13] As Laura Doan has demonstrated, the trial was "*the* crystallizing moment in the construction of a visible modern English lesbian subculture," and the publicity surrounding both the scandalous book and its "mannish" author was a crucial part of "the shift from cultural indeterminacy to acknowledgement."[14] In his account of queer modernism, Benjamin Kahan added that the trial "had the analogous effect for lesbianism as Wilde's trial had for homosexuality—it did not invent a language of lesbianism so much as crystalize an image of the lesbian."[15] The intersecting histories of the vote and the trial made increasingly available two distinct vocabularies—feminist, lesbian—with which to imagine and record the lives of modern women. And the public controversy attached to each image increased the stakes (and, sometimes, the inventiveness) of the biographical acts in this study. Many women writers were very aware of their participation in, and scrutiny under, these vocabularies; for example, just before the publication of *A Room of One's Own* in 1929, Woolf admitted that she feared she would "be attacked for a feminist & hinted at for a sapphist."[16] In contrast to modernist biographers like Lytton Strachey and Harold Nicolson, whose irreverent portraits attacked what they saw as the hypocrisy and foolishness of earlier generations, these writers approached their subjects—their Olivias—with a kind of protective empathy, seeking to preserve rather than flatten their less conventional life stories in intimate biographical acts. As the result of the press surrounding the legal condemnation of Hall's novel, lesbians found themselves newly visible, and close relationships between women were increasingly scrutinized. In the preface of her book about her friend and fellow writer Winifred Holtby, for example, Vera Brittain acknowledges the paradox governing representations of friendship between women: "From the days of Homer the friendships of men have enjoyed glory and acclamation, but the friendships of women," she tells us, "have usually been not merely unsung, but mocked, belittled and falsely interpreted."[17] Brittain here registers both the paucity of the historical record and the modern tendency, especially after 1928, to read all intimate female friendships as potential sexual relationships. This is, in part, why this book focuses exclusively on biographical acts undertaken by women writers, despite the existence of similar projects developed between men and across genders.[18] The very different types of queer feminist biographical acts examined here are all indelibly marked by both the burdens and generative possibilities of this heightened public awareness in the years after 1928.

This book registers these tensions while resisting the temptation to provide a single persuasive account of the relationships described in its pages. As lesbian feminist scholars such as Lillian Faderman, Carroll Smith-Rosenberg, and Sharon Marcus have shown in different contexts, sexual desire pervades friendships between women even as sexual identities remain historically opaque.[19] It simply may not be possible for us, now, to know exactly what it meant for Chloe to like Olivia, then. There is a danger in confidence, in certainty, in the assurance of being right: one "reading" can close down the possibilities of a text and, with it, the historical preservation of identities other than those currently legible to us and preferred by us. For this reason, this project is anchored by my determination to write *about* biography without writing biography itself. My methodology includes close reading and formal analysis, but these readings share space with biographical narrative and cultural history. As Lawrence Rainey once reminded us, stories are simply another form of criticism:

> For many academic literary critics the presence of any story at all has become an object of suspicion. Narrative is thought to be a linear and monologic form that offers factitious coherence at the cost of analytic complexity, storytelling a form of pandering to popular tastes depraved

by mass media. Expository prose, written in rebarbative jargon, is the sign of resistance to the culture industry and the seal of academic integrity. But is it necessary to remind literary critics that a story is not an object that has been merely happened upon? No less than expository prose, stories are complex and contradictory artifacts. The apparent ease with which they may be recounted should not be confused with a resistance to analysis. Stories are analyses—by other means.[20]

Throughout this book, biographical stories *are* analyses, not simply the historical building blocks with which to construct other, more literary-critical arguments. Our use and misuse of the biographical can tell us a great deal about the shifting values of our literary traditions. And while I remain unwilling to ask for a single definitive answer to the question of what it means for Chloe to like Olivia, I am particularly invested in the demonstrated commitments of so many real-life Chloes to the biographical commemoration of their Olivias. In this sense, it does not seem outlandish to think that one of the books pulled down from the shelf by Woolf's narrator might have had an unmentioned subtitle: not just *Life's Adventure* but *Life's Adventure: A Biography*.

Biography, biographical act, biographical practice: throughout this book, I understand these three terms to be part of the same generic framework, and that framework is inclusive of a wide variety of biographical acts and archives. Why, I ask, does what I identify as a common biographical impulse take such drastically different forms? Each chapter details the result of a biographical turn, an impulse toward biographical writing, and the development of a kind of biographical practice, but since the resulting text or archive is not always legible in the same terms as standard biography, I describe the effort born of the biographical impulse itself—no matter the result—as a biographical act. I initially borrowed the term "biographical act" from Charles Caramello, who used it to describe the literary portraiture of Henry James and Gertrude Stein. In Caramello's analysis, the biographical acts of James and Stein were "covers for autobiography," and their literary portraits were mere performances undertaken in order to "construct autobiographical portraits of themselves as exemplary modern artists."[21] Unlike Caramello, though, I do not mean to imply that the coding of this work as biography is always misleading. The writers I study are not *putting on acts*; instead, they are *beginning to take action*, even if their biographical projects cannot always be finished or published during their lifetimes.

These biographical acts are undertaken throughout the middle decades of the twentieth century—a time when the genre was fraught with importance for the future of modernist studies. The height of literary modernism, as an artistic movement, had passed, but the development of modernist studies as a widely recognized scholarly field within universities was still to come. In *Modernism: Evolution of an Idea*, Sean Latham and Gayle Rogers grapple with the long history of the term "modernism" and trace its development, contestation, and revision over the course of the century. In their account, the midcentury consolidation of modernism into an object of professional study first took place in the "full-length studies and biographies of key figures that helped make the authors themselves into embodiments of genius, innovation, and free thought."[22] This foundational biographical criticism was dominated by men writing about men: their paradigmatic examples are Richard Ellmann and Hugh Kenner, whose studies of Joyce and Pound, respectively, "built the core of a high modernist canon around linguistic innovation, difficulty, and autonomy" and provided the grounding for "the new field of modernist studies."[23] While Latham and Rogers go on to acknowledge the parallel significance of classroom-ready anthologies and the establishment of institutional archives for the birth of modernist studies, I want to linger on their observation that critical attention to individual modernist writers, in biographies and single-author studies, is a founding methodology of modernist studies. As several feminist literary critics have suggested, biography had already become the generic terrain on which women battled for their inclusion in history.[24] I extend and elaborate that claim in the context of modernist studies, arguing that these writers take up biography in order to engage in what I call generic activism on behalf of their intimate friends, partners, and companions. They believed that this unconventional biographical work, undertaken in defiance of cultural and generic norms, could eventually transform long-standing social conventions. These intimate biographical practices, which document the trace of desire between women with very different relations to avowal and orientation, feminism and lesbianism, and the work of partnership in private and professional life, are driven by an implicitly pedagogical, future-oriented impulse. In this light, the biographical acts assembled in this book comprise a counterhistory of the field. These projects were not always finished, and they certainly were not understood to be analogous to the big biographical tomes that continue to be named as the founding criticism of modernist studies. Nevertheless, they persisted. And in these biographical acts, these passion projects, these women wrote themselves and their communities into a literary history from which they were being slowly but insistently excluded.

Biography may well seem an unlikely hero. Writers, in particular, have a long history of suspicion toward the genre: W. H. Auden labeled it "always superfluous" and "usually in bad taste," James Joyce envisioned biographers as "biografiend[s]," and Vladimir Nabokov accused them of being "psycho-plagiarists." Even in Latham and Rogers's account of modernist studies' dependence on the genre, the biographical can seem somewhat retrograde. Scholars of modernism routinely employ a wide variety of research methods, many of which rely upon the biographical, and biographically based scholarship has been of long-standing importance not just in the initial formation of the field but in virtually all of the later expansions of that early canon.[25] Yet, especially in our capacity as teachers of modernism, we still tend to imply that the principles of close reading and formal analysis are the most important methods for literary study. For this reason, it has been hard for the field to fully move beyond the long-standing relationship between modernism and New Criticism.[26] And even beyond modernist studies, the necessity of biographical information in other fields of humanities research does not always translate into respect for biographical projects. In his preface to *The Seductions of Biography*, for example, historian William S. McFeely recalls his feelings of surprise and dismay when he first heard himself referred to as a biographer: "About all I knew about that label was that it marked the doom of one's reputation in the historical profession."[27] Real scholars, it would seem—not just literary scholars but historians, too—keep their distance from the biographical.[28]

Scholars of literary modernism, in particular, have only recently begun to acknowledge the extent to which modernist writing itself is saturated by experiments in biographical life writing. Autobiography, driven by changing notions of the interior self, has long been an essential object of inquiry in our narratives (and syllabi) of modernist studies, but, perhaps because of the vehemence with which the most well-known modernist biography—Strachey's *Eminent Victorians* (1918)—rejects not only its subjects but the conventional form of the genre, modernist literary history rarely attends to the interest in biography sustained by so many of its most well-known writers. With few exceptions, scholars have preferred to address other related forms: autobiography, portraiture, the roman à clef, the bildungsroman.[29] Even Latham and Rogers's acknowledgment of the role of biography in scholarly field formation implicitly positions the genre as an early mode of criticism to be eclipsed by more sophisticated theoretical work. As both corrective and continuing conversation, my study highlights the urgency of a critical return to biography studies, especially in the context of modernist, feminist, and queer studies, and it suggests that we should understand the archive as a site of bio-critical action for the writers and subjects long marginalized by dominant disciplinary narratives.

Intimacy and the Archive

Not all of the biographical acts examined in this project are immediately recognizable as biographies. Sometimes biographical impulses find other outlets. Sometimes they fail. One of the basic premises of this book is that the responsible recovery of queer women's life writing requires that we read around the edges of dominant generic form—in other words, that we read biographical impulses, acts, and archives in addition to published biographies. If modernist and midcentury biographical practices could not yet acknowledge the great variety of intimacies between women without what Sylvia Townsend Warner called a "safe margin for every one to be dead in," then the formal structures and governing notions of the genre had to be broken down and rebuilt in other, more capacious ways.[30] In a sense, the formal revolutions of literary modernism in which many of these women had participated in earlier moments in their careers proved to have been a perfect training ground for this later work. Like William Carlos Williams, who argued—in the pages of his own autobiography, no less!—that every form of art "presents its case and its meaning by the very form it assumes" and that "past objects have about them past necessities . . . which have conditioned them and from which, as a form itself, they cannot be freed," many of the writers in this study struggled with the inherited limitations of biographical form.[31] Frustrated by the "past necessities" of the genre, they became amateur archivists, impassioned collectors, and intimate historians, and they pursued projects of collection, collation, and annotation rather than of holistic narrative creation. Each project "presents its case and its meaning" in its expansion of biographical form to include the intimate archive.

In calling these unfinished biographical acts "intimate archives," I highlight the process of archiving as an ongoing biographical practice that pieces together the stories of these authors' most intimate relationships. In Leo Bersani and Adam Phillips's collaborative work on intimacy, they describe psychoanalysis as "what two people can say to each other if they agree not to have sex," and, in a slight adaptation, we can characterize the intimate archive as a collection comprised of what one partner can say about the other once they can no longer have sex—once one partner bears the sole responsibility for making their story together legible.[32] As we will see, this is emotionally difficult work, and the authors I discuss pursue it in full knowledge that they are collating and annotating these biographical acts for an audience that may be several generations in the future.[33] The archive here is, in Jacques Derrida's various formulations, "a pledge," "a promise," and "a question of the future."[34] For this reason, my use of the term "intimate archive" differs from the way Maryanne Dever, Sally Newman, and Ann Vickery use it, in the introduction to their 2009 volume, to refer to "collections of private and, in some cases, highly personal papers that have found their way into public collections."[35] While the intimate archives in my study are also comprised of private papers, there is no confusion about how they "found their way" into their current institutional homes. As biographical acts, they are intimate, not inanimate; rather than understanding them as the passive victims of historical change, I read them as deliberately curated projects.

These archives are intimate for another, perhaps more practical, reason, too. The archival collections of many of the women discussed here are intertwined: the Radclyffe Hall and Una Troubridge Papers are held together at the Harry Ransom Center at the University of Texas at Austin; the Sylvia Townsend Warner and Valentine Ackland Papers are held in the same tiny reading room at the Dorset County Museum in Dorchester, England; the papers of Djuna Barnes and the Baroness Elsa von Freytag-Loringhoven were initially deposited together at the University of Maryland, though they have been separated into different fonds; the Hope Mirrlees and Jane Ellen Harrison Papers, while stored separately in the Newnham College Archives at the University of Cambridge, contain numerous cross-references and must be read together; and, most famously, the archival remains of Gertrude Stein and Alice B. Toklas are filed together throughout the collections of both the Beinecke Rare Book and Manuscript Library and the Harry Ransom Center. In each case, it is impossible to research the life and work of one woman without bumping into the life and work of the other. And although, with the exception of the Stein-Toklas Papers, these archives were not immediately celebrated alongside those of Eliot and Joyce as the foundational archives of modernist literary history, the intimacy of their relationships has been built into the structure of their physical archives.

Throughout this book, I describe these biographical acts as both "intimate" and "queer," and I use these terms in ways that sketch their sometimes ambivalent relationship to the specificities of sexual desire, acts, and identities. Intimacy, like queerness, is suggestive rather than specific. It does not necessarily indicate a sexual relationship, but neither does it foreclose that possibility. Geraldine Pratt and Victoria Rosner describe how the word "intimate" calls forth a "cluster of related ideas: privacy, familiarity, love, sex, informality, and personal connection."[36] Similarly, J. Samaine Lockwood's practice of "intimate historicism" relies on an understanding of the intimate as that which "seems to be about privacy, personal relation, and the domestic."[37] Intimacy usually implies the presence of a relationship: though it is possible to experience intimacy alone, one is more frequently understood to be intimate *with* someone or something—a person, an animal, an object, a group. In Lauren Berlant's account, intimacy "names the enigma of [a] range of attachments . . . [and] poses a question of scale that links the instability of individual lives to the trajectories of the collective."[38] As a theoretical term, intimacy allows for connection—for its own strategic deployment—despite this definitional instability.

The word "queer," like the word "intimate," is useful here because of a similarly unresolvable friction between historical specificity and theoretical abstraction. Several strands of contemporary queer theory have sought to "disconnect queerness from an essential homosexual embodiment" on the basis that "queer maintains a relation of resistance to whatever constitutes the normal," while others see the critical capaciousness of the term as a weakness rather than a strength.[39] In an early *PMLA* article heralding, however ambivalently, the institutionalization of queer theory, Lauren Berlant and Michael Warner demanded resistance to the stabilization of "queer" in favor of the term's "wrenching sense of recontextualization."[40] Eve Kosofsky Sedgwick's "Queer and Now" provides a paradigmatic example of how to imagine the coexistence of multiple valences of queerness. In a now oft-quoted passage, she describes the anti-foundational fluidity of queerness as an "open mesh of possibilities, gaps, overlaps, dissonances and resonances, lapses and excesses of meaning when the constituent elements of anyone's gender, of anyone's sexuality aren't made (or *can't* be made) to signify monolithically."[41] But she also insists that, despite the unpredictable and exciting movement of some queer theoretical scholarship "along dimensions that can't be subsumed by gender and sexuality at all," queerness should not be fully divorced from sexual object choices, practices, and/or identities:

> Given the historical and contemporary force of the prohibitions against *every* same-sex sexual expression, for anyone to disavow those meanings, or to displace them from the term's definitional center, would be to dematerialize any possibility of queerness itself.[42]

The choice to adopt or avoid the term "queer" is thus a deliberate rhetorical strategy. Valerie Rohy, for example, uses "lesbian" rather than "queer" throughout her work as a "strategic anachronism that can illuminate the continuities between nineteenth-century views of female deviance and twentieth-century notions of lesbian identity."[43] While I respect her implicit indexing of Adrienne Rich's "lesbian continuum,"[44] I refer to queer rather than lesbian biographical acts throughout this book precisely because I prefer the broad range of possible intimacies it represents. Only some of the biographical acts in this book are undertaken within relationships we can define with precision. Only some of the relationships between these Chloes and Olivias are known with any real degree of certitude—with the agreement and consensus of both the subjects themselves and the leagues of literary historians who have trailed after them. And it is perfectly fine—responsible, even—to admit we do not know everything about the past. Some queer studies scholars have suggested that the historical gaze of LGBTQ studies has made some sexual histories, identities, and acts legible at the expense of others.[45] While some theorists of queer temporality share Carolyn Dinshaw's critical optimism about the possibilities of a queer "touch across time,"[46] others, like David Halperin and Heather Love, remain wary of the identificatory pleasures of such connection.[47] Indeed, one of the larger goals of this project is to put late modernist and midcentury theorists and practitioners of biography—of early feminist and queer biography, at that—in conversation with more contemporary formulations in queer theory: queer temporalities, queer failures, queer archives.

My contention that the queer feminist literary archive is a form of intimate biography that carries an alternate narrative of modernist literary history is built on the lessons of feminist and queer archival scholarship. Significant academic readerships and para-academic activist groups have developed around concerns about queer, amateur, or otherwise marginalized archives, and this project contributes to this much larger cultural conversation by tracing the fluid boundaries between intimate and institutional modes of preservation.[48] Generations of feminist criticism are indebted to the fundamental idea that the personal is political, or, in this context, that the intimate bears a legitimate relationship to the institutional. Feminist and queer archives value the personal, the private, and the intimate as part of the historical record, and this requires us to read for absence rather than simply acknowledging what is present. As the editors of "Queering Archives," a 2014 special issue of the *Radical History Review*, point out, "the drama of existence is a central, compelling narrative or mystery inhering in queer archives, a drama borne out by countless scholars' efforts to find lost queer things."[49] They go on to describe the queer archive as "a space where one collects or cobbles together historical understandings of sexuality and gender through an appraisal of presences and absences, ... where queer subjects put themselves together as historical subjects, even if done in the context of historical lack."⁵⁰ That lack—that untold, unvalued, unfinished history—is constitutive of queer archives. As many scholars have shown, queer archives have often been preserved—when they have been recognized and saved at all—in private rather than public spaces. Ann Cvetkovich's work on "archives of feeling," for example, asks us to consider the value of "objects that might not be considered archival" alongside immaterial histories that resist documentation because, she argues, sometimes "sex and feelings are too personal or ephemeral to leave records."⁵¹ In this way, the queer archival project is structured by absence—and the question of how to read, preserve, and honor the violence of that absence.

Throughout *The Passion Projects*, unfinishedness is the symptom of this absence. The biographical acts described here are each in a state of arrested development: they were organized but not written, or drafted but not completed, or collected but not narrated, or even, in the case of Woolf's *Orlando*, published but not truly finished. But these are their forms; none will become a more ideal version of itself. Each of these archives, however incomplete, and despite whatever length of time it spent in private hands, is now preserved within the institutional archives of a university, library, or museum. This has taken both advocacy and labor: everything scholars "discover" in an institutional archive has already been processed and catalogued by professional archivists and librarians.⁵² And as Linda Morra reminds us in her work on the "unarrested archives" of Canadian women writers, a writer's personal papers take on a newly public life once transferred into an institutional repository: "while institutional archives might physically hold or 'stop' papers, they also contradictorily allow for ideas to be circulated as researchers gain access to them and render them public."⁵³ In this way, archives are potential sites of queer pedagogy, or what Kevin Ohi has called "queer literary transmission."⁵⁴ While his study focuses on gay male writers and readers, Ohi describes scenes of "thwarted" or "interrupted" transmission as central to a queer literary tradition. Thwarted, interrupted, arrested, incomplete: queerness moves from one generation to the next as an unfinished project.

Passionate Commitments

There is more than one way for something to be unfinished. Writing about Tillie Olsen's novel *Yonnondio: From the Thirties* (1974), Scott Herring has countered its frequent critical description "as a loss, a failure, as an 'if only' wish, and as a thwarted revolution" with the suggestion that Olsen's text represents "an ethos of incompletion" that governed "a sustained act of creativity."[55] Herring calls this "slow writing": "a decades-long revolutionary project that waits for us, refusing to finish wherever 'here' might be."[56] It is slow, in part, because Olsen continued to work on it despite the ongoing pressures of domestic and professional life, but the constitutive unfinishedness of her novel should not be reduced from an aesthetic project to an unfortunate biographical fact. It has taken years for Olsen's unfinished work to be lauded rather than mourned. As Herring wryly points out, "a book never completed took time to become more and more unfinished."[57] And while Herring here gestures toward Olsen's authorial intention, it is also true that *Yonnondio*'s recategorization from tragedy to masterpiece, should it come to pass, will be the result of its reception by readers and critics. As James Ramsey Wallen has noted, "not 'just anyone' is capable of producing" an unfinished work: "Given the vast amounts of scholastic labor that their publications inevitably entail, the mere existence of an unfinished work is usually enough to mark it as a work of genius—or, at the very least, as the work of *a* genius."[58] Like Herring, Wallen acknowledges that most discussions of unfinishedness are underpinned by "a tragic rhetoric of failure."[59] But failure can be a subversive choice rather than a passive fate. In Jack Halberstam's formulation, failure can be "a form of critique" and "a way of refusing to acquiesce to dominant logics of power and discipline."[60] Halberstam's "queer art of failure," like Herring's "ethos of incompletion," is a description of the commitment to unfinishedness underlying each of the passion projects in this book.

Reframed as a defiant commitment in the face of ongoing erasure rather than a lack of dedication, the unfinished biographical acts encountered in every chapter can be categorized as passion projects. Indeed, this book's title—*The Passion Projects*—is not drawn from any one text; rather, it is a term that usefully describes how the concerns and practices I track through the lives of these women are bound together. A passion project is work that its practitioner undertakes for a reason other than professional duty or immediate gain, and so, in this sense, it is characterized by what Dinshaw describes as an "amateur sensibility."[61] The women in *The Passion Projects* are similar to the amateur medievalists in Dinshaw's study in that they are "defined by attachment in a detached world," they "wear their desires on their sleeves," and they undertake projects for which they will never be professionally recognized or paid, projects they may never even finish.[62] The passion project is work that comes at personal cost without the guarantee of a social reward; it is sacrifice that leads to no certain redemption. To undertake a passion project is often to move outside of one's field of expertise or specialization, to labor in a foreign land and to do so for love. It is to pursue desire over practicality, affect over intellect, amateurism over professionalism. It is work in the service of unreasonable pursuits: memory, legacy, the future world. The passion project is a promise to oneself or another that begins in private but continues in an imagined public. And as it originates at that scale, its ultimate goal is an intimate one. This project will, in essence, *matter* because it matters to this intimate, maybe even impossible, audience. And it is perhaps the unavoidable tragedy of the passion project that so many of them remain unfinished. Because they exist outside the lines of ordinary genres, because they strive toward an ethereal goal, because they are frequently last on the existential bucket list, they are often left behind unassembled, askew, incomplete, or unpublished. But even as these projects eschew world-historical ambitions, the purity of their conception lends them a power and potentiality absent from other, earlier works. Their power resides in their queer temporality, their naked emotion, their lateness, even in the way they exist as adjunct to more canonical literary texts. Even in a fragmented archive, these works vibrate with a transhistorical feeling, a *passion* that supersedes their formal disarray or their forgottenness in the eyes of history. The biographical turns of the women in this book—inasmuch as they represent a turning away, however temporary, from the profession of the artist and toward the curating and archiving of love, friendship, and desire—have produced passion projects in this manner. And *The Passion Projects* seeks to excavate them, recognize them, and see the radiant lives left behind in the most intimate, incomplete archives. In every chapter, we will find that Chloe likes Olivia, and she has embarked upon a version of *Life's Adventure* to express it. Following Marcus's suggestion to seek "more than two names and a verb," I query the stakes of a slightly altered phrase: not only "Chloe likes Olivia" but "Chloe *writes* Olivia."

Between Women, Between Generations

Each chapter of *The Passion Projects*—"Intimate Archives," "Abandoned Lives," "Modernists Explain Things to Me," and "The Sense of Unending"—theorizes a specific type of unfinished biographical act and provides several case studies that range across the middle decades of the twentieth century. The book thus forms a loose taxonomy of biographical passion projects undertaken by women during the very period in which women were systematically written out of histories of modernism.

Chapter 1, "Intimate Archives: The Preservation of Partnership," demonstrates that some intimate biographical acts are designed as archival projects to be mined later. Reading the competing biographical preparations of Radclyffe Hall's long-time partner, Una Troubridge, alongside those of her lover, Evguenia Souline, I suggest that these compilers of intimate archives prioritize future researchers over midcentury readers. Drawing on Cvetkovich's notion of the "archive of feelings," I further propose that some queer feminist life stories were intentionally left incomplete—even unwritten. The chapter concludes with a substantial engagement with Sylvia Townsend Warner's late-career life writing. Claiming that the archive of her partnership with Valentine Ackland could not be published without "a safe margin for every one to be dead in," Warner spent years after Ackland's death assembling an intimate archive of their literary life together. Like Troubridge and Souline's letters, Warner's archive was intentionally assembled, collated, annotated, and saved for a more generous future audience.

Chapter 2, "Abandoned Lives: Impossible Projects and Archival Remains," theorizes biographical failure. What happens when it feels impossible to finish telling a life story? This chapter reads two incomplete biographical projects in the context of what Halberstam has called the "queer art of failure": the recognition and reframing of failure as one possible form of the deliberate subversion of heteronormative metrics of success. Djuna Barnes worked for decades to turn the attempted autobiography of her Dadaist friend, the Baroness Elsa von Freytag-Loringhoven, into a publishable biography. Hope Mirrlees compiled a series of half-done drafts, notes, and outlines toward the biography of her late mentor, friend, and intimate companion, the celebrated Cambridge classicist Jane Ellen Harrison. Though their projects were very different, neither Barnes nor Mirrlees would finish their biographies *or* consent to let anyone else take over their projects. This chapter reframes the discourse of failure surrounding both projects and suggests that these so-called failures represent acts of resistance to the normalizing pull of typical biographical narratives.

Chapter 3, "Modernists Explain Things to Me: Collecting as Queer Feminist Response," demonstrates that some impassioned biographical acts and archives range beyond the merely textual. Turning toward three examples of canonizing (if not ultimately canonical) life narratives, I read the midcentury memoirs of modernism-in-the-making written by Margaret Anderson, Sylvia Beach, and Alice B. Toklas as anecdotal archives in which the stories of their relationships are strategically encrypted—and thus preserved—in larger stories of renowned bohemian communities.

None of these memoirs sold well, and none were acclaimed by critics, then or now, as literary achievements in their own right. But the publication of each of these failed projects was silently accompanied by the accumulation and preservation of a collection of modernist artifacts. This chapter thus attends to both textual archives and material collections of art, photographs, and household goods. After taking stock of the relative failure of her memoirs, Anderson's decision to begin what she called her "collection" signaled her transition into this curatorial mode. And reading Sylvia Beach's expansive collection of literary artifacts alongside Alice B. Toklas's dwindling collection of modernist art, I draw on Jeremy Braddock's description of modernist collecting to posit collection and curation, rather than creation and innovation, as late modernist acts capable of turning years of personal witness into public testimony and commentary.

Chapter 4, "The Sense of Unending: Revisiting Virginia Woolf's *Orlando: A Biography*," returns to the most canonical of modernist women in light of these unfinished biographical projects. I reconsider Woolf's 1928 "joke" biography of Vita Sackville-West as an unfinished text, a work that provides a theoretical key for reading the queer temporality of the rest of this book's passion projects. Attending to its (non-)ending in medias res, in which the last page is turned while the subject is only entering middle age, I suggest that valuing the unfinished as an aesthetic category can bring the lessons of queer feminist biographers into sharper focus. The chapter ends by considering how reevaluating unpublished and unfinished work shifts our understanding of modernism's past, present, and future history.

Finally, in the coda, I turn toward the future audience imagined for many of these biographical passion projects. More recent experiments in biographical writing by Lisa Cohen, Jenny Diski, Nathalie Léger, Monique Truong, and Kate Zambreno, I argue, share intellectual and affective motivations with the modernist practices discussed earlier in this book. If the biographical and archival projects I examine hope to assure a future readership for queer feminist life stories, then these contemporary writers volunteer as that readership through the generosity of their attention and the experimental forms of their continued custodianship. I suggest that they write with the affective engagement and sense of generic activism that so many midcentury women harnessed to preserve the lives of their friends, partners, lovers, wives, and companions. In this sense, *The Passion Projects* ends with a generation of women writers who, like their ancestors at midcentury, see the work of writing as inseparable from the work of recovery.

CHAPTER ONE

Intimate Archives

THE PRESERVATION OF PARTNERSHIP

IN THE OPENING of "The Lives of the Obscure," Virginia Woolf describes a "faded, out-of-date, obsolete" library in which "the obscure sleep on the walls." In this silent, dusty room, the books line the shelves like "peaceful graves" and "nameless tombstones."[1] Yet the touch of potential readers contains restorative potential. If these books were to be rediscovered, opened, cared for, and read, one assumes, they might awaken from their long slumber and come alive once more. For Woolf, there is a particular allure to the idea of working on such neglected material:

> For one likes romantically to feel oneself a deliverer advancing with lights across the waste of years to the rescue of some stranded ghost—a Mrs. Pilkington, a Rev. Henry Elman, a Mrs. Ann Gilbert—waiting, appealing, forgotten, in the growing gloom.[2]

Woolf's ghosts are books stranded in a library, but her description of scholarly desire is equally appropriate to characterizations of archival research. The draw of archival desire remains potent in, for example, Carolyn Dinshaw's queer "touch across time," in which contemporary scholars forge "new relations, new identifications, new communities with past figures."[3] At its most romantic, this is a vision of the researcher as a kind of hero who swoops in to make sense of the forgotten or otherwise illegible wreckage of the past. It is a vision of the archive that allows us, as scholars, to make sense out of nonsense, to build a cohesive story out of forgotten fragments, and to rescue marginalized historical narratives from their obscure and often damaged archives.

As Heather Love reminds us, however, focusing on the heroism of archival recovery projects privileges the agency of contemporary scholars and ignores the muted desires of their historical subjects. "In imagining historical rescue as a one-way street," she argues, "we fail to acknowledge the dependence of the present on the past."[4] What if the archive refuses our entreaties for transhistorical communion? What if our would-be subjects turn their backs on us? What if they refuse our touch? Presciently, if we continue a bit further into Woolf's essay, this is precisely the response she describes:

> Possibly they hear one coming. They shuffle, they preen, they bridle. Old secrets well up to their lips. The divine relief of communication will soon be theirs. The dust shifts and Mrs. Gilbert—but the contact with life is instantly salutary. Whatever Mrs. Gilbert may be doing, she is not thinking about us.[5]

In the first few lines, these "obscure" lives seem to look forward to the researcher's touch. They "preen," and they ready themselves for communication. And yet, in an instance of what Jessica Berman has called Woolf's "interruptive style,"[6] the pliable eagerness of the "stranded ghost" in need of rescue is revealed to be a fiction. Woolf's em dash in the middle of the first sentence that promised communication between past and present is an implicit demonstration of archival refusal—what Love asks us to hear as *Noli me tangere* (Don't touch me).[7] The "ghost" in Woolf's archive of obscurity is not dependent upon our contemporary ministrations; indeed, she is not even thinking about us.

But there may be yet another way of understanding our relationship to the archival past. What if the ghosts had us in mind all along? In this chapter, I explore models for this relationship beyond the romance of historical recovery, in which scholars create coherent historical narratives from whatever fragments remain legible to us, or the rejection of historical recovery, in which the archive itself resists what Love calls "emotional rescue." What happens when we scholars, expecting incoherent shards, find intentional collections? What happens when the archive is there, waiting, silenced for years but ready to meet us—a deliberately constructed practice rather than the ruins we visit for scholarly evidence? Sometimes the archive is the purposeful but unheralded work of a collector or a curator, whether amateur or professional. Sometimes what we think of as our fractured, fragmented archives are the remnants of intentional collections that have not, for whatever reason, been preserved or understood as such. And sometimes these archives have stories of their own.

In this chapter, I read two such archives as queer biographical acts that prioritize future researchers over midcentury readers: first, the nearly unpublished biography of Radclyffe Hall written by Una Troubridge, her partner of nearly thirty years, and the competing epistolary collections saved by both Troubridge and Hall's last lover, Evguenia Souline; second, the archival project undertaken by Sylvia Townsend Warner after the death of her partner, Valentine Ackland. These are neither haphazard nor bureaucratic collections of literary remains; rather, they are what I call the intimate archives of partnership. In this context, the intimate archive refers to the accumulation and organization of material about the life of a partner without immediate plans to publish, or otherwise make public, this material. Like Martha Vicinus, who defines "intimate friendship" as an "emotional, erotically charged relationship between two women" while acknowledging that the term is capacious enough to apply to a wide variety of relationships and behaviors, I want the term "intimate archive" to embrace a broad spectrum of representational choices between "published" and "unpublished" work.[8] The pedagogical imperative that drives the writing of biography is no less present if publication must be posthumous, collective, and finished by others, for, as Elizabeth Freeman has suggested, "making other queers is a social matter."[9] The responsibility for Dinshaw's "touching across time" is not one-sided, not merely the provenance of future scholars.[10] Instead, the transmission and translation of queer experience from one generation to later generations is an omnipresent social responsibility: "sexual dissidents must create continuing queer lifeworlds while not being witness to this future or able to guarantee its form in advance, on the wager that there will be more queers to inhabit such worlds: we are 'bound' to queer successors whom we might not recognize."[11] For Troubridge, Souline, and Warner, their intimate archives were constructed with the understanding that their value belonged to the future rather than the present—that, in the words of José Esteban Muñoz, their queerness was about "the rejection of a here and now and an insistence on potentiality or concrete possibility for another world."[12] In these archives, that refusal of the present is bound up in an awareness that the "here and now" had already rejected them, that publication would remain impossible until some future arrival into a more just and open-minded, if always more flawed than utopian, era. The construction and preservation of the intimate archive, despite and because of such rejection, enables a consensual practice of historical recovery. The intimate archivist actively shapes (and sometimes, as we will see in the next chapter, intentionally limits) the conditions of future knowledge.

Intimacy Issues

What do we know about Radclyffe Hall, and how do we know it? Despite the publication of many novels and collections of poetry, Hall's literary reputation continues to be bound up with her most controversial novel. Published in 1928, the same year as Woolf's *Orlando* and Djuna Barnes's *Ladies Almanack*, Hall's *Well of Loneliness* has always had an uneasy relationship to the high modernist literary canon. It has never been out of print, and the cover of my copy touts the novel as "A 1920s Classic of Lesbian Fiction." Cherished by its fans and heralded as a groundbreaking depiction of sexual modernity, it is at the same time snubbed as an aesthetically inferior—or, at the very least, not at all modern*ist*—novel. While not strictly autobiographical, it has often been considered a roman à clef, and anyone writing about Hall has had to contend with this inconsistent slippage between the novel's author and its protagonist. Radclyffe Hall is not Stephen Gordon, but without reading the novel alongside an authoritative account of Hall's life, it can be all too easy to assume that their stories are one and the same.

Writing in 1968, forty years after the *Well*'s British trial for obscenity and twenty-five years after Hall's death, the feminist writer Vera Brittain keenly felt the absence of this critical biography when she agreed to write a recollection of the trial for Femina Books. Brittain remains best known for *Testament of Youth* (1933), her memoir about coming of age during the Great War, but she was also an outspoken feminist intellectual and prolific author who had publicly condemned the charges against Hall's novel in 1928. She, like Woolf, had been one of the forty prominent writers and intellectuals to appear in court as potential witnesses at the *Well*'s trial, although the magistrate did not ultimately allow anyone to testify for the defense. And in a review for *Time and Tide*, Brittain had stood up for the controversial novel on the grounds of freedom of speech: "There is no problem which is not better frankly stated than concealed. Persecution and disgusted ostracism have never solved any difficulty in the world, and they certainly do not make the position of the female invert less bitter to herself or less dangerous to others."[13] Her adamant defense of Hall's novel against charges of obscenity was complicated by her view that lesbianism—or "inversion," as she nearly always referred to homosexuality—was a "dangerous" challenge to the rationality and respectability of feminism rather than an ally in the struggle against patriarchy.[14] Despite Brittain's disavowals, Hall sent her a long letter expressing gratitude for both her presence at the trial and her support in print. But given Brittain's political hesitancy, her selection as the chronicler of the Femina project several decades later was certainly curious.

Since the only biography of Hall available when Brittain undertook this project was *The Life and Death of Radclyffe Hall*, a short book written by Hall's surviving partner, Lady Una Troubridge, Brittain had no choice but to rely on this account of Hall's life. And although her book would focus on the trial, Brittain felt responsible for filling in the historical record to the best of her ability.[15] She begins with a chapter titled "The Life Story of Radclyffe Hall up to *The Well of Loneliness*," and she is sharply critical of Troubridge for telling us "something, but not much, about Radclyffe Hall":

> The facts collected in Una's artless narrative are sporadic, and make little attempt at logical arrangement. Its chief value lies in the evidence that it provides of a selfless, uncalculating affection, of a kind that seldom exists between individuals of either sex.[16]

Her initial impatience with Troubridge's book stems from her conviction that, simply put, it is a bad biography. The narrative is "artless" and illogical, and it provides a highly subjective portrait of their relationship rather than an objective account of Hall's life. Troubridge's intimacy with her subject obstructs rather than facilitates access to Hall's personal history.

It is worth dwelling for a moment on Brittain's complaints about Troubridge's book because they are nearly identical to much of the criticism she herself had received after publishing *Testament of Friendship: The Story of Winifred Holtby*. Brittain and Holtby had maintained an extraordinarily close and dedicated friendship for decades, and after Holtby's early death in 1935, Brittain spent years working on her "testament" to her dearest friend. Ongoing questions about the precise nature of the relationship between Brittain and Holtby had given rise to plenty of gossipy speculation during their lifetime, and the biography did nothing to set the record straight, so to speak.[17] The initial reviews of *Testament of Friendship* reflect this public discomfort with intimacy between women. One reviewer called it "so intimate and personal as to be almost an autobiography of the Yorkshire novelist," which suggests that author and subject seem indistinguishable from one another.[18] Other reviewers found Brittain's methods unprofessional and criticized her lack of "perspective and proportion":

> Why is it that women have not yet started to achieve success in writing biography, at least in its most complete form? The explanation may be

suggested by two words—perspective and proportion. These elements are essential. Paradoxically, the painting of a character demands, above all things, impersonality in the artist. Personal intimacy with the subject and factual resources are materials that by themselves are apt to run all over the canvas. And this is what has happened to Miss Brittain's "life" of her great friend Winifred Holtby. . . . She died three years ago at the age of 37, and her friend continues to mourn her deeply. It is a mood in which biographies should not be written.[19]

Setting aside the repellent sexism with which this review begins, we recognize vestiges of the masculinist modernism of Eliot and Pound in the author's accompanying demand for "impersonality in the artist" and his utter distaste for evidence of "personal intimacy" between artist and subject. For such an obvious display of intimacy to taint the pages of a biography seems to call its very genre into question: the biography written too soon, and by too close an associate, becomes a lament rather than a life story. The critic for the *Times* claimed that *Testament of Friendship* "suffered somewhat from [Brittain's] intimacy with its subject," and a review in the *New Statesman* went so far as to accuse Brittain of writing a solipsistic memorial to their relationship rather than a biography of Holtby herself: "Someone less violently distressed by Miss Holtby's death might have given us a more solid, objective portrait of the many-sided, brilliant woman. . . . The very depth of her feeling made this impossible for Miss Brittain; and as a result, it is not Miss Holtby who is the centre of this study, but Miss Brittain herself."[20] Even critics more appreciative of Brittain's biographical strategy were frustrated by the way she carried it out. For example, an article in the *Sunday Chronicle & Sunday Review* lauds Brittain's dual aims to write "partly as an acknowledgement to her friend, and partly to show that women as well as men can enjoy a deep and noble friendship that even survives the marriage of one of them, in this case Miss Brittain."[21] Yet, even as the reviewer appreciates Brittain's feminist project, she resents the biography's emphasis on the closeness of their personal relationship rather than on the details of Holtby's public life: "I personally want to think of Winifred Holtby as the woman who created the living characters in 'South Riding' not as the earnest undergraduette [sic] who knelt with her head in Miss Brittain's lap, and, in a passion of tears, 'poured out the pent-up torment' of her religious conflict."[22] In these very different reviews, we see the same kinds of complaints rehearsed again and again. *Testament of Friendship*, they claim, was written too soon, by someone too close to its subject, and with too much of a focus on the significance of one relationship.

Over the years, as she distanced herself from the subjectivity and sentimentality of that experiment in intimate biography, Brittain became less and less forgiving of other biographies written by close friends, lovers, and spouses. Her initial assessment of Troubridge's book is consistent with this critical stance. But as she supplements Troubridge's intimate history with details of Hall's personal and professional life, Brittain's tone slowly softens, and she expands upon her earlier commendation of Troubridge's willingness to document "affection" between two women:

> Apart from Ruth and Naomi, those respect-worthy symbols of orthodox friendship, there is little in the Scriptures, or indeed in all literature, to suggest the intensity of love which can exist between woman and woman. But Una Troubridge, for all her simplicity, indicates that it may very occasionally have a quality with which the romance of heterosexual relationships cannot compete. Such love can exist between mother and daughter, sister and sister, or friend and friend; its distinction lies in its intensity, and its freedom from selfishness or the desire to possess.[23]

Notably, her qualified praise is given in language that closely resembles the argument she herself had made in the prologue to *Testament of Friendship*.[24] Like so many of the records of what Lillian Faderman has called "romantic friendships," both of these texts—despite being written nearly three decades apart—begin with a citation of the relationship between Ruth and Naomi, include an exasperated acknowledgment of the paucity of the existing literary record, and emphasize the many possible forms of love between women. Ultimately, Brittain writes, she finds "value in the very artlessness of Una Troubridge's narrative, which makes no attempt to disguise the undivided sincerity of her emotion."[25] Brittain's early disdain for this "simplicity" and "artlessness" is ultimately replaced by a sense of kinship with Troubridge. Like Brittain's *Testament of Friendship*, which had rekindled speculation about the nature of her relationship with Holtby, Troubridge's queer biographical act provides further evidence of "the intensity of love which can exist between woman and woman," and it adds another relationship to the often overlooked and disrespected lineage of Ruth and Naomi.

Claiming Radclyffe Hall: An Almost Archival Story

In a crucial difference from Brittain's book, Troubridge's account was not necessarily intended to be public—or at least not so soon. A few years after Hall's untimely death in 1943, Troubridge, as Hall's literary executor, sought to publish a memorial edition of her works that would include *The Well of Loneliness*, but the Home Secretary informed her that any republication of the novel would run the risk of renewed legal proceedings. Despite this setback, Troubridge felt an obligation to set down Hall's life story in *The Life and Death of Radclyffe Hall*. She claimed that she had been urged by "a number of people" to write the biography because her knowledge of Hall's life, both before and during their relationship, was singular and irreplaceable. "They have warned me," she wrote in her book's foreword, "that if I die leaving it unwritten many things that her readers will want to know, will have the right to know, about a writer of her talent, will be buried with me."[26] So she wrote it, quickly, in 1945. Yet the manuscript remained unpublished until shortly before her own death nearly two decades later. It was, for nearly twenty years, part of Troubridge's intimate archive of her life with Hall, finished but unpublished, complete but unknown. Why?

Despite the fact that it was eventually published, Troubridge's intimate biography of her partner should be understood as part of her consistent practice of writing to impossible, even unimaginable readers: the biography, which itself takes the form of a long letter to unnamed future readers, is counterbalanced by the thousands of still unpublished letters she continued to write to Hall even after her death. She wrote to the future; she wrote to the past. Her queer touch across time all but ignored the present. The biography itself had been undertaken for reasons both personal and political. As Hall's literary executor, she felt responsible for the state of her posthumous reputation, and she was certain that she was the only person who could possibly provide necessary information about Hall to generations of future readers. She seemed to want, too, to prove that she was not ashamed of either Hall's sexuality or her own and to comfort other "inverts." Troubridge and Hall had both been determined that their life together should provide an example to others. This is why, in Troubridge's recollection, they decided together that Hall would write *The Well of Loneliness*:

> It was her absolute conviction that such a book could only be written by a sexual invert, who alone could be qualified by personal knowledge and experience to speak on behalf of a misunderstood and misjudged minority.... I told her to write what was in her heart, that so far as any effect upon myself was concerned, I was sick to death of ambiguities, and only wished to be known for what I was and to dwell with her in the palace of truth.[27]

Unlike Brittain, who had defended Hall's novel despite her complicated reservations about the sexuality of its author, Troubridge was unafraid to acknowledge the legitimacy of "inversion." In one of the journals (known as her "Day Books") she kept throughout her life with Hall, she noted that neither she nor Hall had any patience for the "invert who is ashamed of her kind and cowards can only do harm."[28] And, as she wrote in one of the letters addressed to Hall after her death, the biography was to be an explicit attempt to "cheer and encourage those who come after us."[29] This book, she thought, would be a testament of lesbian life in the early twentieth century—if not quite an "It Gets Better" narrative, then at least a form of "We Were Here" historical graffiti on the wall. Since, she admits in its foreword, she is no "scribe" except for her "addiction to letter-writing," she wrote it in the form of a letter over the course of a single month.[30] The events she describes are ordered chronologically, but despite her avowal to "dwell in the palace of truth" and avoid the pitfalls of what she calls an "expurgated biography" or an "idealized biography," it is a highly subjective account of Hall's life and work.[31] And this partiality reveals a final, more implicit reason for writing it: to minimize the role of Hall's other friends and lovers (especially her last lover, Evguenia Souline) and make it impossible to separate Hall's individual legacy from her long partnership with Troubridge.

In Troubridge's long biographical letter, and in virtually every biography that has been written since then, Troubridge's claim to primacy in Hall's life is incontestable. The pair spent over thirty years together, and their mutual dedication to each other is clear. Yet Hall's relationship with Souline spanned almost the entire last decade of her life, and, as later biographers have shown, this relationship was hardly insignificant. The women even lived à trois for a short time, as Troubridge—like Sylvia Townsend Warner, as we will see later in this chapter—tried to find ways to live with her partner's desire for another woman without losing her entirely. But Troubridge and Souline detested each other, and the torturous arrangement did not last. When Hall's obsession with Souline became unbearable for Troubridge, she appealed to Hall's sense of history and responsibility to posterity. As Hall recounted in a letter to Souline, Troubridge demanded that she consider the effect that news of her affair might have on the lives of other present and future inverts:

> She has reminded me over & over again until I have nearly gone mad, that I have always stood for fidelity in the case of inverted unions, that the eyes of the inverted all over the world are turned towards me, that they look up to me, in a word, that for years now they have respected

me because my own union has been faithful and open. And when she says this I can find no answer, because she is only telling the truth—I have tried to help my poor kind by setting an example, especially of courage, and thousands have turned to me for help and found it, if I may believe their letters, and she says that I want to betray my inverts who look upon me almost as their leader.[32]

This plea worked for a short time before it ultimately failed. Hall would neither stop herself from seeing Souline nor leave her partnership with Troubridge. The situation, awful for everyone involved, continued until Hall's final illness.

Both Troubridge and Souline had long assumed that Hall's estate would be divided evenly between them in her will. In a shocking turn of events, however, Hall drafted a new will only a week before she died, and in this one, she left her entire estate—literary, material, and financial—to Troubridge:

> I devise and bequeath to her all my property and estate both real and personal absolutely trusting her to make such provision for our friend Evguenia Souline as in her absolute discretion she may consider right knowing my wishes for the welfare of the said Evguenia Souline.[33]

It is clear, in the revised will, that Hall still intends to provide for Souline—just as we will see, in chapter 3, that Gertrude Stein's will was imperfectly designed to ensure the material comfort of Alice B. Toklas. While Hall's document stops short of acknowledging the particulars of their relationship, it does emphasize Hall's desire to remain Souline's caretaker and benefactor. Yet Troubridge, who was certainly not Souline's "friend," however much Hall might have wished for this to be the case, was left in complete control of Hall's rather substantial estate. She continued to give Souline a modest allowance, supplemented with occasional gifts, throughout her life, but Souline wrote her many letters requesting a larger share of the inheritance. In one of these letters, Souline characterized herself as "struggling for life, for security in my old age," and reminded Troubridge that Hall had wanted her to be comfortable:

> John [Hall] on her death bed said plainly that she wished us both to be comfortably off if not living in luxury. You seem to disregard the fact that she in her lifetime was inordinately attached to me, and promised me more than once that I shall be well provided after her death. How often she used to say to me: "Evguenia, you can put your piggie-hands in your pig-pocket and whistle, your future is well taken care of." . . .

You know only too well that she wished me to be provided for, even in the event of my marrying. John went as far as telling me she wished my children to be provided for.... Shall I repeat what she said exactly on her deathbed? "I want you both to live happily, in friendship. You'll live if not in luxury—in comfort. But you, Evguenia, shall ask Una's advice."—to which I had promptly replied that I was a grown up woman of forty. John smiled, and patted my hand.[34]

In response, Troubridge wrote a furious letter, outlining her plans for Souline's continued allowance despite the "entirely fictitious and imaginary 'deathbed scene'" she had included in her plea.[35] In contrast to Souline's missive, however, Troubridge's letter seems to be written not only for Souline but for posterity. Conscious that others would someday read their exchange, she reminds Souline that Hall had kept a copy of the "formal letter" she had sent to Souline years earlier, that she (Troubridge) now held that copy, and that she would be keeping a copy of the current exchange, too. She assures Souline that she will "continue the same allowance" that had been guaranteed in Hall's earlier letter, but only as long as Souline has not been "disloyal to John's memory in stating that she made you promises that she did not fulfill."[36] She even adds that Souline's obligation of "loyalty" would last beyond Troubridge's own death: "I have also provided that my trustees (under the same conditions) shall continue the allowance during your lifetime, in the event of my death, but I cannot make it too clear that they will do so at their discretion and only so long as they feel sure that you gratefully respect John's memory."[37] Implicitly, but unmistakably, respecting John's memory meant respecting Troubridge's version of their relationship—a version that minimized Souline's importance to Hall. As it happened, Souline died before Troubridge, but the threat was clear: the price of continued financial assistance was respectful, uninterfering silence.

After Souline's unexpectedly early death, Troubridge finally published *The Life and Death of Radclyffe Hall*, which severely minimizes Souline's role in the last decade of Hall's life. She had already burned most of the letters that had been exchanged between Hall and Souline, just as she had burned, avowedly at Hall's request, the unfinished novel that Hall had been working on in the years before her final illness.[38] With Souline herself gone, Troubridge's narrative of Hall's life, and their long relationship together, was no longer under threat, and she could exhibit the evidence of their partnership however she liked. Troubridge's biography thus performs two important functions. First, it makes a claim for Hall's serious literary significance. Troubridge writes with absolute conviction about Hall's genius and the "beautiful prose which was later to delight so many."[39] Convinced that detailed information about Hall's methods of composition and revision would be of use to future scholars, Troubridge describes the "hours and days of urgent, fertile inspiration, alternating with days and hours of blank, arid inability to string two words together" that set the rhythm of their lives.[40] She writes in detail about Hall's production of what they called "trolley books": books that were "without salient merits and served merely as trolleys to carry her from a fallow period to one of renewed production."[41] And, ironically, given her later decision to burn so much of Hall's unpublished material after her death, she describes her frustration with Hall's propensity for destroying early drafts and her eventual decision to "train" Hall out of this destructive habit: "There came a day when after such a disaster I enacted a solemn promise that never, never again would she destroy anything until we had finally examined it together."[42]

Troubridge meticulously highlights her own irreplaceable role in Hall's creative work, and this is at the heart of her biography's second function. It delivers a narrative of Hall's life in which Troubridge's importance is unquestionable, and it binds their legacies together. Although her veneration of Hall's individual talent is clear, Troubridge's biography—even as it verges, at times, on hagiography—underscores the importance of their partnership to Hall's literary production: the hours spent reading drafts aloud, their collaborative editing process ("writing, reading, dictating, correcting, typing and retyping"),[43] her repeated enactments of the "drama" of affirmation whenever Hall was in need of encouragement, and even her "solitary talent" for titling Hall's books.[44] In this way, the biography makes a claim for both an enduring legacy and an incontestable intimacy.

The Life and Death of Radclyffe Hall is Troubridge's retrospective corrective to the unraveling of her partnership with Hall. "Being now nearly sixty," she writes in an early chapter, "most of my vision works backwards and I can visualize what seemed at the time a mere vortex of impulses and coincidence and tragedy as a pattern that in retrospect seems to have had its definite purposes."[45] With this pattern, the biography attempts to paper over the stress of the final decade of their life together, to edit Hall's last passion for Souline out of historical memory, and to restore the reputation of what she considered respectable inversion to their relationship. Troubridge's decision to truncate Souline's role in Hall's last years was thus both personal and political. In her biography of Hall, she produced a vision of an imperfect but wholly admirable artist, and she also delivered a portrait of that artist as an unshakably devoted partner.

Troubridge understood herself to be in not only narrative but archival control of Hall's legacy. As her own eventual biographer notes, she spent her last years "revising old autobiographical sketches written in the twenties and thirties, and writing new ones" to add to the "body of organized material [compiled] in either conscious or unconscious anticipation of a future biographer."[46] And although her biography of Hall had been written shortly after Hall's death, the fact that she held back its publication until after Souline (and Hall's mother, who had also contested the will) died is telling. She could not have counted on such a fortuitous timeline, so she must have intended for the biography to be part of the intimate archive of her life with Hall that would be discovered by future readers and researchers. Troubridge was much older than her rival; she had almost certainly expected that Souline would outlive her. And although the younger woman was dependent upon her for financial support, Troubridge could not have been certain that an almost complete excision of their relationship from the historical record would not have provoked both legal argument and public scandal. Indeed, she had consulted a lawyer and a publisher shortly after she had written the book in 1945, and both recommended against publication (on both literary and legal grounds).[47] After Souline's death, however, it is understandable that Troubridge would have altered her plans. In one of her posthumous letters to Hall, she admits that Souline's "death of course clears the way for publication of my book."[48] With no one left to challenge her account, and secure in the knowledge that she had burned the letters and manuscripts that would have documented Hall's devotion to Souline, Troubridge found a publisher for the biography. Once in print, her narrative was safely enshrined in literary history. But for this twist, *The Life and Death of Radclyffe Hall* might not have been published until after Troubridge's death in 1963, when it would have been discovered with her day books, letters, and Hall's unburned manuscripts and letters. In this hypothetical history, Troubridge's biography would have been an unpublished biographical act, an archival document of their intimate partnership left waiting with Troubridge's day books for eventual discovery by the "inverts" of posterity. Given that Troubridge's most frequently imagined audiences were the dead (Hall) and the as-yet-unborn (future readers), it is difficult not to think this had been her ideal plan all along.

Yet even after this unexpected publication, her careful arrangement of Hall's remaining manuscripts and letters, and her ongoing revision of their history together in the near daily "Letters to John" written after Hall's death, Troubridge's archival control was incomplete. Our inherited knowledge of Hall's intimate life was not to be fully dependent upon her, after all, for Souline had arranged a meticulous counterarchive. She had saved every single one of Hall's letters. According to several of Hall's later biographers, Souline spent the last months of her life preoccupied by the collation and organization of these letters: transcribing, typing, dating, and ordering them for future publication. She had long believed that publication during her lifetime would be impossible: she assumed Troubridge, as Hall's literary executor, controlled the copyright to the letters while she, Souline, "owned only the paper and ink."49 Yet she felt that they must be published someday, if only to contest what she accurately guessed would be Troubridge's largely libelous version of her relationship with Hall. The epistolary archive she assembled contains 576 letters, a selection of which was eventually published, in 1997, as *Your John: The Love Letters of Radclyffe Hall*. All of Hall's contemporary biographers and critics rely heavily upon this collection, and it provides a welcome counterbalance to Troubridge's construction of Hall's life and legacy. For example, in a 1935 letter sent after finishing *The Sixth Beatitude*, which would be published the following year, Hall credits Souline, not Troubridge, as the major force behind the book:

> My darling love. I have now heard my book read aloud from A. to Z. and think I can say that I am satisfied. Certain small details I have to attend to after a little more consideration, but for the rest I find the work good. Audrey Heath [Hall's agent] told Una (behind my back) that she considers this book of *yours* and *mine* to be equal to my "finest writing."50

In this letter, as in many others, Troubridge is still present in Hall's life, both explicitly (in conversation with Heath) and implicitly (as the voice who read the novel aloud to Hall), but her attempted characterization of herself as Hall's only significant relationship feels increasingly difficult to sustain in the light of the Hall-Souline correspondence.

Despite Troubridge's early commitment to the ephemerality of the intimate archive, her book was eventually published and subsumed as part of Hall's story. Her published biography and unpublished day books have both been consulted and exhibited by biographers and literary critics over the last several decades.

But it turned out to have been Souline who had produced the counterarchive that would be unearthed by future readers. The preservation of Hall's letters was, for Souline, an act of self-preservation as well. This labor, unpublished during her lifetime, could not provide her with material support or widespread recognition, but it did allow for the possibility

[32] CHAPTER ONE

FIGURE 1.1. Final entry in Una Troubridge's Day Book, 1943.

that Troubridge's attempt to erase her from history would be foiled. These letters are an intimate archive born of anxiety, desperation, and fear. The fact that their eventual publication has restored Souline's position within the narrative from which she had been so tenaciously excluded provides no comfort to the dead. But not all intimate archives are so charged with negative affect. In other circumstances, the compilation of an intimate archive might be a transformative, life-affirming act animated by a nearly irrational optimism about readers yet to come. It is to precisely this kind of intimate archival act we now turn.

Sylvia Townsend Warner's "Two Tenses"

In a letter written on April 13, 1970, three years after the publication of her biography of T. H. White and just five months after the death of Valentine Ackland, her partner for nearly forty years, Sylvia Townsend Warner told the *New Yorker* editor William Maxwell that she had "begun to write again":

> No, not a story, not a novel, and nothing for now. An archive. I found that Valentine had kept quantities of my letters, as I had kept quantities of hers. Reading through them, and putting them into sequence, I realised that it is a notable correspondence and the sort of thing

that should be put away in a tin box for posterity. So now I am entirely absorbed in writing the narrative links and explanations and so forth. I am mid-way in the prologue. It is far the best thing I have ever written—and an engrossing agony.... And you, dear William, must be the tin box, since it will count as my Literary REMAINS—absurd phrase. It can't be let out till there is a safe margin for every one to be dead in.[51]

For the next several years, Warner worked on her "archive," getting up early to put the letters in order, supply annotations, and provide the narrative connections that would make their long relationship legible to future readers. During this period, even while she spent her days reliving her early years with Ackland through their love letters, Warner began to notice that she had herself grown old. According to her biographer, Claire Harman, Warner's daily work on this archive allowed her to enter "a life parallel to her daily shadow-life, a brilliant real world in which she and Valentine existed together, where their love lived," and, as if to emphasize this duality, she even kept two separate diaries in 1970.[52] The archive project allowed her to feel closer to Ackland as she drifted, while reading the letters, from her solitary present into the various pasts in which they had been together. One afternoon, while ordering their letters from 1930, the year they had fallen in love, she confessed in a diary entry to feeling Ackland's ghostly presence with her: "Called back by starving cats, I got up in such a riot of joy I forgot the present: but KNEW, KNEW, she had been standing behind me, reading them too. *Vincit omnia.*"[53] Translation: love conquers all, perhaps even our perception of time. During this period (and, as I will show, several others), Warner felt herself to be living in "two tenses," and this allowed her to move freely between a remembered past and a forgotten present, both shared with Ackland. She worked intensely on the project, professing to Maxwell—the *New Yorker*'s fiction editor from 1936 to 1975 and one of her closest correspondents—that she was writing "without the least thought of publication, and intending only equity and accuracy."[54] But despite this disavowal of any plans to publish the letters and supplemental narrative in her lifetime, she was clearly motivated by the thought of posterity: "They can't—yet, at any rate—be published, but I am sure they should be preserved. I am confirmed in this by seeing their effect on the young woman [Susanna Pinney] who puts in a Sunday morning whenever she can, typing them."[55] As she sent installments to Maxwell, he echoed Pinney's effusive praise and Warner's own early judgment that this was her finest work: "in the supplemental narrative ... the simple summation of all the aspects to her love . . . simply exceeds, as prose, anything you have ever written. It is as if you were possessed."[56] Warner's late career is thus marked by two great experiments in biographical form. First, her biography of White, which she began "partly . . . as a dare, [since] seventy is rather an advanced age to begin an entirely different technique," was met with popular and critical acclaim.[57] And, second, the material she prepared for the "tin box" in which to store the archive of her relationship with Ackland was, according to Maxwell, the best prose of her life.

Tin boxes are hardly invulnerable: they can be damaged, lost, even left unopened. But even so, these archives are a sign of faith in—or, at least, hope for—future readership, a sign that, even if a frankly queer biography would not be published without that "safe margin for every one to be dead in," the construction of an intimate archive—an archive that would only later become legible—is possible. Given that the temporal gap between Warner's compilation of this intimate archive and Pinney's partial publication of it stretched approximately thirty years—the typical length of a generation—this archival work demonstrates a queer politics of affiliation and (re)production.[58] What Elizabeth Freeman has referred to as the "bind" between the queer present and future is, for Warner, a double bind: she is bound to successors who, like her young friend (and eventual editor) Pinney, are so moved by these relics of the past that they insist upon their eventual publication, and they are simultaneously bound to their predecessors, the silent and vulnerable subjects of such biographical acts who, no longer living, cannot grant what G. Thomas Couser calls "meaningful consent to their representation by others."[59]

In what remains of this chapter, I show that the biographical archiving process that characterizes Warner's work on these two projects was the dominant compositional methodology of her late period.[60] From the mid-1960s until her death in 1978, Warner's writing changed, both stylistically and generically, and these changes in her aesthetic life are inseparable from the changes in her ordinary, bodily, everyday life. Building on theorizations of lateness by Edward Said, Jane Gallop, and others, I suggest that, in late work, we can see this tension, this calm competition, between writerly life and bodily life.[61] For Warner, for example, her own aging process, when coupled with the long illness and eventual diagnosis of breast cancer in her younger partner, Valentine Ackland, deeply influenced the trajectory of her late passion projects. In this way, the theoretical terrain of artistic and intellectual lateness has a necessary connection to the banalities of physical life: the decline of the body, the approach of death, the sudden realization or slowly increasing sense of mortality. Once we begin to think about a late period, there is no way around the body—and therefore no getting around the life story, either—but the body is not all. The sense we make of late work is not reducible to the time of its composition, but it cannot be explained without it.

Like Said's "late style," Warner's lateness is spurred by the revelation of being out of sync with the present moment. In his writing about lateness, Said assumes that it is connected to something like genius—his examples are all unimpeachably brilliant writers and composers—and he suggests that, for the great among us, "near the end of their lives their work and thought acquires a new idiom, . . . a late style."[62] By contrast, I write about the late period of Sylvia Townsend Warner as a means of exploring a more ordinary sort of lateness: a period of time at the end of life when, for any number of reasons, one trips the wire of mortality, becomes conscious of the slow approach of death, and every intellectual and artistic effort becomes infused with the sense of an ending. This lateness is common, ordinary, and available to those who may well be forgotten, rather than immortalized, by historical narratives. In an extraordinary essay titled "Virginia Woolf in Her Fifties," Carolyn G. Heilbrun described Woolf's literary "transformation," at fifty, as "uniquely female": "To allow oneself at fifty the expression of one's feminism ('the awful daring of a moment's surrender') is an experience for which there is no male counterpart, at least not for white men in the Western world."[63] In contrast to earlier years, the late periods of women writers—and perhaps especially queer women writers—include precisely this "emphatic statement of their sense of self."[64] For Warner, memory was not guaranteed, but she worked to ensure that her present archive would become the future biography of her relationship with Ackland. Shifting Said's exploration of "the relationship between bodily condition and aesthetic style," I suggest that the symptom of Warner's lateness moves from *style* to *genre*. For her, lateness is distinguished, at least in part, by a marked investment in biographical writing.

Although this chapter examines only Warner's late biographical acts, she wrote prolifically throughout her life: all in all, she published five books of poetry, seven novels, and nine collections of short stories (in addition to the short stories she contributed to the *New Yorker* for over forty years), and much of her unpublished fiction has appeared posthumously. And although some of this work was recovered in the 1970s for its feminist and lesbian themes—*Mr. Fortune's Maggot* (1927) and *The True Heart* (1929) remain high on the list of "modern classics" from Virago Press, which explicitly publishes only books by women—Warner is rarely included in discussions (or on syllabi) of British modernism. In recent years, the reprinting of several of her novels in the NYRB Classics series, as well as the publication of new scholarship about her work, has lifted Warner's early fiction into the spotlight, but the biographical writing of her late period has remained in the shadows.[65]

By biographical writing, I mean more than simply published volumes of biography. Warner's only official biography, *T. H. White*, was published in 1967, but she and Ackland were consumed by their end-of-life preparations throughout the decade. For years, they kept themselves busy remaking wills, appointing literary executors, leaving instructions for themselves and others about how to order their posthumous lives and works, ordering correspondence, compiling personal archives, and, in general, preparing ways in which to leave a mark on the world once departed from it. It is tempting to understand these gloomy activities as little more than the remaining tasks of an aging writer (Warner) who, having fallen victim to a selfish seductress (Ackland), had entered into a kind of Faustian bargain— youthful literary potential given freely in exchange for an old age of complacent happiness, complete with vegetable garden and cats. But rather than caricature and dismiss Warner's last years, I contend that these late activities should be read as modes of life writing. In the years of her late period, Warner stopped writing novels and started compiling lives. Her last biographies may have been unwritten, but they were meticulously researched, assembled, and left waiting for a later generation of readers and scholars. For Warner, the archive was not the closet.

T. H. White *and the Idea of Queer Futurity*

While researching her biography of the infamously tortured T. H. White, Warner began to develop a kind of archival consciousness that resembles what Ann Cvetkovich has called an "archival mode of witness":

> To become a "witness" (either literally or more indirectly) to anyone's sexuality is a difficult documentary task, given its frequent privacy or intimacy, and this general secrecy can be further heightened when that sexuality is constructed as immoral or criminal or perverse.[66]

In her analysis of Alison Bechdel's *Fun Home*, Cvetkovich suggests that this archival mode results from Bechdel's inability to learn all of the details of her father's sexuality, and I extend and elaborate this claim in the context of Warner's "witnessing" of White. Even once she was granted access to the remnants of White's scattered archive, Warner did not know what—or, more importantly, *when*—to publish about his sexuality. She became an "avid observer and collector of evidence,"[67] but she had tremendous difficulty constructing a publishable narrative of White's life. During her years of research, she described herself as "living in two tenses," just as, several years earlier, she had experienced the sense of living "in a queer duality" while working on her translation of Proust.[68] The multiple tenses at work in Warner's archival period include what Freeman has called the "queer future tense," in which she imagined her eventual audience, as well as the present tense of her own working life and the past tense in which she sorted through the life of her subject.[69] This is an intimate temporality at work: she is simultaneously alive in her own rapidly aging bodily present and anachronistically embedded in a very particular other moment, whether that moment is part of White's past, the biography's projected future, or her own past relationship with Ackland. In her late period, Warner's "two tenses" mark the belief in a queer posterity—a potential future in which the "disturbing and unassimilable inheritances"[70] of the present have a home—as an organizing force behind her archival and biographical work.

Back in the early 1960s, before she began work on the White biography, Warner was still very sharp and spry, but she had begun to feel her age. All around her, friends and family members had begun to grow old and die, Ackland (with whom she was only recently reunited after a long period of difficulty in their relationship) was not well, and a series of literary rejections had made her doubt her ability and begin to wonder whether "it is only as a cliché they like [her]."[71] During this period, when, according to Harman, "Sylvia wasn't writing well, and knew it," she stoically began to prepare for the end of both creative and physical life.[72] In a 1962 letter to Maxwell, Warner asked him to become her literary executor, reassuring him that his services would be minimal and would not be needed for quite some time:

> I was saying there was no one my ghost would feel easy with, and why not burn the lot, and Valentine said, why don't you ask William Maxwell? And instantly, of course, I saw it was the perfect repose for my ghost and just what I should like. . . . What I would like would be a caretaker for my written remains, and for my diaries. . . . But I don't want to be a Bore or a Burden. Above all, I don't want to be an obligation. Yet if you should incline to it, I would feel very happy. And I would do some preliminary sorting, and make it as easy as I could. By the way, I am not intending to die. It was the mortality of others that made me recast my will.[73]

Though he protested this morose turn in her thinking, Maxwell immediately agreed. At the time, Warner was in comparatively excellent health, and much more concerned about the chronic illness of Ackland than about her own aging body, but she had already begun to worry about self-presentation beyond death. Faced with the "mortality of others," she was forced to consider how best to select the "caretaker" of her own archive, how to assure the preservation of her "literary remains."

Shortly afterward, while at work on several short stories, she was offered the challenge of organizing an entirely separate archive. Early in 1964, Warner was asked to write the biography of T. H. White, a fellow novelist with whom she had corresponded several times. The two had never met, but they greatly admired each other's work, and, after White died on January 17, 1964, Warner described him in a diary entry as "a friend I never managed to have."[74] In stark contrast to Warner's own recent activity, White had not named a literary executor and had merely designated the Alderney Bank as the executors of his estate. When confronted with the enormity of White's literary archive, the bank was naturally rather perplexed, wanted nothing to do with it, and requested that White's agent make all necessary arrangements. Eventually, despite the efforts of said agent to secure the position of biographer for a personal friend, the pro-Warner camp (led by White's friend David Garnett and Michael Howard, of the publishers Jonathan Cape) prevailed, and Warner was agreed upon as a suitable—and particularly sympathetic—candidate for the task. When Howard invited her to begin work on White's biography, Warner tentatively agreed, but the legal difficulties presented by the lack of literary executor stalled the project for several months. Finally, after she had been approved as biographer by all parties, she decided to visit his house before making a final decision to take on the project. In a diary entry from June 5, 1964, Warner described her visit to the "bookroom" at the top of White's "tall house, half-gutted": "I felt it intensely haunted, his angry, suspicious furtive stare directed at my back, gone when I turned round."[75] By the end of her visit, after talking to many of White's friends and neighbors, and spending long stretches alone in White's library with his books and his ghost, she decided to dedicate herself to the biography. From the first instant, she knew that she would wrestle with censors both internal and external: "I shall be in the infuriating quandary of knowing essential elements in the story which it will be impossible to state."[76]

In the three years she spent working on the White biography, Warner struggled to determine what she could—or should—publish about White's various "vices."[77] While researching and drafting each section, she detailed the series of ethical dilemmas presented by the "essential elements" of

White's life story in letters to William Maxwell and David Garnett. In addition to the affinity for fantasy she shared with White, Warner had been chosen as his biographer in part because White's closest friends trusted her, as an openly lesbian writer, to tell his tale generously, openly, and without judgment. In a letter to Garnett shortly after she began work on the project, Warner described the biography's murky position between truthfulness and honesty:

> So far, I only know what I want to do. I won't cheat; and have a beginning idea of what I can't do, which is a bottomless pit. It is a sad revelation . . . that after all the years intelligent people like ourselves have been illuminating English society it is still totally impossible to be honest.[78]

For Warner felt that she could not be entirely honest about White's homosexuality, sadism, pedophilia, and otherwise tortured desires while his partners, friends, and former students were still alive.[79] She was torn: to describe White's personal life in brilliant detail could tarnish his literary reputation and bring libel suits upon both author and publisher; to hide White's predilections from society would betray Warner's burgeoning sense of responsibility to relay the story of White's queer past to a more generous future readership.

Warner hated the idea of altering the biography to spare the feelings of those still living, but she was also reluctant to publish a biography that would allow White's sometimes shocking personal life to eternally dominate discussion of his creative work. For years, she remained "torn in the mind" about several omissions, and in a discussion of White's "flagellatory fantasies" in a letter to Garnett, she demonstrated the relationship between her editorial reticence and her conception of audience:

> The straight ones are childishly prosaic; but there is a Rodiad in augustan couplets which is in his best pastiche hand and full of technical high-spirits. I know in my heart that some should be quoted, if only to confute the moralists who feel that all such pleasures should be taken sadly, must be taken sadly. Yet I don't want the book to be read for a page of scandality since that might make more nourishment for moralists. Oh dear, one writes hoping for a sensible public; and gets on the one hand sympathetic sobbers and on the other hand superior persons with nostrums in their bonnets.[80]

Warner's sense of these "moralists" and "superior persons with nostrums in their bonnets" influenced her work at every step. She felt alternately frustrated by and compassionate toward White's angry ghost, but she knew that

White's story—however besmirched—must be preserved for posterity, for a public that might one day become more "sensible" about sexual matters.

Several passages in the Warner-Garnett correspondence, in particular, reveal their developing reflections about a kind of biographical futurity. Garnett urged her to tell the truth about White as she was drafting the biography:

> Well what I really want to say is that you must write your book without thinking about anyone's feelings. Then when you have completed your masterpiece, you can bowdlerise the 1966 edition, knowing that the whole thing will appear in 1996 and that there will be long reviews saying that you were not only a poet, not only a master of the short story, but the most brilliant & perceptive biographer of the era after the 2nd War & before the final one. Please do this. It is really the only sensible & practical way of dealing with him.[81]

Garnett indicates the possibility of the biography's dual temporalities: first, it would be published in a passable though "bowdlerised" version in 1966; second, it would be republished—in its full, encyclopedic, almost archival glory—to great acclaim in its entirety thirty years later. In this way, the biography could exist in "two tenses," and Warner could avoid both the "sympathetic sobbers" and the "moralists" of the present while still satisfying the "sensible public" of an idealized future.

For her part, Warner preferred to write in a kind of barely disguised code, working with what she called "cunning & dexterity"[82] to fit things into the biography without rousing the ire of the "moralists," but she recognized the limitations of this method. For example, in a letter to Garnett on October 23, 1967, Warner attacked the carefully calibrated first volume of Michael Holroyd's biography of the Bloomsbury writer and irreverent biographer Lytton Strachey: "It is a drudging performance. He has included everything he could & should, and some of the ingredients are marvellous. And it is like a plum-pudding with the brandy forgotten."[83] For Warner, Holroyd's work was perfectly passable, but it lacked the spark of courage. Still, she herself often had trouble bringing the brandy out from the cupboard. While responding to a play involving incest that Garnett had written and sent to her for feedback, she again demonstrated her reluctance to either completely show or entirely withhold the details of private life. On the question of the representation of incest, she described herself as "in two minds":

> I think people should have some elements of private life they keep dark, and that incest could well be one of them. But I also think it a very bad

plan that law, morality & all the rest of it should compel them to keep it dark. And I don't see how this can be amended till the world has grown better manners. Perhaps your parents, your parents poor Tim envied you so much, never said to you: "Don't point." Perhaps you never did point. But it is sound advice and should be given more often and to all ages. In a society which didn't point, the truth about a case of incest would not be all that upsetting and presently not upsetting at all.[84]

Since the world had not yet "grown better manners," Warner's biography detailed a carefully selected version of White's life. She kept some elements of his private life dark while revealing others, and the biography received both critical and popular praise when it was published in 1967. Although she did not follow Garnett's suggestion to write a "masterpiece" and then cut it for publication, she did save her research notes, correspondence, and drafts for future researchers. However frustrating, her work on White's biography led her to develop faith in a queer future in which carefully encoded and meticulously preserved elements of the past could be received without fear of "pointing"—or worse.

The Tin Box: Intimacy, Memory, and the Archive

Although she published only this single biography, Warner's work was characterized by what I have called an archival consciousness long after the publication of *T. H. White*. While writing this biography, she had described herself as "living in two tenses, and very agreeably,"[85] and later, while facing the onset of old age and the increasingly poor health of Valentine Ackland, these "two tenses" shifted as Warner's concentration moved from White to Ackland. Throughout the second half of the decade, Warner and Ackland became intensely focused on the preservation of each other's life stories.

In addition to the epistolary archive Warner collated and annotated after Ackland's death, Ackland herself became increasingly dedicated to preparing versions of their lives for posterity. She had already written a kind of autobiographical lament, *For Sylvia: An Honest Account*, which she gave to Warner on July 4, 1949. This document remained unpublished—a private text written by one partner for the other—until 1985. In the letter introducing the text, she states that she has written this "record of blundering from shame to shame" for Warner, and she signs her name as "Valentine—who loves you."[86] Yet despite its title and explicit dedication to Warner, this memoir of Ackland's life from childhood through her years with Warner reads as though written for broader publication. After the dedication, Ackland begins to address a less personal audience, and her tone becomes more distant as she refers to "the reader," "the author," and "the subject of this book" rather than to the corresponding roles in her intimate relationship with Warner. In the opening paragraphs, she theorizes the "necessary" and "desirable" elements of "an honest account of a life": "first, anonymity, so that the author may be honest, if he can; . . . [second,] that the 'crisis' of the life shall be presented as quickly as possible, before the reader's boredom has set in," and third, "variety, and that is really a matter of presentation on the author's part and perception on the reader's."[87] If Ackland really intended this to be for Warner alone, then the first necessity—anonymity—would have been impossible from the start, and any fear that she might have lost her audience for lack of interest in the material would have been unfounded. Instead, Ackland is writing for posterity, and her memoir delivers an explanation for her life as a functional alcoholic in tandem with an account of her lesbian relationships before—and since—Warner.

Years later, perhaps seeking similar revelations from her partner, Ackland filled several notebooks with detailed notes on Warner's own childhood and youth, despite Warner's later protestations that she would never write an autobiography because she was "too imaginative."[88] And eventually, nearing the end and fearing that she would not return from a hospital visit, Ackland left a long audio recording of her final goodbye to Warner, including detailed instructions for the dispersal and disposal of her personal items.[89] In the last years of their nearly four decades together, Warner and Ackland began to self-consciously produce an archive of their relationship. But unlike Una Troubridge's systematic consolidation of the story of her life with Radclyffe Hall, Warner did not excise Ackland's long affair with Elizabeth Wade White. Instead, this archive included everything. And this archive hurt.

In this "archive of feelings," to borrow Cvetkovich's term for the "both material and immaterial" collection of "objects that might not ordinarily be considered archival," objects that often resist "documentation because sex and feelings are too personal or ephemeral to leave records," Warner placed her faith in a more generous future readership.[90] Her imagination of this readership stands in contrast to Carolyn Steedman's understanding of the historian as the "reader impossible-to-be-imagined" who reads "what is *not there*"—a vision of the historian that has been absolutely essential for the recovery of feminist and queer pasts.[91] Instead, Warner's future audience, as readers possible-to-be-imagined, would be asked to grapple with the additional task of paying careful attention to what *is there*—and to what is spoken, rather than silenced, across generations.

In this way, I read Warner's intimate archive as a deliberate biographical act. In the face of the more than 400,000 words in this collection of letters, its corresponding annotations, and Warner's detailed narrative explanations, her contemporary readers are forced to recognize the unflagging sense of purpose and dedication required to preserve this life history. Warner often admitted feeling this kind of transtemporal duty while at work on other projects. For example, while working on the White biography, Warner had urged David Garnett to preserve the White-Garnett correspondence for posterity, quipping that she "dislike[d] that damned posterity, I shan't be there; but still I feel my duty towards it."[92] She felt that their letters contained a rare quality of intellectual magnanimity, and she gave Garnett tongue-in-cheek instructions for the "two ways" to preserve them: "One is the Box in the B.M. with directions that seven Regius professors must be present at its opening. The other is to publish it. There is something to be said for either."[93] Years later, when faced with this choice in her own life, Warner opted for a version of the first option. After compiling the archive of love letters and hiring Pinney to type them, she sent the top copy to the Berg Collection at the New York Public Library, stored the originals with friends, and kept the second copy with her in her home.[94] Rather than making the eventual opening of this archive into a stuffy scholarly event, however, Warner—in the month before she died on May 1, 1978—asked Pinney to "remove the letters and keep them with [her] until they could be published."[95] Even before Pinney was able to publish any of them, several scholars managed to consult Warner's archive for their biographical projects, including Claire Harman's *Sylvia Townsend Warner: A Biography* (1989) and Wendy Mulford's *This Narrow Place: Sylvia Townsend Warner and Valentine Ackland: Life, Letters and Politics, 1930–1951* (1988). Eventually, in 1998, Pinney edited and published approximately a third of the letters (the collection was far too large to be published in its entirety), along with Warner's connecting narratives and explanatory notes, as *I'll Stand by You: The Letters of Sylvia Townsend Warner and Valentine Ackland*.

Warner's intimate archive, and its eventual partial publication in Pinney's volume, demonstrates the world-making power of epistolary form. In *Epistolarity: Approaches to a Form*, Janet Altman describes the "desire for exchange" as the basic tenet of correspondence, arguing that letter writers enter into an "epistolary pact": "the call for response from a specific reader within the correspondent's world."[96] Written for a particular audience, the letter is always a semiprivate genre. The love letters between Warner and Ackland were privately written and received, but, as published writers, both women may have had the sense that their "epistolary pact" was with posterity as well as with each other. In Warner's archive, the temporal divide present in the initial composition and reception of the letters—that is, the separation of the time of writing from the time of reading—expands into the necessary duality of archival time. The letters, deposited in one era, are then available to be interpreted (and, sometimes, appropriated) by subsequent generations.

The letters stand as a testament to the enduring love between these two women, but they also model a queer politics that would become particularly relevant at the time of their eventual publication in the midst of public debates about marriage rights and queer partnership. Warner and Ackland freely refer to their "marriage" and their "wedded love"; they refer to each other as "wives," "lesbians," and, with increasing intensity over the years, as each other's greatest "Love."[97] Since the publication of the biographies and the edited collection of the Warner-Ackland letters, their relationship has been held up as a model of an idyllic union. As trumpeted on the back cover of Pinney's collection, *I'll Stand by You* is often considered "the most detailed personal account of a lesbian relationship this century." This is an important historical claim, but I contend that the significance of the collection is in the intimacy of the "personal account" rather than in the representation of the "lesbian relationship." The letters and their annotations do much more than deliver a compelling portrait of an early twentieth-century lesbian partnership for the benefit of a late twentieth-century political movement. They are complicated; they are full of emotions both beautiful and ugly. As Warner had once written to Ackland, "the miseries of people who love each other twang in my heart. I can never feel the same sense of compassion for those who don't. My compassion . . . is all mixed with rage, and mitigated by the distraction of raging."[98] In her archive, Warner was committed to making archival space for both rage and compassion, and the exemplary nature of Warner and Ackland's collated story lies in their patient exploration of alternative modes of living—their willingness to attempt life outside of what Lauren Berlant has called the "one plot" of partnered, romantic love.[99]

In addition to its open depictions of lesbian sexuality, the largely epistolary archive contains extended representations of female desire that question the social and historical dominance of the couple form.[100] While composing the explanatory narratives that supplement her collection of letters, Warner forced herself to relive the pain of Ackland's most serious affairs and grave offenses, including the long affair with Elizabeth Wade White that nearly wrenched the pair apart for good. In a letter to Maxwell, she described some of the letters written during that period as "so sad and my memory of the last years so raw that I had to take myself off.... I am perfectly well, but made of damp sawdust. If I were in an hour-glass, *I would stick*."[101] The archive, with its insistent temporal orbit, threatened to draw her permanently away from her life in the present, and several of the narrative annotations were painfully difficult to complete. Yet unlike Una Troubridge, who had nearly erased Radclyffe Hall's other great love, Evguenia Souline, from their story, Warner allowed her rivals to claim archival space.

"Narrative 8," for example, which details the torturous beginning of Ackland's long affair with White and the difficult time the three spent living together in the same house, describes the near impossibility of this (auto)biographical work. Even after the passage of many years, Warner could not "trust [herself] to write a true account of the twelvemonth that followed.... What I remember is so infected by what I felt that it comes back with the obsessive reality/unreality of delirium."[102] According to Pinney, Warner was "proud of [her relationship with Ackland] and wanted it known, though not while she was alive; she would have found it painful."[103] The space of this largely epistolary archive—and its potential publication in some distant future—let Warner relax into a kind of pre-writing: she could be much more explicit about the vicissitudes of her relationship when she understood herself to be setting up the real story for a generous future biographer who would someday fulfill, for her, a version of her own position as the sympathetic biographer of T. H. White. Instead of presenting a coherent historical judgment, her archive deliberately proffers only fragments of the lives of Sylvia Townsend Warner, Valentine Ackland, and Elizabeth Wade White. Rather than write the full story herself, Warner implicitly asks that the letters (written before, during, and after this period) that she has collected and arranged in this intimate archive be allowed to stand as sufficient evidence of the strained, though ultimately devoted, flexibility of their relationship.

In her last years—as she "stayed on alone," in Alice B. Toklas's phrase for life after the death of Gertrude Stein[104]—Warner's solitude continued to cause her pain. If "aloneness," according to Berlant, "is one of the affective experiences of being collectively, structurally unprivileged,"[105] then the act of collating an intimate archive—of collecting, ordering, and annotating a private past for future, public readers—is surely one of the signs of feeling alone, out of sync with both private bonds and public vocabularies. The intimate archivist mourns the past, feels unpublishably alone in the present, and develops an anachronistic bond with the imagined readers, scholars, and subjects of the future. For Warner, the process of compiling this intimate archive was the only immediately possible form of life writing.

I have suggested that we can understand archiving—and the necessarily anachronistic modes of thinking that attend it—as a distinct compositional process of Warner's late period. The construction of the intimate archive is the symptom of this lateness. The "not yet" implicit in the figure of the "tin box" she asked Maxwell to become in order to guard her "literary remains" *is* the temporality of the archive. With reference to José Esteban Muñoz's helpful theorizations of queer futurity, we see that Warner's archive demonstrates her insistence upon "think[ing] and feel[ing] a *then and there*" rather than remaining stuck in the "here and now" of the present.[106] The simultaneity of the "here and now" and the "then and there" recalls Warner's own description of herself as "living in two tenses," and, as I suggested earlier, the "two tenses" that governed her life could slide and shift in ways that did not always privilege the present. After taking on the project of memorializing her most significant relationship, Warner did not send a manuscript out for immediate publication; instead, she prepared the "tin box" for posterity, the intimate archive of the queer biography that, in this case, could not yet be written.

What I am calling the intimate archive is a liminal space, a persistently semiprivate sphere that always maintains the potential—possibly even the desire—to become fully public.[107] Inasmuch as intimacy rests upon the personal, private, and inward-facing relationships between people, these archives remain coded in private, often closeted languages. Yet the act of archiving betrays an effort to translate these vocabularies, to move them outward and forward, in order to provide the possibility of future recognition and communication. The archive is a gesture toward a community to come. It signals hope for a future readership that is related to what Berlant calls an "intimate public": "a porous, affective scene of identification among strangers that promises a certain experience of belonging and provides a complex of consolation, confirmation, discipline, and discussion about how to live as an x."[108] The intimate archive, like the intimate public, provides a space for affirmation, identification, collaboration, and pedagogy across temporal boundaries. Once collected in the archive, the past becomes something that circulates between audiences, something that can be reappropriated and retrofitted to satisfy the sociopolitical demands of future readers. I read Warner's intimate archive as a stalled attempt to hail and promote these transhistorical spheres of "identification among strangers" that confirm the possibility of living "as an x"—that is, as queer women writers and intellectuals.

Archival Scenes: Intimacy across Generations

Warner's intimate archive is a biographical act that demonstrates her attention to the mechanisms by which intimacy is preserved and reproduced over time. This archive shows us that Warner is concerned with both the transmission of queer life stories and the reproduction of intimate scholarly acts across generations. In other words, I read Warner as the curator of our contemporary archival experience in addition to the physical archive itself. To recenter Warner in this way is not to overshadow the important work done by the many librarians and archivists (both volunteers and professionals) responsible for processing, cataloguing, and caring for the materials in the Sylvia Townsend Warner Archive once they were transferred to the Dorset County Museum; rather, it is to ask scholars to be more receptive to the many varieties of labor by which their archival "discoveries" have been prepared for them in advance.

Several years before she began work on the intimate archive of her relationship with Ackland, Warner had written an article—"The American Museum"—in which she reflected on the affective experience of her visit to a newly opened museum in Bath, England.[109] This museum was a curious collection of staged domesticity designed to allow visitors to study "the development of an American lifestyle," but it provoked much more than a reflection on Americana in Warner.[110] She began to consider the work of the curator, and the enormous influence of that individual's (or committee's) unseen editorial hand on her own experience. Reflecting on this difficult curatorial position later, she emphatically praised the "steely selectivity" and necessary "ruthlessness" of the curator(s).[111] In closing, I want to suggest that, like her formative work on White's biography, Warner's almost visceral experience of this domestic archive, as preserved and presented by the museum's curator(s), influenced her later assemblage of the intimate archive of her life with Ackland.

Narrating her inquisitive exploration of the museum, Warner marveled at the curation of not only historical objects but present experience: as the visitor for whom the museum was designed, she had "much more that feeling of walking about in a house than walking past showcases."[112] It didn't feel like a museum, and that seemed intentional. She felt as though she was in someone's home, strolling around and gazing at someone's personal things. This sense of domestic comfort may have been especially surprising because of the building's imposing exterior. If it "had been a Member of Parliament," she jokes, it would "undoubtedly have been painted with one hand thrust into its waistcoat and the other holding a scroll."[113] Once inside, however, the authoritative masculine facade of Bath stone gave way to a succession of more intimate American interiors. Warner felt that the collection resisted the "unassimilable quality of an exhibit,"[114] which is especially curious given the strange temporal organization of the house. First, when crossing its threshold, visitors moved from the very British exterior to a softer, feminized American interior; then, moving through the house, visitors underwent the equally dislocating experience of curated immersion in a new era—something akin to time travel within the walls of the museum. Each room represented the style of a particular American moment, and, "before coming to the next room, one turns the corner of a century."[115] In these interiors, in which women's history was silently preserved, she read fragmented gestures delivered from one generation to another.

Warner's interest in the museum peaked with the Folk Art Gallery, in which she was surprised to find "a folk art that had not stiffened into tradition, but was pragmatic, matched itself to daily life and hailed the known with a cheer."[116] She empathized with the creative ambitions of these largely forgotten artists of the everyday: "Colour and design and ornament can supply a mental stockade against the monotony of such settled lives. So you carved a weathervane, or pieced a quilt, or painted a battle-scene on your barn. You did something that would surpass you, or outlast you."[117] She was compelled by the domestic, the ordinary, "the known," and in the movements taken, in these frequently gendered spaces, away from monotony and toward memory. Buoyed by objects crafted to "surpass" and "outlast," she was intensely moved by the life stories crystallized in these archival exhibits.

Warner's writing about the museum is thus thematically consonant with this chapter's overarching concerns about the preservation of self, intimacy, and the lives of others. Her review of the museum demonstrates her growing interest in the curation of future experience alongside the preservation of current texts and objects. What might it mean to imagine a specifically social future, a version of the future in which viewers or readers are not just politely interested parties but kindred spirits who help to bring it into being? And what might it look like to curate an archive with an eye toward future recovery projects, even while acknowledging the very real possibility that this future might not come to pass?

By describing this as the curation of future experience, I suggest that Warner, even more so than Troubridge or Souline, explicitly and intentionally shaped our eventual experience of her intimate archive. She was concerned not only with the textual objects themselves but with their transmissibility and legibility across generations. Earlier in this chapter,

I read Warner's work on the largely epistolary archive she spent years collecting and annotating as a form of biographical drafting in which she understood herself to be preparing the way for a future biographer who would, one day, inherit, write, and publish the story of her relationship with Ackland. Just as she had become the empathetic biographer of T. H. White, someone would—as soon as there was a "safe margin for every one to be dead in"—pick up her trail of archival breadcrumbs and finish writing their story. Until then, and even afterward, her relationship with Ackland would live in the archive itself. Warner's faith in this future has been rewarded, and much of her archive has been preserved and published. Yet this almost utopian ending nearly didn't happen at all. According to a story told to Dr. Morine Krissdottir (the former curator of the Sylvia Townsend Warner Archive) by Roger Peers (a friend of Warner's and a former director of the Dorset County Museum), the material that is now stored in the archive arrived at the museum in several garbage bags, and because the museum is systemically understaffed, it was slowly processed by well-meaning but largely untrained volunteers over the course of several years.[118]

In the meticulously planned (though largely unpreserved) organization of her archive and its deliberate placement in the Dorset County Museum, Warner took control of the conditions of her own inheritance. She set us up to develop the same kind of archival consciousness that she herself inhabited while working on the White biography. Even the "tin box" that she asked Maxwell and Pinney to become in order to safeguard the story of her life with Ackland was drawn directly from her previous experience. Describing the difficulty of obtaining access to White's diaries, she notes that "the diaries, in a solid yellow tin trunk, . . . are deposited in the Dorchester Museum: and every other day or so I am let in to the Hardy room, where they repose, [to] unlock the trunk, and take relays of them to the library" to read.[119] This is a description of the particular intimacy between the researcher and her primary sources; it is also a description of the arrangement that has structured all research into Warner and Ackland's relationship since her death. Not only did Warner, unwilling to leave the future history of her relationship with Ackland to chance, ask Maxwell and Pinney to become the "tin boxes" in which their story would be kept safe, but she also left instructions that the archive be deposited into the same museum where she read White's diaries. One tin box joins another. Her research experience has become our research experience. Whether or not we find it as "agreeable" as she did, we, too, find ourselves living in Warner's two tenses.

CHAPTER TWO

Abandoned Lives

IMPOSSIBLE PROJECTS AND ARCHIVAL REMAINS

IF THE INTIMATE ARCHIVES examined in the last chapter ultimately deliver a kind of transgenerational happy ending in which we, as feminist and queer scholars, reap the benefits of other writers' careful archival preparations, this chapter attends to another possible ending: the biographical act that becomes an intimate archive accidentally rather than deliberately. In this way, I make space for the historical trauma accompanying so many archival remains. Acknowledging the opacity, messiness, and incoherence of such trauma continues to be a necessary project within queer archival studies. What if the incomplete narratives, hesitantly annotated documents, and textual fragments that comprise an intimate archive are symptoms of failure rather than careful composition and preservation? What if we future readers are not the hoped-for audience but the desperate last ballast against irreparable loss?

This chapter attends to two of these archival failures. Djuna Barnes and Hope Mirrlees were both talented writers who were well known among modernist literati in the 1920s: Barnes's *Nightwood* is now considered a modernist masterpiece, and while Mirrlees is now much less lauded than Barnes, critics have recently read her long poem "Paris" as prefiguring T. S. Eliot's "The Waste Land." In the 1930s, however, both women undertook intimate biographies—of the Baroness Elsa von Freytag-Loringhoven and Jane Ellen Harrison, respectively—that they never finished. At their deaths, both Barnes and Mirrlees left behind substantial collections of biographical material, but unlike the intimate archive left by Sylvia Townsend Warner, these archives have a different, far less hopeful relationship to queer futurity. They do not hail us; their authors and curators have not prepared the way for future biographers and scholars. In contrast to the optimism of Warner's archival ethic, in which she almost seems to wink at imagined future scholars, the archives in this chapter do not expect an audience. They are inscribed with anxieties about loss; they both fear and demand a kind of illegibility. Sometimes, preparing certain lives and relationships for publication, whether that publication is understood to be immediate or eventual, seems impossible. The process of making intimacy legible can be too taxing, or too traumatizing, to finish. Yet in the spirit of what Jack Halberstam calls "the queer art of failure," I want to suggest that these incomplete, unsuccessful biographical acts demonstrate a complex engagement with the overlapping temporalities of shared lives, histories, and audiences.[1] Halberstam suggests that, sometimes, failure is a necessary part of queer life in a heteronormative, patriarchal society: "under certain circumstances failing, losing, forgetting, unmaking, undoing, unbecoming, not knowing may in fact offer more creative, more cooperative, more surprising ways of being in the world."[2] In their present unfinished, forgotten state, these archival lives might still represent ways of writing the history of modernist literature that are more creative, more cooperative, more surprising than those that have otherwise structured the field. Their "failure" makes them all the more meaningful, even if that meaning is not, ultimately, redemptive.

In this way, the incompleteness of these biographical acts suggests a kind of melancholia. In "Mourning and Melancholia," Sigmund Freud describes two possible reactions to the loss of a loved one: the normative response of mourning and the pathological response of melancholia. Mourning ends when the subject severs affective attachment to the lost love object and reinvests the libido in a new object. In stark contrast, melancholia does not end. The melancholic recognizes—and feels—that he or she has experienced a loss but cannot understand or admit the nature of that loss. After the loss of the love object, the melancholic's free libido is not displaced onto a new object; instead, it withdraws into the ego itself: "There, however, it [is] not employed in any unspecified way, but serve[s] to establish an *identification* of the ego with the abandoned object."[3] This is why Freud associates melancholia with narcissistic tendencies. In the world of the indefinitely in-progress biographical act, the writer and her subject are one. Their intimacy is unbroken and unchallenged. The inability to fully, adequately, and publicly mourn the loss of an intimate friendship can thus lead, as we will see in this chapter, to an intense investment in a biographical act that can never be finished. I want to stop short of a reading that delivers a psychoanalytic diagnosis of Barnes and Mirrlees;

rather, I suggest that melancholia provides us with a compelling theoretical structure for understanding the biographical failures of their respective late periods.

If the archival ethic of Warner is a demonstration of what Michael Snediker has called "queer optimism," an ultimately positive affect that is not merely descriptive of Warner's future-focused methodology but present in the content of her prose, then the unfinished projects of Barnes and Mirrlees evince a pessimism about age, sexuality, and intimacy that is equally legitimate.[4] Characterized by silences and omissions rather than testimonies and confessions, these biographical archives—abandoned rather than completed—trouble an easy understanding of biographical experimentation as queer feminist activism.

Djuna Barnes and the "Disquiet Spirit" of the Baroness

The Baroness Elsa von Freytag-Loringhoven, a Dadaist poet and provocateur, died in 1927. She was fifty-three years old, alone in her Paris apartment during an exceptionally cold winter, and the jets on her old gas stove had been left on overnight. There was no note. No one knew for certain whether this was suicide or negligence, and there were even rumors that a departing lover had turned on the gas and then left. In an obituary published a few months later in *transition*, Djuna Barnes, her friend and literary executor, described it as "a stupid joke that had not even the decency of maliciousness."[5] It was a bewilderingly quiet last act from a woman described by her most recent and thorough biographer as "America's first performance artist."[6] After her funeral, Barnes arranged the tribute in *transition*, which included the obituary, selections from letters written by the Baroness, and a photograph of the Baroness's death mask taken by photographer Marc Vaux. A few years later, she began work on a book about her friend, tentatively titled "Baroness Elsa," but although she worked on this biography for several years, she never finished it. And her promise to bring a collection of the Baroness's poetry into print remained unfulfilled when she died in 1982. Why couldn't Barnes finish her book about the Baroness? And why did this incomplete project weigh on her so heavily over the years? In this section, I suggest that the story of Barnes's attempted biography, which has been of comparatively little interest to Barnes scholars, is illuminating both for recent reassessments of her late period and as a kind of anecdotal theory of biographical and archival failure that will be further explored later in this chapter.[7]

The Baroness, as she was called by her contemporaries, was an intense presence in the New York art world in the years surrounding World War I. She was both artist and artwork—a poet and a sculptor, a muse and a model. Born in Germany, she moved fluidly through the avant-garde circles of New York, Paris, and Berlin, but she often chose to write in English, and she felt a special affinity for Americans. She has been described as the living embodiment of Dada's anti-art philosophy: Jane Heap, one of the coeditors of the *Little Review*, wrote that "when she is Dada she is the only one living anywhere who dresses Dada, loves Dada, lives Dada," and *Time* magazine more recently called her "New York's first punk persona."[8] Yet she was largely forgotten after her death, and until the contemporary critical resurgence in her work, she was remembered only in snippets and fragments, here and there, as the eccentric subject of occasional vignettes in the memoirs, letters, and diary entries of other modernist writers and artists. As Barnes recounts in the obituary, only a few of her poems were published during her lifetime, and "mentally she was never appropriately appreciated."[9] Indeed, most accounts of the Baroness focus on her body: she dressed provocatively, incorporating everyday objects into her daily costumes, and she continues to be best remembered for her bizarrely original self-presentation. "With the everyday as her chosen site for revolutionary artistic expression," writes her biographer, Irene Gammel, "she imported life into art, and art into life, thus taking modernity out of the archives, museum spaces, and elite literature to anchor it in daily practices."[10] For example, Barnes herself describes the Baroness as "one of the most astonishing figures of early Greenwich Village life. She had a head like a Roman emperor's, short, sometimes razored, once shellacked, red hair. She batiqued her tailored suits, made earrings from grave-flowers and Christmas tree decorations, and had a voice and a constitution of iron."[11] And in Margaret Anderson's *My Thirty Years' War*, she names the Baroness as "the only figure of our generation who deserves the epithet extraordinary" and notes that the Baroness was one of only two "talents" ever rescued from "the tide of unsolicited manuscripts" received by the *Little Review*.[12] Yet instead of writing more extensively about her poetry, Anderson describes a series of "public emergences" in which the Baroness wore "costumes which resulted in her arrest whenever she appeared on the streets."[13] Anderson's description of the first time she met the Baroness is full of sartorial detail:

> She wore a red Scotch plaid suit with a kilt hanging just below the knees, a bolero jacket with sleeves to the elbows and arms covered

with a quantity of ten-cent-store bracelets—silver, gilt, bronze, green and yellow. She wore high white spats with a band of decorative furniture braid around the top. Hanging from her bust were two tea-balls from which the nickel had worn away. On her head was a black velvet tam o' shanter with a feather and several spoons—long ice-cream-soda spoons. She had enormous earrings of tarnished silver and on her hands were many rings, on the little finger high peasant buttons filled with shot. Her hair was the color of a bay horse.[14]

Later, while upstaging a celebrated prima donna with her own dramatically late entrance, she wore "a trailing blue-green dress and a peacock fan. One side of her face was decorated with a canceled postage stamp (two-cent American, pink). Her lips were painted black, her face powder was yellow. She wore the top of a coal scuttle for a hat, strapped on under her chin like a helmet. Two mustard spoons at the side gave the effect of feathers."[15] And after being repeatedly rejected by William Carlos Williams, she shaved her head, painted it "a high vermillion," made a dress of stolen mourning crepe, and appeared in the offices of the *Little Review* to "exhibit" her head "at all angles" before tearing off her makeshift dress with the claim "It's better when I'm nude."[16] Her poses were legendary, and when she worked as an artist's model, she herself admitted that she "took the hardest poses—nobody would have dared to ask and keep them—because I had given myself my word not to stop—unless I should break down—for ambition and curiosity—to *test my strength*, I had no other aim than that."[17] An extraordinary woman indeed.

By the time Elsa appeared in New York, she was already well into middle age, and when she married Baron Leopold von Freytag-Loringhoven in 1913, she was, unbeknownst to him, eleven years his senior (and still legally married to another man). Their marriage did not last long; when World War I began, the disgraced and secretly impoverished Baron left for Europe, and the Baroness never saw him again. After spending years as a prisoner of war, he committed suicide in 1919. The Baroness was left with a title but without an inheritance, and since she had always depended upon the financial patronage of the men who desired her, she moved deeper and deeper into poverty as she aged. In painter George Biddle's autobiography, he describes the Baroness as an increasingly eccentric "art collector" who, despite the tragic and bizarre circumstances of her life, continued to have "validity":

> She induced me once to visit her collection. It was in an unheated loft near the river on 14th street. It was crowded and reeking with the

strange relics which she had purloined over a period of years from the New York gutters. Old bits of ironware, automobile tires, gilded vegetables, a dozen starved dogs, celluloid paintings, ash cans, every conceivable horror, which to her tortured, yet highly sensitized perception, became objects of formal beauty.[18]

As recent critics have suggested, her "collection" demonstrates the mutuality of influence between her artwork and Marcel Duchamp's famous "readymades." As Dada fell out of favor in the postwar years, however, her provocations were less generously received. Her public appearances were erratic, she worked only occasionally, and her time in New York came to a close.

Barnes and the Baroness met in 1916, when Barnes was still a young stunt journalist and the Baroness was in the high period of her career in New York, but their relationship did not really deepen until 1923, when photographer Berenice Abbott convinced Barnes to help the impoverished older woman. By then, the Baroness was back in Europe, after friends had put together enough money to buy her transatlantic ticket. They were nearly two decades apart in age, but Barnes quickly took on the almost maternal role of the Baroness's benefactor. Much later, in the notes she compiled for her own memoirs, Barnes echoes Biddle's assessment of the Baroness's artistic validity: "She would have been the most sought after woman in Paris had she been wealthy. She knew it, for Paris is a city that makes lions of other nation's *détraqués*, if they can do it in style; she could not."[19] As the pair wrote letters back and forth, Barnes (almost alone among their friends) maintained her sympathy for the Baroness, and she sent her packages with clothing, shoes, books, and money—anything to help alleviate the crushing effects of poverty. She also began to advocate for the Baroness's literary and artistic work.

During these years, Barnes championed the Baroness's poetry to journal editors and publishers, and the two women started to plan a book project together. The Baroness's poetry had never been gathered together and published in a single collection, and Barnes was confident that a volume of her friend's work was a surefire way to help her out of poverty while bringing her some of the critical attention she deserved. She asked the Baroness to write an autobiographical narrative for inclusion in the collection, and she herself planned to introduce as well as edit the volume. In 1924, Barnes completed several drafts of a preface in which she called the Baroness "a contemporary without a country," noting that, "in gathering together her letters, in offering some of her works, my hope has been that a country will inherit her."[20]

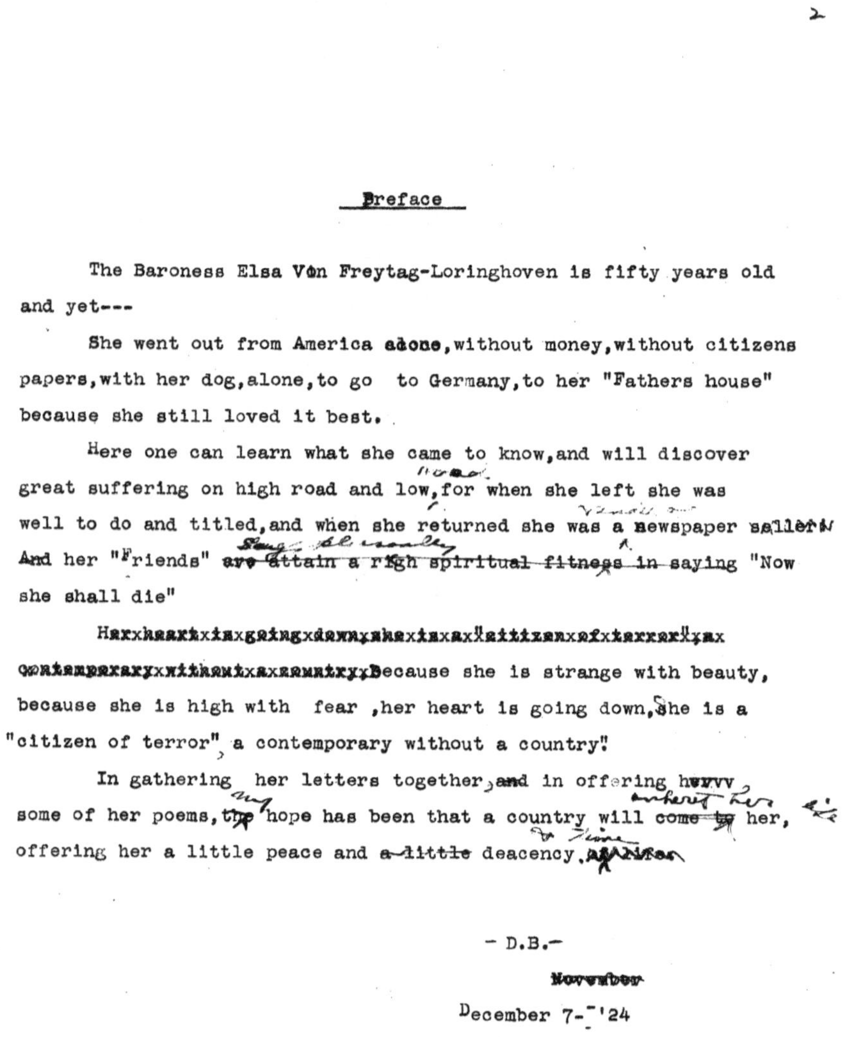

Preface

The Baroness Elsa Von Freytag-Loringhoven is fifty years old and yet---

She went out from America alone, without money, without citizens papers, with her dog, alone, to go to Germany, to her "Fathers house" because she still loved it best.

Here one can learn what she came to know, and will discover great suffering on high road and low, for when she left she was well to do and titled, and when she returned she was a newspaper seller. And her "Friends" are attain a high spiritual fitness in saying "Now she shall die"

~~Her heart is going down, her heart is a citizen of terror, a contemporary without a country.~~ Because she is strange with beauty, because she is high with fear, her heart is going down. She is a "citizen of terror", a contemporary without a country."

In gathering her letters together, and in offering herrvv some of her poems, the hope has been that a country will come to her, offering her a little peace and a little deacency.

— D.B.—

December 7- '24

FIGURE 2.1. Djuna Barnes, "Preface," draft.

These lines betray more than a simple desire to help her friend make some quick money; they make clear Barnes's concern for the Baroness's position within future literary and artistic histories of the period. Her use of the word "inherit" is significant: while playing with a fancifully optimistic assessment of the processes of remembrance and even canonization that might have protected the Baroness's legacy, it mostly serves as a wry, knowing lament that, despite her best efforts, the Baroness would likely remain homeless in history. If the collection remained unfinished and unpublished, who would claim the Baroness and her work? Who would inherit her legacy?

The Baroness, for her part, sent pieces of her autobiography to Barnes through her letters. She composed the narrative in English between 1923 and 1925 while she was living in tenements, charity homes, and even (briefly) a mental institution, and the fragmented prose of her tale reflects the physical disorder of that stage of her life. In several letters, she tells Barnes that she is preparing to begin her life story, and in several other letters, she describes the work of finishing her autobiography as the only thing keeping her alive. "There is only *one* ambition in me now, "she wrote, and that is "to finish my biography."[21] But while she detailed her childhood in Germany, her adolescent rebellion and flight to Berlin's street scene, and her many early love affairs in this "confessional autobiography,"[22] she never finished her account. Interwoven throughout the letters are brief glimpses of her move to the United States, abandonment in Kentucky, subsequent travel to New York and marriage to the Baron, and her later years as a (sometimes quite literally) starving artist, but these snippets are not part of what she understood to be her autobiographical project. Neither the autobiography nor the poetry collection was ever completed, and plans for the volume were abandoned, though several of the Baroness's poems were published individually.[23]

After the Baroness's sudden death in 1927, Barnes found herself in the unexpected and rather overwhelming position of literary executor for her friend's artistic estate. After putting together the obituary for *transition*, she began work on a biography of the Baroness—a project whose ongoing incompleteness would weigh on her for the rest of her life. As she had written in the preface for the volume they had planned together, she wanted the Baroness to be "inherited," and how could this happen unless the story of her remarkable life was eventually published? As the Baroness opined in a letter to Barnes, "I have not become 'known enough' and so I am forgotten."[24] Barnes understood herself to have an obligation to her late friend, and she made a number of inconclusive starts on the narrative in the 1930s. Using the Baroness's autobiographical fragments alongside the archive of their correspondence, Barnes worked intermittently on the biography while she continued to pursue her own creative work, and both *Ryder* and *Ladies Almanack* were published in 1928.

Eventually, T. S. Eliot, who was then an editor at Faber and Faber and who had encouraged Barnes to undertake the biography as a way to make some money for herself while she worked on other literary projects, convinced her that using the Baroness as inspiration for more literary work should suffice.[25] Barnes's most famous work, *Nightwood*, which Eliot himself had accepted for publication with Faber and Faber, came out in London in 1936 (and, with Eliot's now famous introduction accompanying it, in the United States the following year). The Baroness is clearly present in Barnes's novel. The character of Frau Mann, an androgynous trapeze artist from Berlin with "skin that was the pattern of her costume: a bodice of lozenges, red and yellow, low in the back and ruffled over and under the arms," has been described by Gammel as an homage to the bizarre costumes of the Baroness.[26] And, drawing on archival documents, an early article by Lynn DeVore makes a convincing case for understanding the Baroness as one of the most significant models for *Nightwood*'s Robin Vote. For example, Barnes describes Robin as a "somnambule," and, as DeVore demonstrates, this is a term used by the Baroness to describe herself in several of her letters.[27] And there are resonances between Robin and the Baroness that go unremarked by DeVore: Barnes's earlier wish that a country would "inherit" the "hard to know" Baroness is echoed in her description of Robin as someone who "told only a little of her life, but . . . kept repeating in one way or another her wish for a home."[28] Finally, the clutter of objects in the apartment shared by Robin and Nora—"the museum of their encounter"—recalls the strangely documentarian, overstuffed nature of the Baroness's "collection" in New York.[29] By incorporating this tribute to the Baroness into what would become her most renowned work, Barnes encodes her friend's legacy into modernist literary history.

Yet there is evidence to suggest that Barnes still felt she had an unpaid debt to the Baroness, who had once predicted that she would become "a disquiet spirit" after her death if she had not attained some measure of "success" during her lifetime. "If there are haunts," she had written to Barnes, "I'll be one."[30] Barnes may have rightly feared the Baroness was still not "known enough," given that she so clearly shared space with Thelma Wood (an expat artist and Barnes's most notorious former lover) in the character of Robin Vote, and given that Barnes had still not managed to put together a collection of the Baroness's poetry. She repeatedly began, revised, and abandoned the biographical project, only to pick it up again a few years later, and this cycle continued for years. At some point, she went so far as to request the Baroness's death mask for "inspiration," and it later fell—disquietly, no doubt—out of a closet (a closet!) and hit her on the head.[31] Only some of the extant unpublished drafts are dated, but we know that she worked on the biography in the late 1920s, throughout the 1930s, again in the 1950s, and perhaps later still. As Scott Herring has shown, this ability to "imagin[e] her unfinished papers as 'totally new' achievements always in the making" was characteristic of Barnes's late period, when the draft material in her domestic archive grew in startlingly inverse proportion to her scant list of published work.[32] Drawing on

Hannah Sullivan's claim that ongoing and substantial revision constitutes an often overlooked aspect of modernist authorship, Herring observes that, for Barnes, "finishing the drafts was beside the point."[33]

Although Barnes developed this strategy of recursive poetic revision as part of her late-life autobiographical practice, she seems to have been more troubled by its implications for her biographical project. In 1979, after a "premonition" that she would die within months, she called her then-literary executor and unpaid assistant, Hank O'Neal, with a "sense of urgency" about several things she wanted to take care of before her death.[34] In O'Neal's recollection, which he later included in his memoir of his years spent working with and for the reclusive, elderly Barnes, the most pressing task on her list was the publication of the Baroness's work:

> It is urgent that someone do something sensible with her poetry and letters. She wants me to make certain they are published, and the first step is for her to write a letter to the "authorities" at the University of Maryland authorizing me to go through all of Baroness Elsa's papers and make copies. It is unclear why Miss Barnes retains all literary rights to these papers, but she maintains this is the case.... Miss Barnes even tried to work on them many years before but . . . quit before anything was completed. She seems pleased that I will look at the papers and try to make some sense of them; she has even consented to recall, for the record, as much about the Baroness Elsa as possible.[35]

Ironically, Barnes's promise to provide biographical assistance for the volume she wanted O'Neal to produce echoes the Baroness's promise to draft her autobiography for the collection Barnes had tried to put together half a century earlier. It is, perhaps, only fitting that Barnes never gave O'Neal a substantial description of the Baroness's life and works, though she frequently came up in their conversations. Their plans for the Baroness's revival were left incomplete when Barnes broke with O'Neal in 1981, and she died the following year. The remainder of her papers were transferred to the library at the University of Maryland, where they were processed and catalogued alongside those of the Baroness.

Does this constitute success or failure? Every contemporary attempt to tell the Baroness's life story, from the reediting of the autobiography in 1992 to the cultural biography in 2002 to Tanya E. Clement's more recent @BaronessElsa project, has relied heavily on the unfinished biographical acts in this archive.[36] In this sense, Barnes failed neither the Baroness nor the future scholars who would find the materials she saved. Yet she did not seem to trust the future to get it right; as we have seen, she returned to the project of the Baroness and her poetry many times over the course of her life, seemingly stuck between her own apparent inability to move forward with it and her sense of obligation to finish it. As we will see with the case of Hope Mirrlees, such paralysis was not unique to Barnes.[37] Sometimes, a late devotion to the remembrance of one's companion becomes a sustaining passion project, but, at other times, the seemingly impossible labor of finding a country to claim her proves too much to bear.

"The Cult of the Past": On the Late Refusal of Hope Mirrlees

Like Barnes, whose reclusive, relatively unproductive late career is nearly always considered a disappointing mystery, Hope Mirrlees hardly exists in midcentury literary history. Of course, in contrast to the now celebrated Barnes, one is hard-pressed to find Mirrlees in most literary histories of modernism, either. Although she wrote innovative fiction and poetry during the 1920s, Mirrlees has only recently begun to enter our discussions of the period, and when she does, her late period, in which she worked obsessively on biographical projects, is all but ignored. This late period, with its attendant shift toward the biographical mode, marks a distinct change in Mirrlees's intellectual and political ambitions. Like Woolf, with whom she was friendly and whose Hogarth Press published Mirrlees's long poem, "Paris," in 1920, Mirrlees turned to biography in order to revise a historical record dominated and written by men. In the case of Mirrlees, however, these would-be interventions wound up as failed biographical acts. The last fifty years of her life were devoted to two major projects: first, the unfinished biography of her late companion, Jane Ellen Harrison, which remains a collection of notes and outlines in the Newnham College Archives at Cambridge University, and, second, her two-volume biography of the antiquarian Sir Robert Bruce Cotton, of which the second volume remains unpublished.[38] And while she privately published a few collections of poetry during this period, these major works were left incomplete and unpublished at her death in 1978.

Fittingly, perhaps, Mirrlees's own life story is also characterized by silence: the life behind the work (which itself barely survives) is scarcely documented. In this chapter, situated as it is in a book devoted to the study of otherwise strange and unexpected biographical turns, I seek to contextualize Mirrlees's late period in order to understand it as something other than a shameful end to what had promised to be a brilliant career. Despite recent scholarship by Mary Beard, Julia Briggs, John Connor, Nancy

Gish, Sandeep Parmar, Michael Stanwick, and others that has begun to restore Mirrlees's early experimental novels and poems to the modernist canon, little critical attention has been paid to her tenuous position in the milieu of women writers in and after the moment of high modernist literary production.[39] The curious character of Hope Mirrlees survives only in fragments: occasional lines in the letters of T. S. Eliot and the diaries of Virginia Woolf; footnotes in Bloomsbury biographies and institutional histories of Newnham College, Cambridge; and, of course, as the looming, unavoidable, and decidedly controversial figure in the final chapters of all biographies of Jane Harrison, the celebrated scholar of Classics. Yet the responsible recovery of Mirrlees's work for the contemporary modernist canon must reckon with this critically underexamined late period. For, in contrast to Woolf's steady output until her sudden suicide at the age of fifty-nine, and in contrast to the furious pace of Barnes's "geriatric avant-garde," Mirrlees became less productive as she aged.[40] In Anthony Powell's memoir, he describes her as "unmarried, with Bloomsbury associations in early life, though now settled down to a less exacting intellectual condition of comfortable upper-middlebrowdom."[41] If this portrait seems unconvincing—or, at the very least, incomplete—then we must ask why she drastically altered the nature and pace of her work after 1928. I suggest that, after Harrison's death earlier that year, she joined what she once disparagingly called "the cult of the past."

In "The Religion of Women," a short essay published in *The Nation & Athenaeum* on May 28, 1927, Hope Mirrlees describes the "cult of the past" that governs the lives of older women: "A friend of mine has noticed that, if you catch them unawares, the faces of all middle-aged women are sad, . . . as if their bodies divined something that their minds ignored."[42] She argues that, for aging women, time becomes a form of religion: somatically sensing the approach of the end, women begin to embody this encroaching sense of lateness, even as life continues to move forward all around them. Increasingly resigned to the passage of time, they are marked by this admission, this giving up, this giving in to an everyday knowledge of one's own mortality. Crucially, this is more than merely internalized misogyny; for Mirrlees, it is women and poets who share this special sensitivity to the passage of time:

> It is indisputable that nearly all the great tragic utterances about time, and its corollaries, change and death, have been made by men. It is, nevertheless, only the poets, and not the average man, who are haunted by these conceptions. But they do haunt all women. As a general rule, it is love that makes men unhappy, and time that makes women so.[43]

This is a striking reversal of expectations: instead of yet another representation of women's lives as governed by romantic fantasy and delusional domesticity, Mirrlees leaves these comedic narratives to "the average man" and aligns women and poets as joint possessors of the tragic mode. Women and poets alone, she argues, are haunted by time, change, and death. To be sure, Mirrlees, then a forty-year-old woman and poet, was anxious about precisely these things at the time of this essay's publication. While her short piece references Virginia Woolf and George Eliot, Homer and Euripides, and an anonymous pair of "old creatures of the lower middle class," the most important influence on her argument—"Miss Jane Harrison"—is mentioned only once in passing.[44] Shortly after the essay appeared, Harrison was diagnosed with leukemia, and less than a year later, on April 15, 1928, at the age of seventy-eight, the woman with whom Mirrlees had shared her life for more than a decade died. With Mirrlees at her side, Harrison had continued with her intellectual work through the last years of her life, but when she died, so did the visible career of Hope Mirrlees. Once a bright young thing in and around Cambridge, Bloomsbury, and Paris, Mirrlees abruptly stopped her literary work after Harrison's death, retreating from her former intellectual interest in novels, poetry, translations, and essays into the two almost pathologically long biographical projects that would remain unfinished at her death, nearly fifty years later, in 1978.[45]

"More than a Daughter to Her":
Tracing Reputation, Resisting Identity

On or about September 1910, at the age of twenty-three, Mirrlees went up to Newnham College, Cambridge, where she studied Greek for three years. She quickly became Harrison's student, and despite her later characterization of Harrison's "disapproval of [her] exclusiveness as a student," the pair would remain extremely—if indecipherably—close for the rest of Harrison's life.[46] When Mirrlees later drafted a chronological outline of Harrison's life to aid her in the composition of Harrison's biography, she marked 1914, the year after Mirrlees left Newnham, as the year in which their "close friendship starts," although there are several surviving letters and postcards that suggest that they were quite close while Mirrlees was still a student.[47] For Harrison, this would not have been particularly unusual; several of her former students later described her egalitarian friendliness with her students and admired the way "she never paid attention to their respective roles as teacher and student."[48] When Mirrlees later interviewed one of these former students, Victoria de Bunsen, during the course of her research for the biography, she rather admiringly called Harrison "the perverter of [her] youth," explaining that "Jane always spoke to the young as man to man, much too interested in the subject under discussion to consider the effect it might have on them."[49] I return to this particular "effect," and the strong sense of attachment so many of Harrison's pupils (including Mirrlees) developed, in the discussion of "schwärmerei"—a term used to indicate excessive sentiment or enthusiasm, particularly between women—later in this chapter.

After the war, Mirrlees convinced Harrison to leave Cambridge and, in a move that earned Mirrlees the enduring wrath of Harrison's friends, students, and eventual biographers, urged her to destroy all of her personal papers before leaving England. They spent several happy years in Paris studying Russian, undertaking collaborative translations and projects, chaperoning the relative success of Mirrlees's literary work (*Madeleine: One of Love's Jansenists* [1919], "Paris: A Poem" [1920], and *The Counterplot* [1922]), and enjoying the intellectually diverse, sexually adventurous, politically cosmopolitan milieu of the postwar cultural capital before Harrison's declining health forced them to return to London in 1925.

In these years, Mirrlees and Harrison were aware that their close friendship raised eyebrows (or, perhaps more tellingly, did *not* raise any eyebrows in Bloomsbury and Paris), but they did not disclose the precise nature of their relationship. This, of course, did not stop others from speculating about it. In *The Invention of Jane Harrison*, Mary Beard suggests that Mirrlees and Harrison "encoded their relationship within the terms of literary sapphism," and it seems that the literary sapphists, at least, understood it in those terms.[50] In *The Autobiography of Alice B. Toklas*, for example, Gertrude Stein alludes to Harrison as "Hope Mirlees' [*sic*] pet enthusiasm" while describing a luncheon meeting with Harrison and Mirrlees at Newnham.[51] And Stein wasn't alone in her insinuations. In a letter to Lytton Strachey in 1923, Dora Carrington asked him to get to know Harrison and Mirrlees, hinting that their "liaison" would be of interest: "I'm sure they are a fascinating couple."[52] Virginia Woolf, always a discerning observer and capricious commenter on the character—sexual and otherwise—of those surrounding her, seemed to take it for granted that the relationship between Mirrlees and Harrison was not strictly platonic. She and Leonard loved "seeing [Mirrlees] and Jane billing and cooing together";[53] she judged Mirrlees's first novel, *Madeleine*, to be "all sapphism so far as I've got—Jane and herself";[54] she described Mirrlees as having "a passion for Jane Harrison, the scholar: indeed they practically live together, and go to Paris";[55] and, on several trips to Europe, Woolf made plans to pass through Paris, where she often met up with them: "There I shall stay a few days & meet Jane Harrison & Hope Mirrlees who have a Sapphic flat somewhere."[56] (This telling final phrase about their "Sapphic flat" was initially omitted from Woolf's collected letters because they were published while Mirrlees was still alive; in Sylvia Townsend Warner's terms, they hadn't yet landed in that safe space for everyone to be dead in.) Woolf's descriptions of the pair are not proof of anything at all, of course, except that their relationship was written about and discussed by their contemporaries in the sexually open vocabularies and knowing glances of the Bloomsbury set. Emotional and intellectual intimacy, as well as some degree of physical eroticism, were assumed, though sometimes not explicitly vocalized. In a letter written to Mirrlees after Harrison's death, for example, Woolf's sympathy for Mirrlees as a kind of grieving widow is gravely clear, and yet her postscript practically trips over itself in an effort *not* to name their relationship: "Anyhow, what a comfort for you to have been all you were to her."[57]

Similarly, the letters of sympathy Mirrlees received from their friends after Harrison's death in 1928 cast their relationship in alternating terms of physical intimacy and spiritual kinship. Calling Mirrlees Harrison's "real ghostly daughter," an echo of a phrase Harrison sometimes used to describe the place of Mirrlees in her life, Victoria de Bunsen emphasized that she "[felt] first for you—what it must mean—."[58] Agnes Conway, who was writing to Jane when she received news of her death, wrote to say that she "do[es] feel for you & understand[s] what it must be";[59] Mabel Robinson sent her condolences to "the one she loved best, who was more than a daughter to her";[60] and Alys Russell felt the disproportion of her own sorrow: "I cannot tell you how much sympathy I feel for you. For me, it is a very very great loss, but for you it is overwhelming, & I don't see how you are to bear it."[61] Even Mirrlees's brother recognized the importance of their relationship: "I know I can do nothing to help and words are poor comfort but I should like you to know that I realize what an irreplaceable loss she is."[62] Their relationship, while technically left unstated, was understood by everyone close to them to have been almost incomparably intimate.

Harrison's death was a tremendous blow to Mirrlees, and their mutual friends understood this. Yet few could have predicted the ways in which Mirrlees would abruptly change her lifestyle in the years after 1928. Like T. S. Eliot, to whom she is so often compared, she adopted a new religious affiliation in middle age, and her embrace of Catholicism caused her to repudiate much of the work she had done in her younger years.[63] More significantly still, she nearly stopped writing altogether. Between 1919 and 1928, the years she lived (or, according to Woolf, "practically lived") with Harrison, she published three novels, one book of poetry, one long poem, many articles, and, with Harrison, two translations. Between Harrison's death in 1928 and Mirrlees's own death fifty years later in 1978, she published only one book, *A Fly in Amber* (1962), and two ill-received collections of poetry, *Poems* (1963) and *Moods and Tensions* (1976). In her notes toward the Harrison biography, she left the following comment: "With many people intellectual creation is coextensive with the sexual life & ceases with it. This was most emphatically *not* the case with Jane."[64] For Harrison, this observation was declared useless; for herself, however, it may have been quite apt. After Harrison's death, Mirrlees's intellectual life did not entirely cease, but it did undergo a drastic change. Despite the ongoing critical disposition to understand Mirrlees as having stopped serious work after Harrison's death, I highlight the significance of the un- and underpublished biographical acts with which she grappled throughout her late period. When read, republished, and analyzed by feminist and modernist scholars, the work of Hope Mirrlees too often refers only to her early career—1919 through 1928—and ignores her later work in biography. Committed to narratives of triumphant discovery and heroic reclamation, these contemporary recovery projects are perhaps too reticent to admit— and grapple with the stakes of—failure. They may also be too tempted by the romantic narrative of Mirrlees as paralyzed, rather than prodded, by the loss of her partner. This is, in part, what scholars like Heather Love and Jack Halberstam are working against by revising our affective archives of queer history: we need more than proud, triumphant heroes. The conflicted sadness of Mirrlees's abandoned archive tells a very different story.

Unfinished Acts: Facing the Problem of "What to Say & What to Leave Out"

Harrison was a well-respected scholar as well as something of a Cambridge legend, so the question of who would undertake to write her life story was an immediate question. Shortly after Harrison's death, Mirrlees announced her plans to compose Harrison's biography, and she began to collect many of the reminiscences from friends, colleagues, and former students that now comprise much of the Harrison Papers at Newnham. There are several large notebooks containing memories of Harrison as compiled by Mirrlees: most entries are listed under the name of the individual with whom Mirrlees had spoken or from whom she had received information through correspondence, and, interspersed throughout the collection of testimonies, Mirrlees also included her own views and recollections from talking with Harrison about these same people or about the times they describe. On nearly every page in the Harrison Papers, Mirrlees is inevitably present as subject, commenter, or archivist. As Harrison's frustrated biographers and critics have learned, it is impossible to write about her life without leaning, however mistrustfully, on the subjective commentary of Hope Mirrlees. All research into the collection is thus haunted by the question of what else might have been available to us had Mirrlees not convinced Harrison to burn nearly all of her papers a decade before her death, and yet we also owe thanks to Mirrlees and Jessie Stewart (another former student and eventual biographer of Harrison's) for later safeguarding so many of Harrison's extant letters during the Blitz. The Harrison Papers are often understood as raw source material for scholars of Harrison's life and work at Newnham College, Cambridge, but the Papers were entirely assembled and bequeathed by Mirrlees, Stewart, and others—nothing at all was organized or left by Harrison herself. Even before reaching the capable hands of the Newnham College archivists, this archive had become a highly mediated resource, and, as Beard reminds us, "it is precisely because the archival resource . . . that dominates research on Harrison, the collection to which all must turn in (re)writing her life, is so much Mirrlees's creation that it forces its readers into collusion with her vision of the subject."[65] The competing curatorial and annotative voices at play throughout the Harrison Papers help us to understand why Mirrlees's own notes become increasingly veiled, as though she knew, even during the draft stage, that she was writing for a broader audience. For example, she consistently draws attention to the importance of what she alone knows but is unwilling to commit to paper: "One episode the key to JEH's life—indiscreet to mention—*wd* cripple her word—She would have hated it published."[66] For Mirrlees was not the only person to begin work on a biography of Harrison, and she was anxious to prove that, no matter how long the public had to wait to read it, her voice occupied a position of utmost privilege.

Not long after Mirrlees began her research, Stewart also began work on a memoir about Harrison. At first, Stewart and Mirrlees amiably decided to combine their efforts, splitting the enterprise down the middle, with Stewart working on a Cambridge-centered intellectual history drawn largely from Harrison's writings, and Mirrlees dealing with Harrison's personal life. For a while, this joint decision worked well, and in the spring of 1932, Mirrlees wrote optimistically about the project: "I feel so relieved and pleased about Jane's 'Life'—it's a lovely plan."[67] At the end of that very year, she was brimming over with so much inspiration that she stopped all other work: "I decided to put my other book [probably *A Fly in Amber*] aside & start right off on Jane's—& I am now full of it! . . . I'll start on the 'frame' of her life, if you will do her writings & then we can compare notes."[68] As they soldiered on, sending packets of Harrison's letters back and forth throughout the 1930s and 1940s, they began to diverge in their views about the future of the project, especially regarding the uses of the letters themselves.

Despite her initial enthusiasm for the book, Mirrlees started to hesitate about the prospect of publishing so much of Harrison's private world. As everyone who has read them knows, the letters are full of pet names, inside jokes, and private enthusiasms: the written correspondence of Harrison and Mirrlees constructs an elaborate fantasy world in which the women are alternately walruses, bears, and sea creatures, and in which they refer to themselves as "elder" and "younger" wives. (Though it is tempting to seize upon such intimate vocabulary as irrefutable evidence of a romantic or erotic relationship between the two women, scholars would do well to remember Carolyn Heilbrun's statement about the letters written between Vera Brittain and Winifred Holtby: "They write to each other what may sound like love letters to a world attuned only to affection between courting men and women.")[69] Meanwhile, as Mirrlees became increasingly critical of Stewart's plans for completing her book, the pace of her own work began to slow. Finally, in 1943, she decided to cease work on her half of the project altogether:

> I am afraid you [Stewart] think I have been very dilatory over Jane's Life, but I never really felt any need for dispatch. I remember your once saying that if one wanted to have a free hand with the letters, the more of the people concerned who were dead the better. And that certainly applies to the other aspects of this Life. In fact the problem of what to say & what to leave out is a very difficult one. And my inability to resolve it is one of the reasons that has decided me to abdicate. You see, I knew that Jane was extremely reserved about her own past. And one feels that she would have disliked its being made public. And yet if one does not do so, the life looses [*sic*] what she would have called its "pattern."[70]

I return to the significance of such "patterns" later in the chapter, but this paralyzing indecision about "what to say & what to leave out" is the central issue of the unfinished, unpublished biography. Like Warner, Mirrlees knew that she could not yet tell the entire story. But in contrast to Warner, who felt that her relationship to Ackland was already clearly and securely legible as wife, intimate companion, and loving partner, Mirrlees repeatedly emphasizes the primacy of her relationship with Harrison without making the nature of it clear.

Mirrlees was also reluctant to break with Harrison's own previously published inclinations toward silence, her own prior decisions about "what to say & what to leave out." In Harrison's *Reminiscences of a Student's Life*, which was published by the Woolfs' Hogarth Press in 1925, she apologized for her silence on several key periods of her life and for her omission of "the men and women who influenced me most—my real friends" because they were still alive.[71] This did not leave Mirrlees in an easy situation. She did not want to share too much of Harrison's private life with the world, but it was unbearable to her that her silence should be taken as ignorance on the subject. Archly critical of Stewart's manuscript and insistent that only she, Hope Mirrlees, truly understood the real Jane Ellen Harrison, she haunted Stewart's attempts to finish her book (and her many unsuccessful attempts to publish it before it finally appeared, in 1959, as *Jane Ellen Harrison: A Portrait from Letters*). As Beard astutely notes, she was "unwilling to write her own intimacy *out* of the story, but unwilling to write it *in* either," and, for years, she remained "caught on the knife edge between Bloomsbury-style exposure and the alternative rhetoric of reticence":

> Hence . . . her constant claim to a unique right to speak of Harrison's private world—and, at the same time, her constant refusal to do so; her repeated parade of the intimate secrets she knew but could not say, the things that Harrison had told her but that she could never make public. Or at least not yet.[72]

Indeed, many of the drafts and outlines Mirrlees compiled are filled with references to what Mirrlees knows but cannot say. A constant editor of her own creative process, Mirrlees wrote and then struck out the names of any potentially compromising—or compromised—individuals, often leaving only letters to refer to them, as in "The C——— Letters." She almost compulsively interrupted her own notes, especially when she feared herself to be coming up against one of Harrison's personal boundaries. After an entry in the "Outline of Life" corresponding to 1905–6 that details Harrison's "terrible mysterious breakdown," for example, the following is crossed out (though, unlike some of Mirrlees's more violent editorial marks, it remains just barely legible): "I don't know how much or how little I may say about the next important episode—I was told about it in confidence, & must obtain the permission of one of the people concerned."[73] Similarly, just before the start of the entry for 1910, Mirrlees again breaks in (and again crosses out the following words): "In regard to Jane's private affairs during the next few years, I do not feel at liberty to speak. I was told about them in confidence."[74] Her reticence is both quietly boastful and clearly tortured. She claims the right to speak—or, in this case, not to speak—on behalf of her companion on the basis of intimate companionship rather than kinship or conjugal partnership. Because of this uncontested intimacy, Mirrlees was both the only person able to communicate the truth about Harrison's life *and* the only person who felt responsible to uphold Harrison's own vetted version of her public image and life story.

After Mirrlees stopped work on the biography in 1943, several of Harrison's other friends and former students rallied behind Stewart and angrily demanded to know what Mirrlees had been doing for so many years: "What an amazing creature Hope is! Why didn't she give in her hand long ago instead of waiting 16 years? Hasn't she written *any*thing?"[75] While Harrison's Newnham crowd largely supported Stewart's continued effort to finish her project, several others, including potential publishers such as Leonard Woolf, urged Mirrlees to resume work on the biography. After reading Stewart's manuscript, Woolf described it as "so incoherent" and "so obscure that it is out of the question to make a book out of it," and he innocently suggested asking his old friend Hope Mirrlees to edit the material: "I feel that she would be quite capable of taking the material and making something of it."[76] And D. S. MacColl, an influential art critic, similarly implored Mirrlees to reconsider the task, referring to her work on the Harrison biography as her "sacred duty":

> Will you think me impertinent if I urge that you should devote yourself to that task before it is too late? I don't know, of course, what work you are engaged on, and therefore have perhaps no business to talk; but if you don't get this, shall I say, sacred duty performed I don't know who is competent to take it on. Few now survive from the earlier days and the ranks become thin even of your period of close companionship with her.[77]

Thus the informal critical consensus was that Mirrlees must be the one to write Harrison's life, and even Stewart, while continuing to press on in her revisions to the manuscript and search for a publisher, agreed that Mirrlees alone could bring certain aspects of Harrison's story to light. In a letter dated May 5, 1946, she admitted Mirrlees's privileged position in

Harrison's life: "One point is to me crystal clear that you alone can do the personal life & you have got it all there, waiting to be brought forth—I do not see why you should tell the Secret. *'Pourquoi rompre ce glorieux silence?'*"[78] Mirrlees would not finish her book, but after Stewart finally published her version with Merlin Press in 1959, she again fantasized about her own, more intimate, portrait of Harrison: "A little memoir of Jane is beginning to form up in my mind."[79]

She never finished this "little memoir of Jane," of course, and we are left, instead, with her curated preservation of the Harrison Papers, which she donated to the Newnham College Archives in 1973. (Stewart had donated her own papers and letters relating to Harrison in 1964.) There are over 240 pages of notes, outlines, and drafts toward Mirrlees's biography of Harrison, but researchers who delve into these "muddled," "repetitive," and "at times incomprehensible" pages in search of what Stewart had called "the Secret" will be sorely disappointed.[80] Like Hugh Vereker's "complex figure in a Persian carpet" in Henry James's "The Figure in the Carpet," this "Secret" remains shrouded in "glorieux silence."

We cannot know the precise nature of the relationship between Harrison and Mirrlees. We can, however, recognize what David Kazanjian has called, in a markedly different context, the "scenes of speculation in the archives we recover."[81] And we can surely find a reflection of the various modes of female friendship, companionship, and intimacy considered possible in the early years of the twentieth century. If Mirrlees was, as Beard suggests, "caught on the knife edge between Bloomsbury-style exposure and the alternative rhetoric of reticence" as she struggled to tell Harrison's life story, she was surely not alone in her attempt to maintain this awkward balance between Victorian "romantic friendship" and more modern discourses of lesbianism.[82] Most critical accounts of her draft biography focus on her descriptions of Harrison's early love affairs, nearly all of which were with men. (In using "nearly," I cautiously follow the lead of Mirrlees herself, who wrote first that "all her love affairs were with men," then crossed that out and replaced it with "*nearly* all her love affairs were with men.")[83] Most scholars read this archive as a depiction of Harrison's juvenile affairs with a succession of male scholars before the final period of her great happiness with Mirrlees. Rather than retrace the story of the young Harrison's heterosexual love affairs, I now turn to the descriptions of female friendships and passions that fill the pages of Mirrlees's notebooks and early drafts.

In the several sections of the biography that she managed to complete, she describes the strange consistency with which Harrison's female friends developed almost obsessively passionate feelings toward her. Over and over again, Mirrlees refers to these relationships as "schwärmerei": "For biological reasons, the [crossed out: youthful] schwärmerei of a girl for a member of her own sex when it comes to an end inevitably leaves a sense of grievance, of having been cheated"; "all her life Jane was tormented by people having schwärmereis [sic] for her"; "nobody could continue a friend of Jane's on an intense basis unless they conceded their schwärmerei"; and so on.[84] According to the Oxford English Dictionary, "schwärmerei" refers to "religious zeal, fanaticism, extravagant enthusiasm for a cause or a person; an erotic attachment, esp. of one woman or adolescent girl for another; a 'crush.'" For Mirrlees, and for the authors of most of the OED's other citations of "schwärmerei," the term refers to a zealous, passionate, possibly erotic, yet somewhat illegitimate or immature attachment. Schwärmerei occurs between women; even more often, schwärmerei is what happens between immature women or girls. Significantly, it is also used in several of Freud's descriptions of relationships between women, most notably in "The Psychogenesis of a Case of Homosexuality in a Woman" (1920). First used (in English) in 1845, the word has largely fallen out of contemporary usage, but even at the height of its popularity—and that of its other forms, *schwarm* (n.), *schwärm* (v.), and *schwärmerisch* (adj.)—the term was not common.[85]

In dwelling on this term, I suggest that Mirrlees's frequent use of "schwärmerei" marks the other half of what she knows but will not say: not simply the embarrassment of Harrison's early passion for the already engaged Henry Butcher or the humiliation of her later desertion by Francis Cornford (which other scholars, including Stewart, have already discussed at length), but the less commonly noted passionate nature of her relationships with several key women in her life. Throughout her notes for the Harrison biography, Mirrlees seems to go to great lengths to show that such relationships between women were ordinary occurrences. Before she went up to Newnham, Harrison had studied at Cheltenham Ladies' College, and when Mirrlees interviewed friends of hers from that time, they all spoke of "her passion for Miss Dorothea Beale [the principal], which was returned."[86] Later, while taking notes on the recollections of a friend (Elinor Paul) from her student days at Newnham, Mirrlees parenthetically interjects her own commentary after Paul's description of a woman who, while unhappily married to a "self & brutal" man, "worshipped Jane": "It is by no means an unusual relationship, an almost romantic friendship between a married woman with children & a young girl."[87] And, unable to resist the temptation to discuss Victoria de Bunsen's playful description of Jane as the "perverter of [her] youth," Mirrlees immediately recounts another story:

Gwen Darwin told me that when she was very young she began to teach herself Greek. Jane heard of this & told her if she cared to come into her room sometimes on Sunday mornings she would help her. The first morning Sappho turned up in the conversation, & Jane discovering that Gwen knew nothing about Sapphism told her all about it.[88]

These anecdotes, and others like them, suggest that Harrison had many friends and admirers among the women at Cheltenham and Newnham, but also, and perhaps more significantly, they show that Mirrlees paid careful attention to descriptions of Harrison's other relationships with women. Her observations about these relationships are often very similar to the kinds of observations their Bloomsbury and Left Bank peers would make about the "open secret" of the relationship between Mirrlees and Harrison. Mirrlees's notes toward several sections of the biography sometimes read like a careful catalogue of Harrison's most intimate female friendships. This long-standing interest in Harrison's relationships—and Mirrlees admits she only knew about several of them through what she called "assiduous pumping"[89]—itself demonstrates a kind of schwärmerei. Even as the unfinished biography bears all the mournful signs of late work—as well as the devotional refrains of the "religion of women"—it is also marked by this supposedly unseemly, even immature, attachment.

Furthermore, there is a clear link between this schwärmerei and the necessarily obsessive work of intimate biography. The effort and sustained attention required to complete any large scholarly project is immense. Moreover, the modes of attachment we move through in the work of scholarship—perhaps especially in identity-based recovery projects, though doubtless elsewhere as well—resemble the schwärmerei described, though never explained, by Mirrlees. We become overly attached to, and in some cases defined by, our scholarly work. In the case of intimate biography, when the scholar-biographer must treat the companion whose loss she still mourns as the object of study, dedication to the project can become almost religious in nature. In this sense, collecting, annotating, and assembling such an intimate archive—especially if that archive would never be finished—might all be considered melancholic forms of schwärming. Unable to fully and maturely mourn—and move on from—Harrison's death in 1928, Mirrlees entered a long period of melancholia in which she channeled her sense of loss into the biographical project. Like many melancholics, Mirrlees was well aware of whom she had lost, but perhaps not fully cognizant of what she lost in her, and, as we have seen, she felt unable to name—or even, perhaps, to fully recognize—the nature of her attachment to Harrison. And so that biographical project, like melancholia itself, would not, could not, end.

For the fifty years after Harrison's death, Mirrlees worked off-and-on on this biography. During this time, despite her inability to bring that project to completion, she also began a second biographical project. Rather than write the life of someone close to her, however, she chose to undertake a historical biography of Sir Robert Bruce Cotton, one of the most well known of the English antiquarians of centuries earlier. In contrast to the way Sylvia Townsend Warner developed a kind of biographical consciousness during her work on the T. H. White biography, Mirrlees worked first on the more intimate project before taking on the biography of Cotton. If Warner's intimate archive was the result of her earlier biographical theory and practice, Mirrlees's later project functioned as a kind of release valve for the obsessive, frustrated biographical practice she developed while working on the Harrison biography. As she grew older, and the years spent on each project began to weigh on her, she developed a fervently religious zeal about her role in each biographical project. Despite entreaties from friends and colleagues, she would not finish the Harrison biography, but she used her new training in that project's genre to transfer her obsession for her subject to a new object in her next—and final—biographical act.

Historic Preservation and Biographical Extravagance: The Case of A Fly in Amber

We do not know why Mirrlees began to write the Cotton biography. Her remaining letters and papers show us that she was very enthusiastic about the project, even as her pace of composition slowed significantly over the years, and we know that T. S. Eliot was largely responsible for shepherding the first half of the biography into print, but the archive at Newnham College gives us no real clue as to why she was drawn to Cotton in the first place. I have suggested that the melancholic work of intimate biography fueled her interest both in the genre and in the obsessive scholarly practice necessary to produce it. In this reading, even this later volume is a response to Harrison, and to the void left by her death in Mirrlees's intellectual and emotional life.

Several chapters into the first volume of *A Fly in Amber: Being an Extravagant Biography of the Romantic Antiquary, Sir Robert Bruce Cotton*, Mirrlees reflects upon the oddity of her title. "Cotton is the fly," she explains, "and the period in which he lived is the amber. In some of the chapters there is 'much amber'—too much, perhaps. But I trust that it is not the cloudy variety and that the fly can always eventually be discovered."[90] Mirrlees continues to reference this "amber" throughout the book. Introducing the next chapter, she admits that she would like to spend more time analyzing particular passages from Cotton's letters, but the genre will not admit this: "But, alas! This book is not the Baltic Sea, and the amber-capacity of each chapter is strictly limited."[91] In a sense, this is simply a different way of naming the "Life and Times" biographies so popular in the nineteenth century, in which the life of the biographical subject reflects upon the larger times of the nation and historical period. Yet, for Mirrlees, these two elements of the biographical project do not always work in perfect harmony: here, the amber is sometimes cloudy, and it can overwhelm any clear sense of the subject's individual life trajectory (let alone the subject's character). Indeed, one can easily feel, while reading Mirrlees's book, that it is nearly all amber, and this is even more the case in the second, unpublished volume, in which Cotton—still nominally the subject!—does not even appear until the second half.[92] Curiously, Mirrlees had not always thought of amber as "the period" in which her subject lived. In her notes for the Harrison biography, Mirrlees gives amber primary importance by associating it with Harrison: "Jane was amber—one of the life-giving substances; I myself on the other hand owe my whole picture of the universe to her, & everything about me that is not ignoble."[93] Amber, here, is not the social fabric but the subject herself. Harrison's life is the amber in which Mirrlees finds herself caught; amber, the color of her energy.

Throughout the Cotton biography, Mirrlees contrasts the work of what she calls the "romantic antiquary" with that of the historian, arguing that antiquaries have the "two-fold task" of both "preserving the present" and "restor[ing] the past."[94] It is clear that Mirrlees feels a similar burden in her biographical work. Like the romantic antiquaries of whom she writes, she values "a sense of period"—an expression coined, she thinks, by Roger Fry to "denote the ability of seeing an age ... which of necessity must be neither too near our own nor too far away from it ... in perspective."[95] For both romantic antiquaries and successful biographers, "the minutiae of the past appear to be both close at hand and also in the golden distance. Moreover, one of the concomitants of a sense of *period* is a sense of *humour* in reference to the past."[96] She writes about her struggle to balance life and times, fly and amber, minutiae and golden distance in one coherent narrative arc:

> Happy the biographer who can discover this fatal implication in the beginning and end of his hero. Otherwise the history tends to be merely

a chronicle. There must be some spiritual logic, some hint of pattern, a few significant incidents of which, from time to time, we hear the echoes; in short, there must be a plot. But the old word for plot is fable, and when a biographer cannot discover a plot he has to invent a fable.[97]

She strives for something more than a "chronicle," even if she must speculate occasionally by straying from the historical into the aesthetic in search of "some hint of pattern." The discovery or invention of pattern differentiates the mere chronicler from the historical artist. For Mirrlees, her unfinished biographical acts became a way of keeping the past simultaneously close at hand and in the fabled, golden distance. Years earlier, while working on the Harrison biography, she had realized that this yearning for aesthetically pleasing narrative plots was also at the root of what she called "Jane's Intellectual Urge" for pattern:

> I have suddenly realized that Jane's itch was really aesthetic—what she admired was pattern. Where she differed from the purely literary artist was in medium. She admired Dörpfeld's theories, in the way a lover of letters admires, say, Virginia—i.e. for the beauty of the pattern. The conclusions drawn from vast learning by a brilliant & constructive intellect were what satisfied her aesthetic sense—truth was not her aim. As in all art there were restrictions, of course, & Unities which had to be observed, e.g. one was not allowed to invent the facts.[98]

Yet one could certainly embellish them, as Virginia Woolf had suggested while writing about the usefulness of the "creative fact" for modernist biographers, and one could refuse to police the boundaries of their potential significance.[99] Inspired by Harrison's "intellectual urge," Mirrlees's grand, somewhat indulgent search for—and sometimes creation of—the "pattern" of Cotton's life is part of why she called her book an "extravagant biography": "I have . . . used extravagant in its obsolete sense of *vagrant, wandering out of bounds.*"[100] Throughout the biography, she continues to flag her own careful attention to "obsolete" words and meanings, as though underscoring her ability, as in Warner's "queer duality," to live in multiple historical times simultaneously.[101] And if, to find that ever-desirable "hint of pattern" in Cotton's life story, she was sometimes forced to tip the scale in favor of amber, that was all to the good.

In a sense, I am forced to make the same choice now, as I speculate about the relationship—the "hint of pattern"—between the two projects that constitute Mirrlees's melancholic late biographical turn. As she assembled and annotated documents from Harrison's life, she (like Una Troubridge) was as much a curator as a biographer. And as Mary Beard and other scholars have shown, the editorial and curatorial choices made by Mirrlees during these years have had an incontestable influence on all future histories of Harrison's personal life and professional work. Before Harrison's death, Mirrlees was responsible for the burning of nearly all of her Cambridge papers; after her death, she became responsible for saving everything that remained. This is a striking reversal of roles.

In this light, it is important to remember that Cotton remains of particular interest to historians of English literature precisely because he is responsible for the preservation of singularly valuable historical and literary documents. After the Dissolution of the Monasteries between 1536 and 1541, Cotton was one of the first antiquaries to begin to purchase, collect, and preserve the old books and manuscripts that were being destroyed across all of England. As Mirrlees later put it, if "zeal in the salvaging of manuscripts be the sign of a true antiquary, then Cotton is the Simon Pure."[102] His famous library, comprised of books, manuscripts, medallions, and coins, has since formed the basis of the contemporary British Library, which still retains the idiosyncratic classification system from Cotton's library.[103] Significantly, Cotton saved an incredible number of documents from the doom of the bonfire: narrating this literary holocaust, Mirrlees describes the great "loss to letters" as many "thousands of innocent, beautiful and edifying books" were deemed popish poison and suffered "like butterflies with wings broken or torn off by little wanton boys."[104] At Oxford, "a large proportion of the manuscripts found in the neighbouring monasteries was burned in a bonfire.... And many manuscripts not totally destroyed suffered indignities that might have been invented by Panurge himself had he been let loose in a monastic library."[105] Cotton's library thus housed an impressive portion of the remainder of what was not burned or otherwise destroyed during these years. And he knew better than anyone else the locations of all other surviving manuscripts.[106]

Hope Mirrlees thus turned her attention to Cotton—the man responsible for saving so many of our most important literary manuscripts from early modern bonfires—during the very years she found herself unable to complete her biography of Harrison, whose personal papers she had urged into a bafflingly histrionic bonfire so many decades earlier. This is, as Mirrlees and Harrison would surely agree, a "hint of pattern" that should help us to read the plot, if not the fable, of Mirrlees's late biographical turn. After Harrison's death, she began these two biographical projects and joined what she had, only a year earlier, disparagingly called the "cult of the past."

CHAPTER THREE

Modernists Explain Things to Me

COLLECTING AS QUEER FEMINIST RESPONSE

WHEN MARGARET ANDERSON and Jane Heap decided to close the *Little Review*, the profoundly influential modernist little magazine they coedited from 1914 to 1929, they made plans to publish an unconventional final issue.[1] Something different; something unexpected. But for a magazine that had published some of the most daringly experimental literature ever written, what could possibly qualify as unconventional? In the course of its fifteen-year run, the *Little Review* had published an astonishing number of the writers now associated with high modernism: Sherwood Anderson, Djuna Barnes, H.D., T. S. Eliot, Elsa von Freytag-Loringhoven, James Joyce, Ernest Hemingway, Amy Lowell, Mina Loy, Gertrude Stein, and William Carlos Williams, among others. Given such visionary editorship, it is perhaps surprising that what they decided to pursue for the magazine's final issue was not really literature at all. Instead, in Anderson's words, they solicited a collection of life writing from "the artists of the world."[2] As advertised in the cover's top right corner, the issue promised "confessions and letters": "more than fifty of the foremost men in the arts tell the truth about themselves in this number."[3] To set this truth-telling in motion, Anderson and Heap designed a questionnaire. The issue itself was comprised of responses to the following:

QUESTIONNAIRE

1. What should you most like to do, to know, to be? (In case you are not satisfied.)
2. Why wouldn't you change places with any other human being?

3. What do you look forward to?
4. What do you fear most from the future?
5. What has been the happiest moment of your life? (If you care to tell.)
6. What do you consider your weakest characteristics? Your strongest? What do you like most about yourself? Dislike most?
7. What things do you really like? Dislike? (Nature, people, ideas, objects, etc. Answer in a phrase or a page, as you will.)
8. What is your attitude toward art to-day?
9. What is your world view? (Are you a reasonable being in a reasonable scheme?)
10. Why do you go on living?[4]

Rather than solicit new voices for a conversation about future literary and artistic production, they asked established artists to assess the recent past by answering these ten questions. Most of the questions assume a retrospective position, an understanding of oneself as having passed one's prime and entered a more mature, or even late, period. The phrasing of the second question—"Why wouldn't you change places with any other human being?"—makes the arguably outrageous assumption that none of the polled artists *would* consider trading places with anyone else. And the eighth question—"What is your attitude toward art to-day?"—practically invites a kids-these-days response of condescending dismissal. Yet despite a few questions so bland one would not be surprised to encounter them in Anderson's midwestern high school yearbook, the questionnaire ends with a characteristically caustic bang: "Why do you go on living?" Responses varied widely in content and form. Some, like Djuna Barnes, declined to address the questions at all except to disparage them. Others, like Dorothy Richardson, answered at length. In a pair of farewell editorials, Anderson and Heap addressed their own questions indirectly. Heap described the decision to end the *Little Review* as an inevitable consequence of answering some of the questions herself: "It is a matter for speculation whether anyone who has tried to get at real answers would dash into print with the results. I at least am keeping my answers for my own use and enlightenment."[5] And Anderson, too, noted her weariness of sanctimonious assertions about the artist's ability to transform the world: "I am not interested at the moment in transformation. I want a little illumination."[6] Their long-standing faith in the transformative social power of aesthetic experimentation and provocation had dimmed. To seek "illumination" is a fundamentally different mission—a more humble, if no less necessary, task. At the end of their editorial run, their questions for their long-standing contributors were largely retrospective in nature. The last issue of a journal devoted to experimental fiction was filled with writing about people's actual lives: what they had done, what they were doing now, what they wanted to do eventually.

For Anderson, the closing of the *Little Review* marked an important transition in her intellectual trajectory. Although she had already turned over the editorship of the magazine to Heap in 1923, it was only after this last issue was published in 1929 that she fully made the biographical turn that would characterize the rest of her literary production. As it turned out, after putting together that final number, she would spend the rest of her life preoccupied by various forms of life writing—not only about her life but about the lives of her closest friends and companions. But her *Little Review* days would reverberate throughout the years to come. She had spent the first portion of her life as an editor who, in Jessa Crispin's appropriately illuminating description, "hung the transatlantic wire that allowed electricity to flow between worlds, allowed French literature to influence American, British to influence Russian."[7] She had been convicted of obscenity after publishing portions of James Joyce's *Ulysses*, and she was directly responsible for the initial publication of much of what we now consider canonical modernist literature. Her significance to the history and development of transatlantic modernism is hard to overstate, yet it is often devalued. We have no biography of Margaret Anderson. A collection of her letters has not been published. She is present only tangentially in the biographical, cultural, and literary histories of the early twentieth century. And while this is equally true of someone like the poet and novelist Hope Mirrlees, who most often appears in contemporary scholarship through a series of footnotes and brief references in work primarily focused on other modernist writers, the ongoing devaluation of Anderson's work—editorial and otherwise—is still shocking.

Or perhaps it is not shocking at all. As Sarah Blackwood has argued, editing remains a form of undertheorized and underappreciated intellectual "carework."[8] While she acknowledges that literary history is rife with examples of editing as a masculine expression of mastery, connoisseurship, curation, or power struggle, Blackwood ultimately suggests that the "often invisible" editorial process should more often be considered a form of service work, and that, especially when that work is performed by women (as service work so often is), it is routinely devalued in favor of narratives of individual productivity and irrepressible genius. Editorial labor is carework precisely because, when done well, it is "often erased *in the very moment* of its acknowledgment: think here of the author of a monograph thanking those who have made this 'great work' possible. The more aligned editing becomes with feminized worlds of teaching, service, and care, the less cultural capital such work accrues."[9] In Blackwood's account, editorial labor and other forms of collaborative intellectual work are routinely devalued, to the ongoing detriment of women in particular, by the dominant "strictures of liberal individualist understandings of authorship."[10] These observations about the gendered misrecognition of contemporary editorial practices have a long history. As Jayne E. Marek details in *Women Editing Modernism: "Little" Magazines & Literary History*, the contributions of women editors and publishers to modernist literary history are routinely minimized: "discussions of women's work are usually predicated upon the work of associated men, or upon the assumption that women's accomplishments occurred in spite of their personalities rather than because of them."[11] And even when women's editorial, archival, and other paraliterary work is recognized as constituting a significant contribution to modernist literary history, the literary and artistic projects of women—unlike those of T. S. Eliot or Ezra Pound, for example, who were also important editors—are often relegated to the minor and considered less worthy of sustained attention. In this light, it is unsurprising that even Crispin, founding editor of the online literary magazines Bookslut.com and Spoilamag.com and author of a literary memoir purportedly devoted to modernism's "dead ladies," tempers her praise of Anderson's inspired editorial work by prefacing it with the disclaimer that Anderson "produced no important writing of her own."[12]

This chapter is about three women who are commonly understood to have produced no important writing of their own: Margaret Anderson, Sylvia Beach, and Alice B. Toklas. An editor, a bookseller-turned-publisher, and a secretary-companion. They are minor figures, in the sense that most people learn about these women through their relationships with other, more major modernist writers: Anderson as the editor of the *Little Review*, Beach as the self-proclaimed "midwife" of James Joyce's *Ulysses*, and Toklas as the "wife" of Gertrude Stein. But without denigrating the significance of these relationships, what happens if we recenter these women? Not just in terms of their significance to the history of Anglo-American modernist cultural production in interwar Paris but because of their midcentury contributions to what Kate Zambreno has recently referred to as the "modernist memory project."[13] What can we learn from what they themselves produced?

With this recentering in mind, the structure of this chapter acknowledges and continues a model of life writing that has been particularly influential within the history of queer feminist cultural production: the compilation and juxtaposition of three women's lives. To take just a few examples: Gertrude Stein's first published book, *Three Lives* (1909), contains the stories "The Good Anna," "Melanctha," and "The Gentle Lena." Feminist writer and activist Kate Millet's only documentary feature film, *Three Lives* (1971), which was produced by an all-woman crew, focuses on the reminiscences of three women: Millet's sister, Mallory Millet-Jones; chemist Lillian Shreve; and artist Robin Mide. And Lisa Cohen's *All We Know: Three Lives* (2012) performs the dramatic recovery of Esther Murphy, Mercedes de Acosta, and Madge Garland, three women who, in very different ways, were adjacent to modernist cultural production but are frequently forgotten by contemporary modernist studies. While the first two chapters of this book were each devoted to a pair of passion projects—the intimate archives of Una Troubridge and Sylvia Townsend Warner; the failed biographies attempted by Djuna Barnes and Hope Mirrlees—this chapter takes the shape of a triangle. In calling attention to this shape, I do not mean to suggest the dramatic messiness we might expect from the "love triangles" of Radclyffe Hall, Valentine Ackland, and others. Instead, taking my cue from Geometry 101, I read this triangle as a strong formation, one that is difficult to break and, with any luck, impossible to ignore.

This chapter's triangle contains the lives—and life writing—of Anderson, Beach, and Toklas. While the relative "importance" of their prose may be the subject of ongoing debate or casual dismissal, each of these three women published and otherwise prepared substantial biographical acts in the middle decades of the twentieth century. These memoirs of the so-called Lost Generation—Anderson's *My Thirty Years' War* (1930), Beach's *Shakespeare and Company* (1959), and Toklas's *What Is Remembered* (1963)—garnered generally positive reviews in most major publications, though their reviewers tended to assert their historical rather than literary value. Largely anecdotal in nature, these books are frequently considered to have been compiled rather than written, edited rather than created. In each case, the extensive labor of their editorial "carework" is elided and rendered invisible.

Beyond their published books, these women were also each actively, if differently, arranging for the preservation of their collections of modernist literature, artwork, and ephemera. As Sean Latham and Gayle Rogers have detailed, part of modernism's midcentury consolidation relied upon the "aggressive campaign [of institutions such as the Harry Ransom Center, the Yale Collection of American Literature, the University of Buffalo, and the University of Tulsa] to collect the archives of modernist writers."[14] And in *Collecting as Modernist Practice*, Jeremy Braddock has argued that, especially during this period, collecting was a "mode of public engagement modeling future . . . relationships between audience and artwork."[15] Braddock is most interested in thinking about art collections (that were privately collected but publicly exhibited) and what he calls "interventionist" literary anthologies, but his theory of collecting as public engagement provides a useful frame for understanding the modernist collections of Beach, Anderson, and Toklas. Furthermore, taking into account Braddock's convincing description of a "collecting aesthetic" as "one of the paradigmatic forms of modernist art," I suggest that this is what we see in the midcentury memoirs compiled by the women in this chapter.[16] Each of these books is, essentially, a textual collection: an edited group of fragmented anecdotes, a gathering together of pieces of our literary past in an effort to shape our future reception of it.

This chapter considers these projects—life writing and collecting—together, in inextricable relation to one another, as the consuming passion projects of each woman's late period. In this triangulated reading, the life writing and collecting of Anderson, Beach, and Toklas are late genres that preserve a counterhistory of modernism grounded in women's lives. During the same midcentury moment that the first histories of modernism were published—histories that established the overwhelmingly masculine modernist canon that, despite our best efforts, still persists today—these biographical acts demonstrate queer women's resistance to their own impending marginalization and even exclusion from the dominant narratives of late twentieth-century literary history.

Modernism's Midwife: Sylvia Beach's Unfinished Jobs

Before returning to an extended discussion of the passion projects that dominated Margaret Anderson's late period, I first turn to the more well-known figure of Sylvia Beach. Famous both for founding Shakespeare and Company, her bohemian bookstore in interwar Paris, and for publishing James Joyce's *Ulysses* when no one else would, Beach had by 1925 become, in literary critic Eugene Jolas's estimation, "probably the best known woman in Paris" and "certainly one of the most important figures in contemporary letters."[17] From that height of literary celebrity, Beach's profile slowly faded over the years. Her Shakespeare and Company never reopened after World War II, and she never published anyone other than Joyce. But she had published modernism's most scandalous novel, hung out with Hemingway, met "the ladies with high collars and monocles" at

Natalie Barney's salon, and refused to sell her last copy of *Finnegans Wake* to a Nazi.[18] By the middle of the century, she had stories to tell.

And tell them she did. In 1959, four years after the suicide of her partner, Adrienne Monnier, Beach—then seventy-two years old—published *Shakespeare and Company*, a collection of remembrances and vignettes about the years she spent at the helm of the Left Bank bookstore and lending library of the same name. She had begun the work many years earlier, at least in part because she hoped she might make some money out of it (remember that publishing Joyce almost destroyed her, financially), but it was slow going, especially as Monnier's health grew worse and she required constant care. The project took many years. In Princeton University's collection of Sylvia Beach Papers, a nearly blank notebook labeled "Notes for Memoirs" contains the following set of questions and answers:

Questions	Answers
What about your memoirs? ...	Working on 'em —
When do you think they'll be finished? ...	Dunno—
When are they coming out? ...	When they're finished—
Do you think they'll ever be finished? ...	I wonder—
Aren't they just about finished? ...	I guesso—[19]

The possibility that she would never finish the book certainly seems to have crossed her mind. The tone of this miniature self-interview is playful, even mocking, a literary version of Abbott and Costello's "Who's on first?" routine. But its circularity is also darkly Beckettian, its structure resonant with the now infamous last lines of *The Unnamable*: "I can't go on. I'll go on."[20] What's more, her questions betray an anxious uncertainty about the status of a properly finished work. She avows that they will come out "when they're finished," but when asked about when that will be, she replies in three different ways that each refuse the idea that the question has a stable premise: "Dunno—," "I wonder—," "I guesso—," all followed by dashes that extend her ongoing difficulties in finishing the project down to the granular, grammatical level of the sentence itself. What does it mean to call something finished? How does one know when to stop finishing it? Her reluctance to answer such questions once helped to produce the final form of *Ulysses*, as Beach famously allowed Joyce to continue making changes to the novel throughout several sets of proofs. Why should she hold herself to a different philosophical standard regarding the hairline difference between finished and unfinished work?

Still, after Monnier's death, she seemed to feel an increased responsibility to complete the book, even going so far as to suggest, in an unpublished, undated manuscript page, that finishing it had become her primary reason for living:

> Can see no remedy at all for the swooping down of death on someone you love. What preceeds [*sic*] it for a long or short time and the ridiculous ceremonies however simplified accompanying the internment of "deceased", the regrets rightly termed "eternal", the realization that the person is gone for good, without giving you another chance to do things better and not be so inattentive to what's really important—yet you were given plenty of time—years to improve!
>
> Maybe—surely she had something more to disclose if you had listened closer.
>
> This feeling of incompleteness is one of death's worst cruelties. Sometimes you wish you had left with her as she suggested—she knew what living without her was going to be like. She knew everything—Adrienne.
>
> But leaving my jobs unfinished, I seemed to feel it important to tidy up before going—why were years not enough to clear away rubbish—why and how and when and where did it accumulate? Been playing around all my life—butterflying and skimming—"vierges folles."[21]

Though filed in with other undated drafts of *Shakespeare and Company*, this heartbreaking page never made it into the published text. Like Toklas's *What Is Remembered*, which ends with Stein's death in 1946, Beach's book ends with Hemingway's "liberation" of Shakespeare and Company (and then "the cellar at the Ritz") at the end of World War II.[22] Though *Shakespeare and Company* does begin with an autobiographical sketch of Beach's childhood and adolescence before she moved to Paris, it abruptly stops without a similarly autobiographical conclusion covering the years between the end of the war and the book's eventual publication. The story stops, but Beach's life went on, and the absence of this continued narrative imparts a "feeling of incompleteness" entirely separate from "the swooping down of death." Instead of writing about those years, Beach chose to formalize that feeling, to stay behind after Adrienne's death and publish the book after tidying up, after clearing up, but before actually finishing it. That "feeling of incompleteness" haunts even the "finished," published version of *Shakespeare and Company*.

Yet though initial reviews were positive, and the book remains in print, Beach's formal and stylistic choices have been all but ignored. Just as Beach is most commonly remembered as merely the "midwife" of *Ulysses*, her memoir is usually valued for its content—for what it can tell us about the lives of canonical modernist figures like Joyce, Hemingway, Pound, and Stein—rather than as a deliberate formal experiment in its own right. So what do we see if we shift our focus onto the form of *Shakespeare and Company*?

An early critic called it "a charming, gay astringent scrapbook," and this description of *Shakespeare and Company* as a "scrapbook" rather than a more conventional autobiography is sound.[23] As Ellen Gruber Garvey argues in another context, scrapbooks could serve as "adjuncts to professional careers," contribute to the material culture of fandom, or, in a more political vein, allow "people in positions of relative powerlessness" to make "a place for themselves and their communities by finding, sifting, analyzing, and recirculating writing that mattered to them."[24] If we look closely at *Shakespeare and Company*, we see a book in which the artistic work of the disenfranchised modernist author may be reimagined as curation rather than creation. It is full of personal anecdotes, quotations from letters, annotated photographs, hand-drawn cartoons and other images, and reproductions of significant manuscript pages and publications.

In his introduction to the most recent edition, James Laughlin describes Beach's compositional strategy like this: she "put the name of a person or a topic at the head of the page and then type[d] in what was remembered about him or it. No need to worry about structure or chronology."[25] This is somewhat of a caricature. Beach's volume moves in a roughly chronological order from her childhood adoration of Paris to her settlement there after World War I all the way through to Hemingway's return to the Left Bank. But Laughlin is correct that Beach didn't worry all that much about a strict structure: in a letter to a friend, the infamous modernist patron, editor, and political activist Harriet Shaw Weaver, she explained (too hard on herself, as usual) that she was "given to dwell endlessly on something of no importance, then rattle along in an airy way when [she] should be paying attention."[26] Like Alice B. Toklas and Margaret Anderson, as we shall see, Beach was drawn toward the anecdotal mode as that which falls somewhere between the literary and the historical, between the pliable whimsy of fantasy and the uncontroversial hardness of fact.

The anecdote thus opens up the possibility of composition as curation rather than creation. I am suggesting, here, that Beach—like Anderson,

Toklas, and so many of the other women in this book—was working in a late archival mode of artistic production. She was trying to get it right, trying to tell the story of her life as an American expat in literary Paris. It was the story of modernism's "Lost Generation," most obviously, but it was also *her* story, *her* bookshop, *her* partnership with Monnier (to whom the fragmented memoir was eventually dedicated) that would be preserved in its pages. She was sometimes frustrated by the corrections several well-meaning friends made to her drafts, especially after her publishers decided to put out a small portion of her work-in-progress as a "Christmas gift book" in 1956. Titled *Ulysses in Paris*, it, like the eventually completed memoir, would be considered a book about Joyce, not about Beach. In a letter to Weaver, who had written to correct an "erroneous account" published in this excerpted text, Beach responded, in what I can only imagine is an exasperated tone, that she "should never have written memoirs without a memory" and that she should probably have Joseph Prescott, the Joyce scholar who was then working through her private collection, finish them for her. "He," she went on, "is a walking file cabinet, everything neatly in its place."[27]

Beach understood that she herself wasn't exactly a "walking file cabinet," but at the same time, she was rapidly transforming her home into something remarkably akin to a file cabinet. During the years in which she worked on her memoir, she was actually working on two other major archival and curatorial projects. First, aware of her advancing age, she was busy "making a minute catalogue" of her library in order to arrange for its sale and preservation: "I have been hurrying myself a bit these last weeks," she wrote, "slicking up my memoirs and cataloguing or at least trying to, some of my library which might have to be moved across the Atlantic one of these days. This is a job I would have preferred to do after, not during, the one on my book, but owing to circumstances I had no choice."[28] This "cataloguing" work makes her not only the publisher of *Ulysses* but also one of the first and most crucial Joyceans, as much of the Joyce material available at SUNY Buffalo today has survived because of Beach's dedicated preservation efforts.[29] Second, she assisted the U.S. Embassy in Paris with the preparation of a monumental 1959 exhibit about the expat writers of the 1920s called "The Twenties: American Writers and Their Friends in Paris." By all accounts, this exhibit could not have taken place without Beach's willingness to loan out her personal collection: nearly all of the six hundred items displayed belonged to her.[30]

In Beach's late career, we thus recognize the cultivation and demonstration of an archival consciousness. In the last few years of her life—what she called her "official period"[31]—she was (a) writing a memoir, (b) "cataloguing" her massive archive of literary material, and (c) curating a major cultural exhibit filled with artifacts from her personal collection. In this chapter, and in this book as a whole, I suggest that we must understand these activities as interrelated modes of turning years of personal witness into public testimony and commentary. This is the act of collection, of curation—rather than creation and innovation—as modernist artistic work.

So, Sylvia Beach: collector, curator, chronicler of modernism. Given this frame, it is no wonder that her name has come to stand for not only Shakespeare and Company but Shakespeare, Joyce, Hemingway, Stein, and Company. Although Beach's memoirs, letters, and surviving archive are mined more for evidence about Joyce and other major writers than for information about Beach's own life, the story of Beach and Monnier's relationship is legible to us today in large part because their story was preserved in the larger narrative of the artistically renowned bohemian community in which they lived and worked. Her stories about Joyce dominate the pages of her published memoir, but her long companionship with Monnier is quietly and casually evident on nearly every page—and on so many of the pages edited out of the initial publication, like that mournful description of how she remained alive after Monnier's death only to "tidy up." In the published book, Monnier is everywhere: in the index, the only list of entries longer than the list of entries about Joyce is the list about Monnier. The first bookstore described in its pages is not her own but "the little gray bookshop of A. Monnier."[32] And her description of their first interaction demands more (though not much more!) than surface reading:

> I was disguised in a Spanish cloak and hat, but Adrienne knew at once that I was American. "I like America very much," she said. I replied that I liked France very much. And, as our future collaboration proved, we meant it.[33]

Throughout the rest of the book, Beach moves casually between a singular and plural first-person perspective. In a section titled "The Thirties," for example, a single paragraph contains the following lines: "Many of my friends had gone home.... But we still had a few of our best friends around the Quarter, at least for a time."[34] Monnier's name does not appear anywhere on this page. But she is still unmistakably present, the inextricable other part of the "we" Beach uses throughout the book.

Furthermore, it is not just their relationship that she preserved in her book's pages. Reading *Shakespeare and Company* today, even in its condensed, edited form, reveals the many ways in which Beach collected the names of so many modernist women writers who were being slowly forgotten as male scholars left them out of their accounts of the period. For example, marking the death of Mary Butts, she notes that "all of her books that had appeared disappeared, too; they seemed to go out of print after she died."[35] And in writing about the singular literary genius of Djuna Barnes, she reminds her readers that "she doesn't seem to have been given her due in books on writers of the period. Certainly she was one of the most talented and, I think, one of the most fascinating literary figures in the Paris of the twenties."[36] I could go on: years before feminist literary critics began the important work of recovery and reclamation that continues today, there was, speckled throughout Beach's memoir, a collection of small but insistent notes about Natalie Barney, Bryher, Radclyffe Hall, Mina Loy, Katherine Anne Porter, Gertrude Stein, Alice B. Toklas, "Saint Harriet" Weaver, and other modernist women writers and artists. This is collection as modernist practice, yes, but it is also collection as a specifically queer feminist modernist practice.

If, as Ann Cvetkovich cautions, the queer "archive of feelings" is comprised of ephemeral, unpublished, even unfinished "objects that might not normally be considered archival," then we must learn to think about the queer modernist archive differently.[37] What have we inherited, and from whom? Who has been disinherited in the process of preserving the archive of literary modernism? The question of what is in any given collection of archival evidence is only ever the first question. Who did the collecting, and why? Who collected this as evidence of what, exactly, and whose stories are rendered invisible? Part of our work now, in relation to the fragmented archival present of modernism's queer feminist history, is to learn to recognize—and thus, in a way, inherit—the collections undertaken, if not fully published or wholly preserved, by the women we might think of (with reference to Sara Ahmed's powerful formulation) as the aging killjoys of our past.

The Queer Disinheritance of Alice B. Toklas

In this section, I address the life and late work of someone we might think of as having been rendered invisible in plain sight: Alice B. Toklas. If you've read any Gertrude Stein, the odds are good that you've picked up *The Autobiography of Alice B. Toklas*, the 1933 best seller written "as if by her secretary-companion."[38] Surely, you might think, someone immortalized in Stein's most well-read book does not require recovery? Her infamous recipe for "Haschich Fudge" notwithstanding, however, the odds are substantially less good that you've read any of Toklas's own writing.[39] We know that Toklas wrote many, many letters during and after her long relationship with Stein. Despite repeated suggestions from her friends, however, she refused to write anything like a memoir for some time after Stein's death in 1946, reasoning that she didn't need to do it because "Gertrude did my autobiography and it's done."[40] Eventually, in 1954, she published *The Alice B. Toklas Cookbook*, which was followed four years later by *Aromas and Flavors of Past and Present* (another cookbook, though she later distanced herself from this one due to editorial squabbles), and finally, in 1963, she published *What Is Remembered*.[41] This last title is, in fact, a memoir—during the process of composition, it had several titles, including *Conversations with Miss Toklas* and *The Autobiography of Alice B. Toklas by Alice B. Toklas*.[42] Yet despite the fact that Toklas had outlived Stein by many years, *What Is Remembered* ends abruptly with Stein's death. The last sentence? "Then the whole afternoon was troubled, confused and very uncertain, and later in the afternoon they took her away on a wheeled stretcher to the operating room and I never saw her again."[43] Like Beach's *Shakespeare and Company*, the end of Toklas's book feels like an abrupt interruption, an incomplete ending. It is as though Toklas's life—her real life, her reportable life—ended at the moment of Stein's death, and that is so often how we continue to think of Toklas: either with Stein or not at all. But of course Toklas's life did not end with Stein's, and, in this section, I want to call attention to the way our literary inheritance of Stein depends upon the material disinheritance of Toklas. Given this queer disinheritance, I suggest that Toklas's midcentury life writing signals not only an unsuccessful attempt to salvage her dwindling finances but an extralegal, affective claim on Stein's estate and legacy. If we tend to only remember Toklas now as Stein's partner, this writing insists that we remember their relationship as an actual, if not necessarily equal, partnership.

After a lifetime as Stein's "secretary-companion," Toklas became her secretary-archivist in the years after her death. Continuing the work they had begun during the last years of their life together, she meticulously catalogued and collated Stein's unpublished manuscripts so that they could be both published and preserved according to the terms of Stein's will. Stein wanted everything published, and she wanted everything archived at Yale. Even before Stein's death, they had already sent enough material to Yale that there had been a serious exhibition on Stein held at the Beinecke in 1941. According to Donald Gallup, curator of the Yale Collection of American Literature, Stein had been "very much interested" in the tremendous success of the exhibition and promised to send them even more material after the war.[44] Yet Carl Van Vechten, who served as Stein's official literary executor, was "staggered" by the amount of work this entailed: in a 1947 letter to Toklas, he admitted that he "had no idea there was so much, and I am practically convinced if you want to carry out Baby's wishes in toto it will be necessary to sell a picture (or two)."[45] Eventually, as we know, everything made it to Yale, and almost everything made it into print. But the last part of his sentence—"it will be necessary to sell a picture (or two)"—is particularly telling. Stein's literary archive was donated, not sold, to Yale, and the posthumous publication of Stein's unpublished work was financed in large part by Stein's estate. Stein and Toklas had shared a life together for decades. They were partners, companions, wives. Yet, after Stein's death, Toklas's life was thrown into turmoil.

Although Stein's will ostensibly provided for Toklas, it provided detailed instructions for her own legacy first. The second paragraph bequeaths Picasso's portrait of Stein to the Metropolitan Museum of Art; the third paragraph bequeaths "all my manuscripts, and all my correspondence and photographs which may have any artistic or literary value, to the Library of Yale University"; and the fourth paragraph bequeaths to Carl Van Vechten "such sum of money" as he would, "in his absolute discretion, deem necessary for the publication of my unpublished manuscripts."[46] Toklas—then sixty-nine years old—was almost an afterthought:

> All the rest and residue of my Estate, of whatsoever kind and wheresoever situated, I give and bequeath to my friend, ALICE B. TOKLAS, of 5 rue Christine, Paris 5°, to her use for life and, insofar as it may become necessary for her proper maintenance and support, I authorize my Executors to make payments to her from the principal of my Estate and, for that purpose, to reduce to cash any paintings or other personal property belonging to my estate.[47]

Upon first glance, this appears as though it should have been sufficient to ensure Toklas would be comfortable throughout her remaining years. However, Stein seems not to have accounted for the ease with which a person of such a legally ambiguous (that is, queer) relationship to Stein could be bullied out of the support that was rightfully hers. While greed is more than enough to explain Toklas's effective disinheritance, it is surely not too much of a stretch to affirm that sexism and homophobia were its catalysts. It is difficult to imagine, in other words, that Stein's husband—had she had one—would have been so effectively marginalized after the tragic death of his beloved wife. And, in any case, Stein certainly failed to adequately estimate the cost of such voluminous posthumous publication. In a letter to Toklas, Van Vechten worried—rightly, as it turned out—about "the cost to your comfort of the expense [of publication]," but Toklas urged him to follow Stein's wishes, no matter the impact on her own quality of life.[48] Van Vechten describes the "endless amount of work" it will take to publish all of Stein's work, but he specifically notes that he was "not afraid of that." Instead, what made him nervous was "the cost to your comfort of the expense, UNLESS YOU ARE WILLING TO SELL SOME PICTURES."[49] After publication costs, the principal of the estate was left to nearly nothing—in the vocabulary of Stein's will, it was far more "residue" than "rest." Even after substantially cutting down her living expenses, the increasingly unhealthy and elderly Toklas was left with a choice: either sell some of the modernist paintings they had collected together or descend into poverty. For a long time, she desperately tried to avoid selling that "picture (or two)" even though, as their value increased (she had twenty-eight Picassos!), she couldn't raise the funds necessary to insure them properly. She finally agreed to write her memoirs; alas, they did not do well enough to guarantee her financial security. Eventually, feeling as though she had exhausted all other options, she agreed to sell some paintings, but as the court-appointed estate lawyer informed her, "the Stein children [that is, Gertrude's brother's children], as remaindermen, have objected to the sale of any pictures without their prior consent."[50]

Stein's relatives contested Toklas's right not only to sell paintings included in the estate but to make further donations to Yale on her own behalf. In a letter to Toklas written when the "residual Steins" attempted to reclaim Toklas's gift of "two little chairs," Gallup asked, "Aren't they going to admit that you had the right to own anything at all yourself?"[51] The answer, unfortunately, was a resounding no. Toklas died nearly penniless, her right to inherit the Stein estate—even the paintings they had collected together, even the items she had purchased or created on her own—hotly contested by several of Stein's relatives (the widow of her nephew, Allan Stein, in particular), to whom the estate would pass after Toklas's death. Yet our inheritance of Stein's queer modernism— the many volumes of Stein's work and the Stein collections at the Beinecke and the Ransom Center—exists in large part because of Toklas's self-sacrificing preservation work. (Unlike the arguably similar work of Hope Mirrlees, the skill and faithfulness of this archival work are evident in the degree to which—and ease with which—Toklas can be made to disappear from it.) As Gallup detailed in the Yale *Gazette*, the Beinecke's Stein collection is "a monument as lasting as marble," and much of it was made available "through the kindness of Miss Toklas."[52] Even as Toklas was finishing work on this "monument," she was being materially disinherited and denied the provisions explicitly made in Stein's will to assure her lasting comfort.

This is queer disinheritance. Despite the forthright publicity of the long relationship between Stein and Toklas, and despite the explicit legal protections Stein extended to Toklas in her will, the estate came under intense familial pressure from Stein's blood relatives. As the value of the remaining Picassos and other paintings continued to rise throughout the century, Toklas was both an obstacle and a threat to their eventual inheritance. They attempted to remove the artwork from Toklas's care in several ways: for example, since she could not keep up with the rising insurance premiums on the artwork without selling some of it in order to insure the rest of it (and they objected to such sales after discovering that Toklas had sold several paintings below market price), they asked the court to take the art away from Toklas for safekeeping.[53] This claim, made on behalf of the future inheritance of their children, works on the logic of what Lee Edelman has called "reproductive futurity,"[54] and it effectively disinherited Stein's chosen partner. In 1960, while Toklas was spending time in Rome for her increasingly fragile health, the Steins sued for removal of the paintings from her Paris apartment; they won, and the paintings were moved into a vault at the Chase Manhattan Bank. Finally, in 1963, at the age of eighty-six, Alice B. Toklas was kicked out of her Paris apartment. The building was being sold, and while she was given the option to buy the apartment she had shared with Stein, she could not afford to do so. The "residual Steins" were naturally not among the friends who banded together to try to stop the eviction and, when that failed, find her a new home.[55] She died in poverty in 1967.

Toklas's story demonstrates the vulnerability of queer estates, literary and otherwise. Despite their "legendary" relationship—which, as art historian Alice T. Friedman contends, survives not only because "they made their private lesbian relationship a matter of public consumption" but because "they created and preserved their own archive of texts and photographs as a way of proving their existence"[56]—Toklas was materially disinherited. But queer literary inheritance has always required other, extralegal forms of world-building. Life writing is one way of ensuring what Kevin Ohi has called, in another context, "queer literary transmission": "the conveying of knowledge in pedagogy, the transmission and material preservation of texts."[57] As a couple, Stein and Toklas built the archive of their lives together; as a widow attempting to continue on alone, Toklas—once described by Janet Flanner as "the most widowed woman I know"[58]—continued to assert her connection to Stein by writing it, again and again, into history. In some of the uncorrected proofs to *What Is Remembered*, Toklas seems to have considered ending her book with a discussion of Stein's will. Explicitly stating that "Gertrude Stein had left me in the life tenancy of the flat and the pictures," she describes how she went on to live without expectation after Stein's death:

> The portrait by Picasso she left to the Metropolitan Museum, who wrote me that they were making her a benefactor of the museum. Someone told me that was what they did to anyone who left them a picture or pictures to the value of seventy-five thousand dollars, which was the first indication to me of the enormous value of the Picassos. Gertrude Stein had never wanted to know the value of the pictures; she said that it was not her affair.
>
> I picked up my life as I could, not expecting in the least that I should live. It seemed so natural that if Gertrude were not going to be here I wouldn't either.
>
> The years since, one year after the other, have been sad but not unkind. I have been attended to by friends, too numerous and too generous to mention, and I have been blessed with the comfort of the Church.
>
> Until quite recently I had the pleasure of Gertrude's collection of pictures. Now they are gone. When I returned to Paris from Milan last year, after taking the baths at Aqui for arthritis, the pictures had been removed from my apartment because of the risk of theft. As my sight has grown dim and my memory of the pictures is still vivid, I suffered little from their loss.[59]

In this version of *What Is Remembered*, Toklas implicitly acknowledges the loss of her inheritance—"Now they are gone."—but ultimately makes light of it. Her memory, her archive of feelings, remains with her, even if the physical traces of their life together were stripped from her possession, one by one. But this is not how the published version ends. Instead, *What Is Remembered* ends with Stein's death, and Toklas never grows old alone. After assisting Van Vechten in fulfilling Stein's desire for preservation and publication, Toklas' midcentury life writing continued to affirm the importance of their relationship above all else. In her illuminating study of Toklas's three autobiographies, Anna Linzie rightly observes that, "in its content and temporal scope, . . . *What is Remembered* almost entirely stays within the frame established by *The Autobiography [of Alice B. Toklas]*."⁶⁰ But rather than read this as a shortcoming, Linzie calls it one of Toklas's "tricks of evasion": "keeping in mind [her] talent for disguise and camouflage, this . . . need not indicate that she is *sadly* missing from her autobiography, or that her autobiography is failed, but rather that her agency in the text resides precisely in the right to remain silent."⁶¹ In a "trick of evasion" that thumbs her nose at the residual Steins—I suffered so little, we might imagine her saying, that I will not even acknowledge their loss in print—Toklas herself removed her impoverished, largely solitary, late period from literary history.

Others—particularly other queer women writers—found such omissions scandalous, however, and they wrote her right back in. In the next section of this chapter, I return once more to Margaret Anderson, whose late "Collection" contains an account of a conversation she had had with journalist Janet Flanner after Stein's death:

> I congratulated her on the article she had written in the *New Yorker* about the fate of Gertrude's famous paintings, regretting that they hadn't been left to Alice Toklas.
> "You gave so many interesting details about Gertrude's will that I suppose you were swamped with appreciative letters", I said. "Not at all", Janet said—"not one. No one seemed to care. Over here we all felt it shameful that Alice had the right only to sell one or two in case she badly needed money." "Shocking", I said.⁶²

No one else cared. But they did. Flanner wrote not one but two accounts of Toklas's disinheritance in the *New Yorker*, the second of which seethed with a barely controlled rage over Toklas's all-but-forgotten legacy. She noted that it was only through Toklas's "penury and self-denial, plus her driving determination," that the volumes of Stein's unpublished work were printed by Yale University Press.⁶³ And, after Toklas's eventual death, the collection of paintings and drawings "which Alice had fought so bitterly to keep in tact [*sic*] as a memorial to [Stein], became the property of Allan Stein's children and was dispersed by them without sentiment."⁶⁴ Some of this, writes Flanner, became "the nucleus, in December of 1970, of a spectacular exhibition [at the Museum of Modern Art]—'Four Americans in Paris: The Collections of Gertrude Stein and Her Family.'"⁶⁵ I have a copy of the catalogue for this exhibition. It is gorgeously bound in red leather with gold lettering. Four black-and-white photographs—the four expat Americans, Stein and "her family"—adorn the cover.

Alice B. Toklas is not among them.

Beyond Biography: Margaret Anderson's "Collection"

Unlike Alice B. Toklas, whose midcentury life writing explicitly attempted to make "what is remembered" about her synonymous with what is remembered about the life she shared with Stein, Margaret Anderson spent the entire second half of her life trying to establish her own independent identity. She was only forty-four years old when the last issue of the *Little Review* was published, and she would spend the next forty-three years attempting to produce what generations of critics have almost uniformly failed to see as "important writing of her own." Only a year later, in 1930, she published *My Thirty Years' War*, the first in a three-volume autobiographical series that would eventually include *The Fiery Fountains* (1951) and *The Strange Necessity* (1962). In addition to this trilogy, she also published *The Unknowable Gurdjieff* (1962), an account of her studies with George Ivanovich Gurdjieff, a mystic philosopher and spiritual teacher.[66] And, in the final years of her life, she wrote a lesbian novel loosely based on her own experiences; although she could not find a publisher in her lifetime, the manuscript would eventually be rediscovered, edited, and posthumously published under the title *Forbidden Fires* (1996). While Anderson did not herself identify any of these books as explicitly biographical projects, they are all varieties of life writing: personal narratives that open into stories about friends, colleagues, and, sometimes, an entire generation of artists and writers.

In one view, it is easy to see Anderson's life as divided into two separate phases: the first, editorial and "important," from roughly 1914 to 1929; the second, retrospective and "unimportant," from 1930 until her death in 1973. But this quick categorization misrecognizes the ways in which her personal memoirs—and, later, her personal "Collection"—were themselves massive editorial projects. The entwined passion projects of life writing and collection pushed back against the rapid consolidation of modernism as a predominantly masculine movement—a history that was beginning to take shape in literary criticism such as Edmund Wilson's *Axel's Castle: A Study of the Imaginative Literature of 1870–1930* (1931) and generational autobiography such as Malcolm Cowley's *Exile's Return: A Literary Odyssey of the 1920s* (first published to little acclaim in 1934 with the subtitle "A Narrative of Ideas" and later republished in 1951 with the subtitle "A Literary Odyssey of the 1920s"). Wilson's book described W. B. Yeats, James Joyce, T. S. Eliot, Gertrude Stein, Marcel Proust, and Paul Valéry as "the culmination of a self-conscious and very important literary movement."[67] And while Cowley's book was slightly more inclusive, Sherwood Anderson is the only "Anderson" in either index.

By then, however, Margaret Anderson was accustomed to being overlooked and underappreciated. In the opening paragraph of *My Thirty Years' War*, she describes the ongoing "war" of her title: "I have never been able to accept the two great laws of humanity—that you're always being suppressed if you're inspired and always being pushed into the corner if you're exceptional. I won't be cornered and I won't stay suppressed. This book is a record of those refusals."[68] Omitted from the rapidly calcifying histories of modernism, the inspired and exceptional Margaret Anderson compiled her own.

But despite generally positive critical reviews, her books neither sold well nor made much of an impact. They were valued almost entirely for their anecdotes about more famous figures, and, today, they are out of print. In a review of her collected memoirs in the *New York Times Book Review*, Alfred Kazin paid Anderson the sort of dubious compliment that continues to shadow her legacy: "I believe everything that Margaret Anderson says precisely because she is not a writer but a rhapsodist without guile."[69] This critical consensus that Anderson was "not a writer," that she, in Crispin's later phrasing, "produced no important writing of her own," continues to shape her legacy. As feminist historian Elizabeth Francis has shown, the category of the dilettante editor and that of the expat lesbian constitute the "two distinct frames of reference" that have contributed to Anderson's marginal historical position. For literary historians, Francis suggests, Anderson has been "primarily understood as a dilettante who happened to be in the right place at the right time, surrounded by the right people, especially Ezra Pound, to publish groundbreaking modernist writing."[70] And when not categorized as a dilettante editor, she has been claimed by feminist and queer historians most interested in her membership in the expatriate lesbian community in interwar Paris. The effect of these histories, Francis demonstrates, is that Anderson's "unconventional womanhood has been the basis for her dismissal as a serious modernist figure and a source of celebration."[71]

Anderson chafed against this critical dismissal. Kazin's claim that she "could have become anything except a great writer" clearly irked her, as she had written a novel but, due to its explicitly lesbian themes, could find no one willing to publish it.[72] In an unsent response to Kazin, she admitted that she was "rather grieved by your insistence in regarding me as a non-writer. Of course I've never regarded myself as a real writer, but lately I've begun to think that I was becoming one, and now you strip me of that excitement. All the letters I receive about my books praise my way of *writing*—'Your phrasings, your style—it is almost as if you had created a new form', and so on."[73] But while she questioned the nearly incessant devaluation of her prose by professional literary critics, she simultaneously admitted her own sense of herself as working in a different "realm." In a letter to publisher Coburn Britton, she remarked, "You see, cher ami, that I'm more *appreciator* than *creator*. I never think of myself as a writer, but as a *discusser*."[74] As someone who had, over half a century earlier, founded the *Little Review* in order to "spend [her] time filling it up with the best conversation the world has to offer," Anderson continued to see herself as primarily a "discusser"—an editor by both calling and trade.[75]

Rather than concede that this constitutionally curatorial nature was somehow inferior, however, Anderson proudly identified herself as an "appreciator," an elevated amateur, even a dilettante. As noted elsewhere in this book, contemporary critics have undertaken a similar reassessment and reclamation of the virtues of amateurism. Carolyn Dinshaw, for example, recognizes the value of "various ways of knowing that are derived not only from positions of detachment but also—remembering the etymology of amateur—from positions of affect and attachment, from desires to build another kind of world."[76] And Marjorie Garber reminds us that the categories of "amateur" and "professional" occupy an ever-shifting but inextricable relationship in which "they produce . . . [and] define each other by mutual affinities and exclusions."[77] Artistic and literary worlds require both amateurs and professionals, appreciators and creators, discussers and writers. As Anderson once explained at length, they work in different, sometimes (though not always) complementary, ways:

> A dilettante is a person who knows all those "small, perfect things" that scholars know nothing about. I, as a dilettante, know everything that intellectuals don't know, and intellectuals know everything that I don't know. Intellectuals and scholars have no interest in the discriminations that I love; they understand nothing about them, don't want to listen to them; aren't even *capable* of hearing them.[78]

Although Anderson had earlier referred to herself as a "discusser," she here highlights her equally profound gifts as a listener. She can hear things that intellectuals do not even notice. An accomplished pianist herself, Anderson's theorizations of artistic discernment often employ musical comparisons. For example, in a further illustration of the dilettante's particular capacities, Anderson recounted a story about Brahms's infamous critical appreciation of a young pianist's recital: "I *hate* what you play," he is said to have pronounced, "but I *love* the way you play it. You never hurt the sounds." This is an unexpectedly synesthesiac explanation. How can sounds get hurt? To some, this will seem like nonsense. But this is Anderson's point. Not everyone—not even every so-called expert—is capable of recognizing, much less understanding, the difference between sounds that are "hurt" and those that are not. For Anderson, however, this distinction is crucial to the proper recognition of the dilettante as "the kind of person who always knows when the sounds are hurt":

> An intellectual doesn't know, or care, whether the pianist hurts them or not—he doesn't hear the hurt, or care if the pianist hurts the sounds; all he wants to hear is the music, well played or not. All these subtle matters are my obsessions, my manias, my greatest joys and my everlasting rewards. Since scholarly critics are always ready to regard such distinctions as "trivial", they call people like me dilettantes. We are, I suppose, and we're happy to be.[79]

And so, faced with an unrelenting critical chorus that demeaned her work as a series of trivial obsessions undertaken by a flighty woman who could not possibly compare to the geniuses she published in the *Little Review*, she deliberately turned away from the prospect of publishing more books. "My books have never sold," she admitted, and "I can say (almost literally) that I've never made a penny on a book."[80] In her last years, she began to imagine other forms of intellectual work. She knew that memoirs of modernism, especially those featuring the most famous contributors to the *Little Review*, were always likely to make some (much-needed) money, but she refused to do it on principle: "I realize of course that there is a ready-made advance sale for any book of gossip about the 'great names' of our L.R. contributors of the 20's. But I've done all that in 'Thirty Years' and it no longer has any interest for me."[81] Instead, the project she took up in this period—her last obsession, her final passion project—would be "*about something* more important than anecdotes."[82] She had long harbored plans for the "note-books of quotations of 'great prose'" she had collected throughout her life, and, at first, she wanted to "arrange them as a sort of anthology with ... comments running through."[83] Soon, however, she began to eschew any publication plans at all, and, in a letter to Michael Currer-Briggs, a British manuscripts dealer, she wrote, "I am instinctively opposed to regarding or presenting this ... as a BOOK."[84] Like Sylvia Townsend Warner, who chose to put together rather than publish the intimate archive of her life with Valentine Ackland, Anderson addressed herself to the tasks of collection, compilation, and annotation.

She called it her "Collection": a meticulously annotated, if chaotically curated, set of letters, transcriptions, photographs, and unpublished writing (by Anderson herself as well as her closest friends). Delighted by the possibility that she might be able to sell it all together as a coherent collection to a university library interested in the preservation of modernist literary history, she worked on it, off and on, for years. The University of Wisconsin had purchased Jane Heap's papers for a substantial sum, she reasoned, so why not cushion her final years with a similar sale? As she soon realized, however, such collections usually consist of original letters and manuscripts, and she herself had (unknowingly, and, as it turned out, tragically) made the mistake of keeping very few such documents over the years, never "imagin[ing] that anyone would want to read them": "I fall short on 'originals'. In L.R. days I never thought of *buying and selling*, I was naive enough not to keep any letter that was badly, obscurely handwritten. I would make typed copies and then throw the original away—even if it came from Joyce."[85] She valued the conversation itself, the art and the ideas, not the objects.

Without these now precious manuscripts, Anderson's "Collection" held little appeal for most libraries and university archives. Yet in a letter to Elizabeth Jenks Clark containing earnest instructions about how to "*edit your life*" toward artistic activity, she describes the discovery of "how to make my COLLECTION papers really interesting: something which I think has never been done before. Very exciting, probably rejectable, but what does that matter? To do it is what matters. I shall be my own master, in my own realm."[86] Anderson here specifies neither the details of this discovery nor the nature of this realm, but the significance of total editorial control is perfectly clear. In her *Little Review* days, she and Heap had been reluctant to accept substantial sponsorships of the *Little Review* for fear it would compromise their editorial independence. Half a century later, Anderson continued to emphasize her desire to do the "really interesting," "exciting" thing, no matter what the cost.

In an arrangement she unfortunately did not live to witness, the Collection is now part of the Elizabeth Jenks Clark Collection of Margaret Anderson at the Beinecke Rare Book and Manuscript Library of Yale University. To describe it as "really interesting" and "exciting" is an understatement. The Collection is meticulously arranged; there is a title page, an extensive introduction, a short preface, and then many folders full of annotated material. In the introduction, Anderson notes three primary disadvantages of the Collection.

First, she acknowledges that there are very few original letters and manuscripts from the most famous contributors to the *Little Review*. This poses a problem for any potential sale of the Collection to a university archive: "But of course any University wants to buy the originals! Copies can be faked, invented!"[87] Since she had routinely typed copies of incoming handwritten correspondence throughout her life, and the original copies were irrecoverably lost, her hands were tied. She could only insist that her transcriptions were "exact copies, comma by comma," and convey her hope that the "vitality of the material contained in—and copied from—the originals will somewhat compensate for their disappearance."[88]

Next, she describes the impossibility of exact chronology. "Nearly all my correspondents," she notes, "left their letters undated."[89] While her own letters were more precise, she found it virtually impossible to reconstruct a completely accurate order of events. Yet she assures her readers that this hardly matters: "In sorting out these letters and trying to put them into some kind of order, I've not felt that strict chronology is of great importance."[90] The precise timing of events hardly mattered; her perception of their importance, and their interrelatedness, was key.

Finally, Anderson explains that her "chief correspondents" were women because "the men I knew years ago happened not to belong to the type which I classified as great conversationalists."[91] Remember that, for Anderson, who had started the *Little Review* in order to fill it with "the best conversation the world has to offer," the phrase "great conversationalists" indicates far more than a certain adroitness with witty banter. Great conversationalists are great thinkers, great artists, great writers. Conversation equals passionate ideas. This third "disadvantage" of the Collection is thus the result of her general dismissal of men as "great conversationalists." To make this point impossible to ignore, Anderson immediately got specific. She named names. Directly after the description of the Collection's "disadvantages" is a list of men's names—the same names that routinely appeared in both literary histories and the kind of gossip books she refused to write—with corresponding notes about their relative appeal as conversationalists. With this list, she wasn't just privileging her memory of conversations with her female friends; she was tearing down the legends being built all around her in other midcentury memoirs of modernism. I quote only a few particularly telling examples from the twenty-nine names on her list:

> Beginning with Sherwood Anderson, he and I could talk for hours, but we never conversed.
>
> Dreiser? I would have felt that I was talking with a stick.
>
> Hart Crane never said anything I wanted to hear.

William Carlos Williams seemed to me rather unauthentic, in some way exaggerated, in some way not strong.

Hemingway always impressed me as an immature, though informative and entertaining [*sic*]; but his personal world couldn't have been more remote from mine.

Ditto for Scott Fitzgerald. Once at midnight, in a drunken daze, he tried to break down the door of my hotel room, insisting that I was wrong about him and that we should talk. I knew that we shouldn't.

Joyce, in all our meetings, was the least conversational man I ever met. Once I heard someone suggest a topic which he hoped would fire him, but which received only a blank blind look. "The subject doesn't interest you, Mr. Joyce?" "Not in the slightest", Joyce answered. During such blockages Jane and I would turn our attention to Norah, and then he would become at least partially alive.[92]

This dryly hilarious list spans almost four full pages of the introduction. The sheer volume of it is impressively insistent; in going on and on (and on), Anderson seems to agree with Sara Ahmed's description of collection as a "empowering" feminist act.[93] I think this is right, and I'll go a step further. If the rest of the Collection constitutes Anderson's last great passion project, then this list is a kind of killjoy's preamble—Anderson's modernist burn book. Like the "burn book" popularized in 2004's *Mean Girls*, this list was not designed for publication or circulation, but, at the same time, it was never understood to be entirely private. Anderson showed it to visiting friends, and she clearly imagined that future researchers would eventually read her testimony. She gamely acknowledges her own culpability: "some of these hindrances and stoppages may have been my fault. Perhaps I even sounded like a prig." This may be true. Throughout the list, Anderson's faults are at least as visible as her brilliance. But when I first encountered this list in the reading room of the Beinecke, surrounded by portraits and busts of mostly male writers, I immediately thought about how hard Anderson would have laughed (and perhaps cried) at Rebecca Solnit's *Men Explain Things to Me* (2014). In the titular essay, first published in 2008, Solnit describes the infuriatingly common experience of what has recently become known as "mansplaining," though she herself does not use that term:

Men explain things to me, and other women, whether or not they know what they're talking about. . . . Every woman knows what I'm talking about. It's the presumption that makes it hard, at times, for any woman in any field; that keeps women from speaking up and from being heard when they dare; that crushes young women into silence by indicating, the way harassment on the street does, that this is not their world. It trains us in self-doubt and self-limitation just as it exercises men's unsupported overconfidence.[94]

It is impossible to imagine myself into Anderson's world without thinking seriously about the unceasing aggressions, micro and macro, that she faced for years—and which continue to affect her posthumous reputation. Anderson did not publish this list of bad conversationalists—the men who explained things to her, no doubt—but she left it for us in a place of prominence. It is surely not an accident that the last name on the list is Ezra Pound, the man most frequently given credit for the genius of the *Little Review*'s inspired publication record.[95] Anderson closes this section of her introduction by addressing the former foreign editor of the *Little Review*:

> I can express all I want to say by explaining why I never had an impulse toward real talk with Ezra Pound. "Real," to me, means: what revealing personal-information is going to be divulged? Ezra was a talker of talkers, but not the kind I thrive on. What I sought has been described by Wallace Stevens in a poem:
>
> It would have been like lighting a candle,
> Like leaning on a table, shading one's eyes,
> And hearing a tale one wanted intensely to hear.
>
> For me, Ezra would be the person most unlikely to meet such a test. I can no more imagine him leaning on a table and telling a tale than I can imagine him talking with an American housewife about her domestic problems.[96]

Instead, the figures leaning across Anderson's table, and whom she wanted to commemorate with her Collection, were women: friends who "talked as everyone does about little things, but . . . *conversed* about all those things 'counter, original, spare, strange' that are too unprevailing in ordinary communication."[97] These friends—the luminaries, the ones "always lighting candles"—were Jane Heap, the friend and former lover with whom she had coedited the *Little Review*; Georgette Leblanc, the French soprano with whom she lived from when they met in 1924 until Leblanc's death in 1941; and Dorothy Caruso, with whom she lived from when they met in 1942 until Caruso's death in 1955. Anderson contends that she had "never heard other people saying or thinking the things these friends thought, and . . . never found their thoughts in books."[98] Indeed, most of the Collection is dedicated to her annotated history of these three lives and supplemented by tales of the group she identified as her "principal characters": Heap, Leblanc, and Caruso but also Janet Flanner, Solita Solano, Monique Serrure, A. R. Orage, Gurdjieff, and, as noted in "A Short Preface," the more recent friendship of Elizabeth Jenks Clark, who would eventually be responsible for placing the Collection, along with the rest of Anderson's personal papers, into the Beinecke.

Though devoted to "conversation," the Collection is less a transcript than a work of queer feminist collage. The layout of one early page contains almost no text at all (figure 3.1). Instead, it resembles a traditional photo album: four portrait photographs, one in each quadrant, with names and dates below each photo. The 1918 photos, taken when they were still in a romantic relationship, seem to gaze across the page at each other. And while we might expect that Anderson would have positioned the 1927 photographs so that they would be looking elsewhere, since, by then, they were no longer a couple, she intentionally reversed the upper order so that, again, they are turned toward each other. What's more, the album-like, four-quadrant layout of this page is never repeated. The kinship between its two subjects, placed in an inescapable orbit around each other, is singular. And though the "principal characters" share space in the Collection, Heap's "conversation" similarly dominates its pages.

Most of the Collection is a more complicated mixture of images, typed text, and handwritten annotation. For example, another page contains a black-and-white photograph of Heap that takes up at least two-thirds of the page (figure 3.2). In contrast to the images discussed above, where the layout twice suggests that she is staring at (or at least toward) Anderson, Heap here looks directly at the camera. She is seated in an armchair; her hair is cut short, and she is wearing a tuxedo. Her gaze is formidable, even challenging. Her brows are furrowed. And she is not smiling. Anderson's purplish-blue ink credits the photograph—which was taken in 1927, the year before the newspaper publication of a similarly styled portrait of Radclyffe Hall would result in a crucial shift in lesbian legibility[99]—to the now legendary photographer Berenice Abbott. Layered on top of the bottom right corner of the photograph is a slip of paper containing a typed quotation by Elspeth Champcommunal, a mutual friend. The names of Heap and Champcommunal are underlined in Anderson's red ink. In

FIGURE 3.1. Manuscript page from Margaret Anderson's unpublished "Collection." *Top*: Anderson in 1918, then Heap in 1918. *Bottom*: Heap in 1927, then Anderson in 1927.

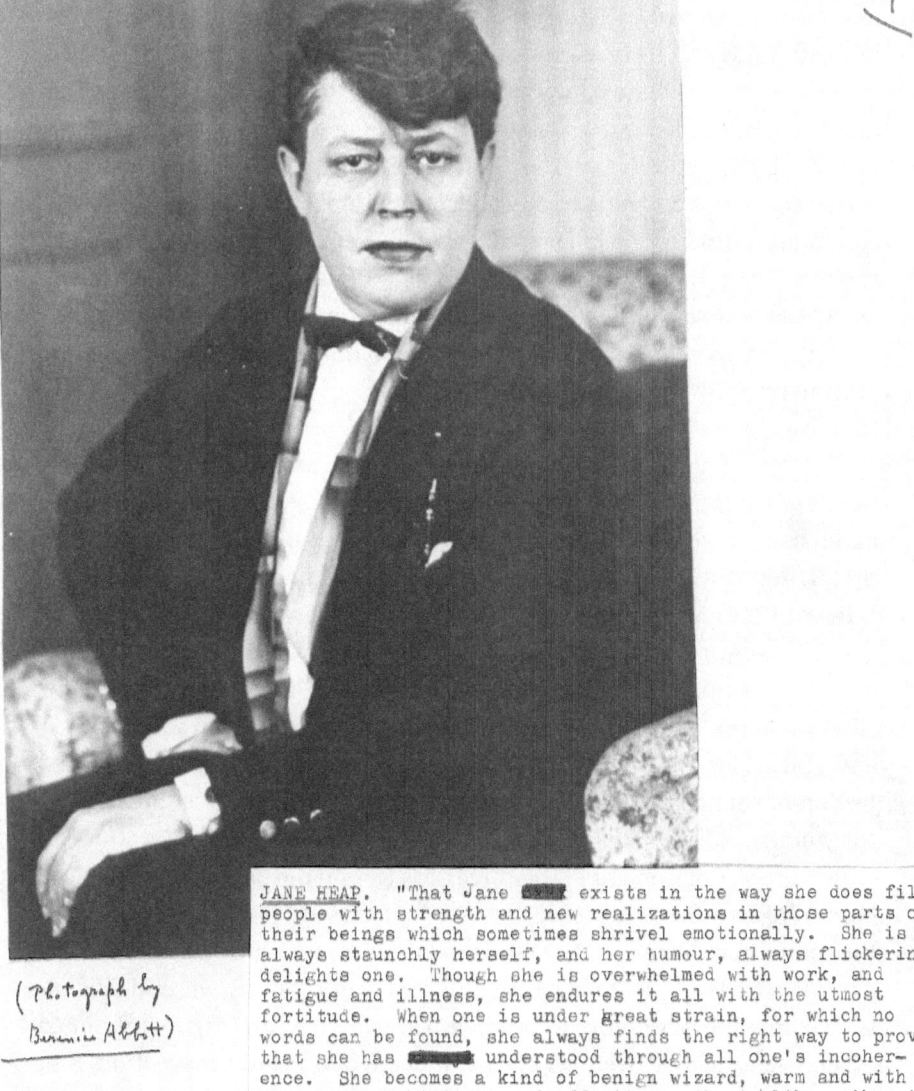

(Photograph by Berenice Abbott)

JANE HEAP. "That Jane ▨▨▨ exists in the way she does fills people with strength and new realizations in those parts of their beings which sometimes shrivel emotionally. She is always staunchly herself, and her humour, always flickering, delights one. Though she is overwhelmed with work, and fatigue and illness, she endures it all with the utmost fortitude. When one is under great strain, for which no words can be found, she always finds the right way to prove that she has ▨▨▨▨ understood through all one's incoherence. She becomes a kind of benign wizard, warm and with a mysterious kindness and affection. She is like a 'home' in herself, full of a loving security which banishes ▨▨▨▨▨ tensions, so that one becomes, momentarily, a new being". Elspeth Champcommunal.

FIGURE 3.2. Manuscript page from Margaret Anderson's unpublished "Collection."

the selection chosen by Anderson, Champcommunal describes Heap as a "benign wizard": "That Jane exists in the way she does fills people with strength and new realizations in those parts of their beings which sometimes shrivel emotionally. She is always staunchly herself, and her humour, always flickering, delights one."[100] On their surface, these lines are banal, but in Anderson's repositioning of them, they signal a shared vocabulary—not a code, necessarily, but an implicit agreement. Champcommunal's description of Heap's "always flickering" personality recalls, in the context of the larger Collection, Anderson's earlier description of her friends as "always lighting candles"—a phrase that, in its origin in Wallace Stevens's late poem, "Two Letters," signals not only the spark of a vivacious personality but the retrospective, even nostalgic, image of a group of old friends gathered together once more.[101]

But Anderson's was a nostalgia for unruliness, antagonism, and revolution. On another page (figure 3.3)—this one all text and no images—she juxtaposes three distinct memories of Heap's legendary "conversation": first, a description of Heap's response to the abdication speech of King Edward VIII and the "drudgery" of inheritance laws; second, an excerpt from a letter in which Heap bemoans the inability of certain *New Yorker* writers to acknowledge that "everything in the world has changed" during "the war years" (presumably, World War I, though one cannot be sure); and, third, Heap's response to the banning of *Ulysses* for the nominal protection of young women: "If there's anything I really fear it is the mind of the young girl."[102]

Anderson's placement of the three passages on the page does not follow chronological order. Instead, they are juxtaposed together—Down with the monarchy! Down with established cultural institutions! Down with paternalistic law!—in a showcase of both Heap's historic wit and Anderson's contemporary ability to produce a searing feminist argument out of otherwise unrelated archival scraps. Indeed, upon closer inspection, it is this latter feat that provides the animating logic of the page's composition. Anderson's collage makes it impossible not to see this act of curation as itself a kind of creation. The page begins with Edward's abdication, a literal patriarch disavowing his inheritance (and its earthly and ethereal power) in favor of "love and freedom." It continues, after this account of the voluntary decentering of the head of church and state, with Heap noting that the war itself had shifted the "center of gravity" of modern times. And, finally, it contains an acerbic paean to the "minds of young girls." This page is a scrapbook of the masculine Heap's intellectual charm, but it is also a micronarrative—following a jumbled, backward chronology—of feminist

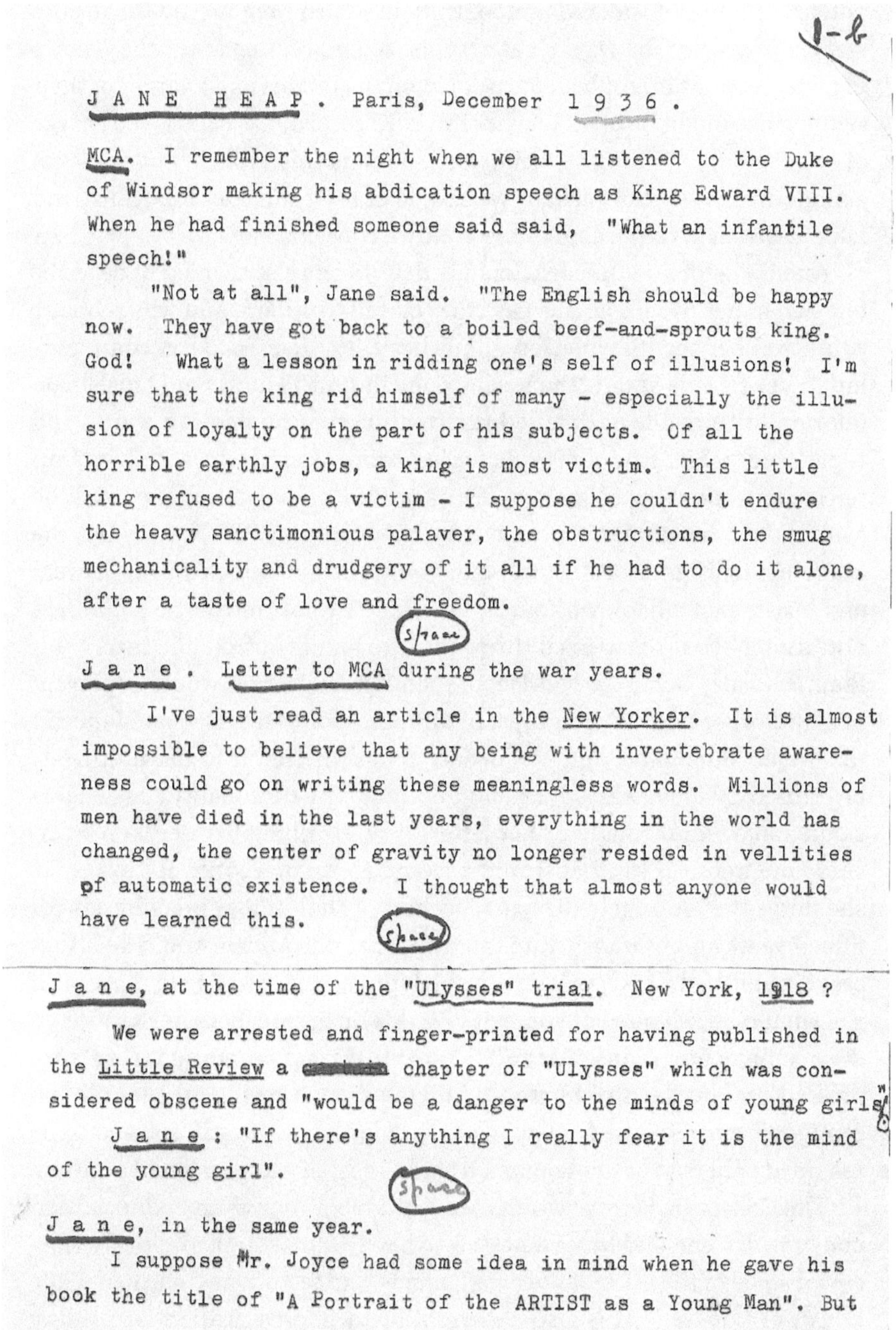

JANE HEAP. Paris, December 1936.

MCA. I remember the night when we all listened to the Duke of Windsor making his abdication speech as King Edward VIII. When he had finished someone said said, "What an infantile speech!"

"Not at all", Jane said. "The English should be happy now. They have got back to a boiled beef-and-sprouts king. God! What a lesson in ridding one's self of illusions! I'm sure that the king rid himself of many – especially the illusion of loyalty on the part of his subjects. Of all the horrible earthly jobs, a king is most victim. This little king refused to be a victim – I suppose he couldn't endure the heavy sanctimonious palaver, the obstructions, the smug mechanicality and drudgery of it all if he had to do it alone, after a taste of love and freedom.

Jane. Letter to MCA during the war years.

I've just read an article in the New Yorker. It is almost impossible to believe that any being with invertebrate awareness could go on writing these meaningless words. Millions of men have died in the last years, everything in the world has changed, the center of gravity no longer resided in vellities of automatic existence. I thought that almost anyone would have learned this.

Jane, at the time of the "Ulysses" trial. New York, 1918 ?

We were arrested and finger-printed for having published in the Little Review a ~~certain~~ chapter of "Ulysses" which was considered obscene and "would be a danger to the minds of young girls"

Jane: "If there's anything I really fear it is the mind of the young girl".

Jane, in the same year.

I suppose Mr. Joyce had some idea in mind when he gave his book the title of "A Portrait of the ARTIST as a Young Man". But

FIGURE 3.3. Manuscript page from Margaret Anderson's unpublished "Collection."

potentiality in the wake of a modernity in which men are no longer the "center of gravity," by way of catastrophe or choice. Certainly, these sorts of juxtapositions might be read as incidental, and this explanation of their significance might be open to what David Kazanjian has called "the charge of overreading."[103] But given Anderson's foundational role in putting forth a modernist aesthetic, perhaps we should at least consider following, and taking seriously, the stream of her archival consciousness.

Anderson found it unconscionable that no one else seemed to be as interested in her friends as she was. She refused to understand why scholars contacted her for information about her *Little Review* days, complaining to her friends about "the boring contributors [Hugh Ford] insists on quoting, with floods of detailed information that no one can want," and explaining *"why I insist on Jane's mind being shown,* (since it always interested me more than Ezra's or Joyce's or Eliot's)—meaning: the [*sic*] she could talk about things of which they knew nothing."[104] She derides the academic insistence on "factual questions, none of which I can answer," and insists that a book without "all the Jane I want" must also contain "a note saying that your refusal threw me into an uncontrollable rage."[105] If their scholarly books erased Heap, then her Collection would represent her, and other neglected figures, in all their glory. But her confidence in the project fluctuated, and her anxiety about whether it would ultimately be refused by universities for being "nothing but 'personality'" resurfaces again and again throughout her letters.[106] Describing her decision to include the manuscript that would become *Forbidden Fires*, for example, she notes the "strangely dizzying" feeling of "holding in one's hands for fifteen years an unpublished manuscript that one *knows* would be a success if published. It is like being pushed into a corner and held there, as if you should be ashamed of yourself."[107] This imagery echoes her refusal, in the opening paragraphs of *My Thirty Years' War*, to be "cornered" or "suppressed," as the "laws of humanity" dictated must be the case for all "exceptional" and "inspired" people.[108] Decades later, she still refused to be ashamed of herself or her talented friends, most of whom she had outlived.

The Collection is thus simultaneously a biographical and editorial act, one in which she understood herself to have "(almost unconsciously) corrected some of the mistakes of arrangement and techniques" she had made in earlier books.[109] It is also a work of historic preservation containing photographs, images, and newspaper clippings; short quotations, longer stretches of commentary, and entire unpublished manuscripts written by her friends; and, through it all, Anderson's own annotations and unpublished manuscripts, both typed and handwritten in several colors of ink.

It was a long "labor of assemblage."[110] Her letters describe the extent to which the project took over her living quarters while she worked on it.[111] Turned down by publishers and refused by universities, she nevertheless persisted in preparing her Collection, however unfinished or unpublished, for posterity. Unlike many of the other collectors and biographers profiled in this book, it is even possible to speculate that Anderson considered this unpublished, unsellable, largely unseen archive to be the ideal form for her recollections and remembrances.

For this reason, any estimation of Anderson's importance for feminist modernist studies is incomplete to the extent that it does not address her unfinished, unpublished work—that which was undertaken behind the scenes, out of the public eye, and which only sometimes becomes available to be inherited by contemporary queer feminist modernist scholars. Like the editorial and preservation work of Beach and Toklas, Anderson's role in publishing "groundbreaking modernist writing" has been systematically demeaned by generations of critics. But while Beach referred to her own late period as her "official period," and Toklas intentionally worked to ensure that she would only be remembered, however dismissively, through her relationship with Gertrude Stein, Anderson's late period was defined by a decline into relative obscurity. And while Beach contributed many original manuscripts to our archives of modernist literary history, and Toklas's determined stewardship delivered not only manuscripts but artwork into our museums, Anderson left us with nothing quite so tangible. Just "personality," as she would put it, to be inherited by "the minds of young girls."

CHAPTER FOUR

The Sense of Unending

REVISITING VIRGINIA WOOLF'S
ORLANDO: A BIOGRAPHY

IT MAY COME as a surprise to encounter Virginia Woolf yet again at the end of this book. After three chapters about a wide variety of archival passion projects, all of which focus on incomplete, unfinished, or unpublished work, the return in this chapter to what may now be the most published, most canonical oeuvre in queer feminist modernist studies might seem counterintuitive. But unlike Gertrude Stein, who, as we saw in the last chapter, left explicit instructions in her will regarding the publication of her remaining manuscripts after her death, Woolf left only two notes—one for her husband, Leonard Woolf, and one for her sister, Vanessa Bell—and a fully drafted but unrevised novel, *Between the Acts*, which was published posthumously later that year. She was not yet finished, but she could not go on. And although virtually everything—not just *Between the Acts* but her diaries, letters, stories, and essays, too—would eventually be collected and published, her suicide on March 28, 1941, cast a shadow of unfinishedness over the history of modernism, and queer feminist modernism, in particular. What else might she have written? What else might we have inherited?

In this chapter, I return to Woolf's most legendary passion project—*Orlando*, her 1928 "biography" of her lover, Vita Sackville-West—in order to suggest that even finished, published books might sometimes prompt us to read them in light of what I call the unfinished aesthetic of queer feminist modernism. Learning to read *Orlando* this way is to learn to read beyond its ending. Feminist literary critic Rachel Blau DuPlessis famously uses the phrase "writing beyond the ending" as a way to describe narratives that subvert dominant patriarchal ideology and provide women characters with an array of possible life choices other than those that end in either marriage or death. In the twentieth century, she suggests, women writers "invented strategies to sever the narrative from formerly conventional structures of fiction and consciousness about women."[1] These "postromantic strategies" are most clearly visible in a novel's final chapter—even its final pages.[2] All endings contain the trace of ideological conflict, however well resolved, but the narratives DuPlessis examines are powered by the discovery that their women authors (and, sometimes, their protagonists) exist outside generic conventions. As a result, their attempts "to make fiction talk about women and their concerns, especially when a woman is the speaking subject, may necessarily lead to a radical transformation of narrative structures."[3] What can we learn about the larger social world from the narrative resolution attempted in its fiction? What does it mean when the kind of resolution expected in any given genre—marriage at the end of a romance, for example—never arrives? In DuPlessis's reading of *Orlando*, the "culturally plausible ending" of marriage occurs before the end of the book, and the rest of *Orlando* is "Woolf's swift panorama of the kinds of fiction and values that are now possible":

> At the midnight stroke with which the book ends, undeclared revelations are implied: of love united with quest, of the end of sexual polarization, of an erotic affirmation of sexualities, and of the critique of all institutions of gender, from unmanageable dresses to narrative conventions.[4]

And DuPlessis is right. This is all here, however implicitly, in the novel's final pages. But what if Orlando's story does not end with the close of the book? What if attending to whatever we find "beyond the ending" is not only a writerly practice but a readerly responsibility, too?

In this frame, reading *Orlando* requires us to adopt an archival sensibility, a willingness to understand and appreciate its complicated material history as both critique and gift. For, as we shall see, although it was initially attempted as a joke, *Orlando* ultimately entered the world as a queer feminist intervention—one that was possible to generalize for generations of future readers but that was also unmistakably geared toward a very particular audience at the time of its publication: Vita Sackville-West. Officially dedicated to "V. Sackville-West" and known as a playfully fictionalized biography of its dedicatee, the book ends before its protagonist's death, when Orlando, "now thirty-six," has just reached "the oncome of middle age," that "strange" time when "nothing is any longer one thing."[5] And on October 10, 1928, in a careful coordination of these strange temporalities, Woolf sent Sackville-West a specially bound copy of *Orlando: A Biography*, which would be published by the Woolfs' Hogarth Press the next day. Although Woolf had finished the manuscript in March of that year and had completed her revisions to the proofs in September, *Orlando*'s publication date remained firmly set for October 11, the same date on which the last chapter of *Orlando* is set. By sending the book on the tenth, Woolf ensured that Sackville-West would be reading it on the eleventh. In its final pages, the story of the mysteriously middle-aged Orlando overlaps, for a single day, with the real-life story of the thirty-six-year-old Sackville-West. The impeccably precise timing of this gift implicitly demonstrates that the book ends neither with the "culturally plausible" marriage of its protagonist nor with the DuPlessian "undeclared revelations" contained in its closing image of a wild goose flying away at the last stroke of midnight. Instead, *Orlando* ends, if it does, with its transformation, on publication day, from private manuscript to public text. But the finality of this ending, too, is perpetually called into question by the unfinished, ongoing life story (and, eventually, legacy) of Sackville-West herself. Woolf's gift of the manuscript carried on their private tradition of publication day jokes—the year before, for example, Woolf had sent her a "dummy copy" of a first edition of *To the Lighthouse*, inscribed as her "best novel," that contained only blank pages[6]—but this time, the specific timing of her gift, especially given its subtitle, meant that Woolf had intentionally arranged for Sackville-West to finish reading *Orlando* and then immediately begin to live out the rest of Orlando's story.

The carefully staged intermingling of fictional and historical lives in such a deliberately intimate gift provokes a set of crucial questions for this chapter. Can we take *Orlando*'s subtitle—"A Biography"—seriously as a provocation to think about the politics of genre? What is the significance of Sackville-West as both subject and recipient of *Orlando*? And what might it mean to read *Orlando* as an unfinished biography? Given the timing of the gift, we might ask, does the book really end at all? Is it possible to separate the text from the life underpinning—and continuing beyond—it? Sackville-West had claimed a few days earlier that she would "hardly exist" until she received her copy.[7] And immediately after her first, breathless reading of *Orlando*, she even mimicked the harried, rushed tone of the last chapter—in which Orlando is "terribly late" and "violently struck" by the chimes of the hour—in her letter to Woolf: "There are a dozen details I should like to go into, . . . but it is too late today; I have been reading steadily all day, and it is now 5 o'clock, and I must catch the post."[8] If, throughout the novel, its protagonist often resembles Sackville-West, here we see that Sackville-West, after reading *Orlando*, sounds like . . . *Orlando*. To read *Orlando* beyond the ending is thus to read Sackville-West's life as more than historical inspiration. It is to read *Orlando* as a text left unfinished by Woolf, no matter its publication status—and, in this way, it is to recognize it as a text that emphatically, even angrily, refuses to know the endings of women's lives in advance. In this chapter, I contend that reframing *Orlando* as a constitutively unfinished text directs our attention toward a more general unfinishedness of queer feminist modernism—an unfinished aesthetic that appears not just in the necessarily ongoing projects of recovery and reconstruction but in the supposedly finished, polished aesthetic objects we value, too.

Queer/Late/Modernist Biography

Since Nigel Nicolson's proclamation of *Orlando* as "the longest and most charming love letter in literature," we have witnessed a relentless critical desire to read *Orlando* as the encoded, otherwise untellable story of a private love between two very public women.[9] These readings are both necessary and valuable, but they make it easy to forget that, at the time of *Orlando*'s publication, Sackville-West's status as the inspiration and model for Orlando would not have been known to anyone but those familiar with Bloomsbury gossip. The implicit claim that *Orlando* is only a love story limits Sackville-West's importance as biographical subject and reduces the formal difficulty of *Orlando* to scarcely more than a set of references to "the love that dare not speak its name," which, once decoded, becomes unworthy of study except as biographical evidence. It is to read *Orlando* as merely a more ornate version of what critics appraised *Shakespeare and Company*, *What Is Remembered*, or *My Thirty Years' War* to be: that is, no more than a delivery mechanism for interesting information. In this way, one queer reading actually diminishes the larger stakes—both feminist and queer—of the text.

While *Orlando* has long held the attention of scholars working at the intersection of modernist and queer studies, I want to suggest the expansion of these approaches to *Orlando* through renewed attention to genre: specifically, to the book's often overlooked subtitle, "A Biography." Woolf's revision and expansion of generic codes in *Orlando* make it a uniquely important text to revisit in light of contemporary theorizations of queer temporality. Throughout this chapter, I foreground what I think of as *Orlando*'s queer time in relation to biographical form, and I demonstrate the resonances between Woolf's critique of the generic conventions of biography and contemporary critiques of the institutions of what Lee Edelman has called "reproductive futurism." Queer temporality studies critique understandings of time as a naturalized, internalized, bodily performance of the too easily accepted social scripts that govern our lives, asking us instead to recognize and resist—in our scholarly practices as in our lives—the standard, heteronormative, biologically driven temporal organization of our world. Carolyn Dinshaw, for example, holds out the possibility of what she calls "touching across time"—collapsing it, even, through the vectors of desire that connect marginalized subjects in different historical periods.[10] This is a non-linear version of history in which time holds the potential to twist and pull in unexpected directions as, in Elizabeth Freeman's phrasing, "some minor feature of our own sexually impoverished present suddenly meets up with a richer past, or as the materials of a failed and forgotten project of the past find their uses now, in a future unimaginable in their time."[11] *Orlando* is hardly failed and forgotten, but I suggest that, in reading its modernist frustration with normative temporality as *queer* frustration with the mandates of *hetero*normative temporality, we open up productive new avenues for understanding *Orlando*'s cultural work.

Biography, as a literary genre, is the gatekeeper par excellence of reproductive time, and it is difficult to extract oneself—or one's subjects—from the pull of biographical form. In what I take to be a representative critique of the genre, Terry Eagleton issued a complaint about the exasperating "paradox about biographies":

> We read them to savor the shape and texture of an individual life, yet few literary forms could be more predictable. Everyone has to be born, and almost everyone has to be educated, oppressed by parents, plagued by siblings, and launched into the world; they then enter upon social and sexual relationships of their own, produce children, and finally expire. *The structure of biography is biology.* For all its tribute to the individual spirit, it is our animal life that underpins it.[12]

Eagleton implicitly names reproductive time as the temporal logic of standard biographies, and his contemporary impatience with the chronological predictability of biological form seems to have been learned from Woolf and other modernists, for whom such impatience was axiomatic. In Juliette Atkinson's recent reassessment of Victorian biography, she asks literary critics to reconceive of the relationship between Victorian and modernist biography as a "dialogue" rather than a "rupture."[13] Yet Woolf certainly understood herself to be part of a high modernist rebellion against Victorianism, and she used *Orlando* to criticize what she saw as the usual structure, methodology, and general assumptions of these typical Victorian biographies. While critics such as Atkinson, David Amigoni, and others now recognize a broad spectrum of nineteenth-century biographical practices, the chorus of modernist outrage over the previous generation's stereotypically long, impersonal, supposedly objective lives—in which "the fundamental reason for writing a man's life was that he was admirable"[14]—was thunderous. In a discussion of Harold Nicolson's *The Development of English Biography* (1927), Amigoni links the genre of biography with the "business of pedagogy."[15] Biography-writing was—and perhaps continues to be—motivated by the desire to instruct and educate future generations. The history of biography may well be a history of the textual memorialization of great individuals, but it is also a history fueled by a drive to teach the readers of biographies how to emulate—or avoid—the lives of others.

From the perspective of modernist biographers, this pedagogical imperative was too often weighed down by superfluous details and buried under extraneous evidence. Woolf, among others, accuses Victorian biographers of writing an "amorphous mass" of "innumerable words" that fail to "choose those truths which transmit personality."[16] Their books tell of events rather than character, and they emphasize achievement, action, decisions, and conflict rather than the tumultuous inner lives of their subjects. In Sidney Lee's delivery of the 1911 Leslie Stephen lecture at Cambridge, he even praised this methodological preference for action and external events, claiming that "character which does not translate itself into exploit is for the biographer a mere phantasm."[17] Yet these biographies were often criticized—even in their own times—for consisting of little more than a list of exploits. An anonymous review published in October 1857 reveals frustration with biographies that "swell almost to bursting with minute details, under the process of accumulation," and demands "a portrait, not an inventory of the features possessed by the subject."[18] This call for a "portrait" demonstrates the desire for artistic expression as a necessary supplement to historical research.

This artistic element is precisely what modernist biographers sought to deliver.[19] For example, in his 1934 biography of Goldsworthy Lowes Dickinson, E. M. Forster clearly reverses the priorities Lee had set forth two decades earlier: "the movements of a tourist's body are not worth recording unless they generate movements inside his mind."[20] Modernist biographers used "exploit" and external "movements" only as much as they were useful in the discovery of character, and they were prepared to "admit contradictory versions of the same face."[21] Moreover, they welcomed contradictory plottings of the same life. A. J. A. Symons, who would go on to write the meta-biographical *Quest for Corvo: An Experiment in Biography* (1934), declared his objection to the dependence upon chronology as the inviolable structuring principle of biography in a 1929 lecture delivered as part of the "Tradition and Experiment in Present-Day Literature" series:

> Constructed on the simple formula of chronological sequence, they begin, for the most part, with their subject's birth, and describe his curly headed innocence, his sailor suit. Chapter 2 and 3, which show no diminution of the one or discarding of the other, are headed "Schooldays" and "Alma Mater," and precede "Early Manhood" in which a passing reference to "wild oats" shows that the author has also experienced much! and then chapter 5, "Marriage," sets us on the trail for home. "Life in London," "Early Work," and "Later Work" lead naturally to "Last Days": a deathbed scene, several moral reflections, a list of the books or acts of the victim, and one more biography is on the shelf, probably to stay there.[22]

If biographies tell individual life stories, so the modernist critique goes, then there is no reason why all biographies must follow the same deadening, if factually accurate, formal structure. For both modernist and contemporary critics, the major problem with biography is its seemingly inviolable progression of the body through time: a biography details its subject's birth, education, inheritance, marriage, children, and death. Crucially, this complaint is reiterated again, almost word for word, in the work of Jack Halberstam, who has defined queer time as "the perverse turn away from the narrative coherence of adolescence-early adulthood-marriage-reproduction-child rearing-retirement-death."[23] If, as I have suggested, the archival passion projects and biographical acts of these midcentury modernists laid the groundwork for the ethics of recovery that would later animate feminist and queer approaches to literary history, then this transhistorical attack on the suffocating conventions of biography might well be the most crystalline articulation of their methodological touch across time. The normative understanding of the human lifetime that is the object of this shared critique undergirds the generic structure of standard biography.

Orlando's subtitle signals that Woolf's passion project is an active intervention into the theory and practice of biography, and throughout the book, she protests the tyranny of such temporal logic: "an hour, once it lodges in the queer element of the human spirit, may be stretched to fifty or a hundred times its clock length; on the other hand, an hour may be accurately represented on the timepiece of the mind by one second."[24] Instead of capitulating to Symons's "simple formula of chronological sequence," she imagines an entirely new—and unfinished—life trajectory for her subject. Before beginning work on *Orlando*, Woolf had had a sudden realization about how she could "revolutionise biography in a night,"[25] and *Orlando* is the result of her lifelong interest in reforming— even revolutionizing—the writing of lives. Although the book is clearly identified as "a biography" and was, at least initially, shelved accordingly in bookstores, *Orlando* resists easy categorization: its subject lives more than three hundred years and experiences this absurdly long life first as a man and then as a woman, and we learn nothing about Orlando's birth or eventual death. Since the story of Orlando's life is fantastic, it has proven difficult for critics to read *Orlando* as a serious undertaking, but Woolf's persistent attention to biographical conventions, even as she repeatedly breaks them, should make it impossible to understand *Orlando* as only co-incidentally or insignificantly related to the genre. At minimum, *Orlando*'s subtitle highlights the importance of life writing—and biographical writing, in particular—for Woolf's larger project. As a generic hybrid, *Orlando* combines elements of satire, fantasy, social criticism, and the novel, but Woolf's subtitle insists that *Orlando* must be read as a biographical act. To dismiss the importance of biography in light of the generic capaciousness of the novel form necessarily underestimates the gravity of Woolf's engagement with the genre.

Despite her insistence on its subtitle, however, *Orlando* made Woolf nervous. In a diary entry written shortly before its publication, she worried about the effect that the book's ambiguous genre would have on the reading—and, crucially, buying—public:

> We may sell a third that we sold of The Lighthouse before publication— Not a shop will buy save in 6es and 12es. They say this is inevitable. But it is a novel, says Miss Ritchie. But it is called biography on the title page, they say. It will have to go to the Biography shelf. I doubt therefore that we shall do more than cover expenses—a high price to pay for the fun of calling it biography. And I was so sure it was going to be the one popular book![26]

This brief passage reveals the dissonance between Woolf's initial confidence in the commercial viability of her project and her sudden anxiety about the "high price" of her choices after the Hogarth Press actually began to try to sell it. She intended for her first biography to be both "truthful" and "fantastic," and although she admitted that she "began it as a joke," she suspected that she "went on with it seriously."[27] Her designation of *Orlando* as a biography sparked an implicit conversation about genre between the publishers and the booksellers expected to stock *Orlando*: What is a biography? Why is *Orlando* called a biography? Had she finally written her "one popular book"? And why should people buy it? As it turned out, neither Woolf nor her booksellers needed to worry: advance sales were poor, but *Orlando*, as she predicted, turned out to be her biggest commercial success. The reading public adored her playful caricature and rebuke of Victorian biographical conventions.

Orlando unrelentingly mocks these conventions. As her narrator-biographer rushes to avoid any "odious subjects," pleading that we must "let other pens treat of sex and sexuality,"[28] Woolf implicitly criticizes the unwillingness of so many biographers to write about sexual matters. In this way, she echoes Sigmund Freud's criticism and correction of biography in *Leonardo da Vinci and a Memory of His Childhood*: "If a biographical study is really intended to arrive at an understanding of its hero's mental life it must not—as happens in the majority of biographies as a result of discretion or prudishness—silently pass over its subject's sexual activity or sexual individuality."[29] As if to illustrate the "discretion or prudishness" of most biographers, Woolf indicates that Orlando's "change of sex" provoked an uproar all but ignored by her biographer:

> Many people, taking this [lack of surprise on Orlando's part] into account, and holding that such a change of sex is against nature, have been at great pains to prove (1) that Orlando had always been a woman, (2) that Orlando is at this moment a man. Let biologists and psychologists determine. It is enough for us to state the simple fact; Orlando was a man until the age of thirty; when he became a woman and has remained so ever since.[30]

For Woolf, questions of sex and sexuality should neither be brushed under the table as "simple facts" nor left for the scientific scrutiny of "biologists and psychologists." Instead, these difficult questions about the inner life of the subject should be part of all biographies—especially biographies of women, in which the genre's historical "demand for action" must so often remain unsatisfied.[31] Criticizing her narrator's frustration with Orlando's experience of life as a woman, Woolf mocks the brutish willingness of so many biographers to ignore passive, unconventional subjects of biography: "If . . . the subject of one's biography will neither love nor kill, but will only think and imagine, we may conclude that he or she is no better than a corpse and so leave her."[32] This, Woolf suggests, is how biographers have left women out of history.

Woolf spent much of her life trying to write—and encouraging others to write—women back into that very history. Although *Orlando* is the first of her three major texts to carry the subtitle "A Biography," Woolf had been interested in the genre of biography for the entirety of her intellectual life. Biography and other forms of life writing were practically in her blood. Her father, Leslie Stephen, was the first editor of the *Dictionary of National Biography* (*DNB*), and she spent much of her childhood observing his struggle to finish that monumental undertaking.[33] Calling it "dramatically eclectic," Colin Matthew, the first editor of the *Oxford DNB* in the 1990s, praised Stephen's *DNB* for including "several categories of subjects which in the 1880s were quite outside 'scholarly' interest, particularly sportspeople, murderers, journalists, actors and actresses, deviant clergymen, transvestites, fat men, old women, and . . . agnostics and secularists."[34] Despite this characterization of the original *DNB* as remarkably inclusive, the fact remains that the overwhelming number of those deemed worthy of inclusion were men. In the library of Woolf's childhood home, as "in all the libraries of the world," as she would later write, "the man is to be heard talking to himself and for the most part for himself."[35] Stephen was a difficult and overbearing father, and in "A Sketch of the Past," Woolf reflected that, if he had lived longer, "his life would have entirely ended [hers]. What would have happened? No writing, no books;—inconceivable."[36] In their domestic life, Stephen was a patriarchal, repressive figure, but he was also an eminent Victorian man of letters, and he (and his library) could hardly be other than an important intellectual influence on Woolf. As Ruth Hoberman suggests, what Woolf called "the great Victorian fight . . . of the daughters against the fathers" was for her "waged in relation to biography, . . . [and] in her writing about it and experimenting with it, she was redefining her relation to her father and, on a larger scale, the relation of women to history."[37] According to Ellen Hawkes, Woolf read *Three Generations of English Women* as an adolescent and, at the age of fifteen, began her own "history of women."[38] (We might think of the manuscript of the young Virginia Stephen's "history of women" as the ghostly ancestor of the unfinished passion projects in this book.) Though she finished neither that project nor the other histories of women—"say of Newnham or the woman's movement, in the same vein"[39]—that she proposed to write after the completion of *Orlando*, her early journalism is filled with reviews of recently published biographies that, when read together, suggest a developing theory of biography. *Orlando*'s genre is, therefore, part of an ongoing feminist argument.

Woolf's revolt against Victorian biography was feminist before it was modernist. But she was nevertheless part of a wave of modernist biographers who employed a strategic blend of fact and fiction as a way to lift their subjects out of their drearily sequenced lives. In Harold Nicolson's *Some People* (1927), for example, real people are slightly disguised and historical events are distorted and redistributed among fictional stories. As suggested by the vagueness of its title, the book blurs the line between factual biographical sketches and romans à clef, ultimately suggesting that real facts and experiences are less important than impressions and inner feeling. It heralds the power that our stories about people, whether true or false, hold to define our views of them.

Woolf reviewed *Some People* in an essay called "The New Biography" (1927) in which she outlined the ways in which biographical practices had begun to change in the twentieth century. She observed that her contemporaries seemed to recognize their own legitimate narrative presence in their works, and that they were artists rather than mere historians: unlike previous generations of biographers, the new biographer "chooses; he synthesizes; in short, he has ceased to be the chronicler; he has become the artist."[40] Where too many earlier biographies were characterized by the worship of great men, the twentieth-century biographer no longer needed to be "the serious and sympathetic companion, toiling even slavishly in the footsteps of his hero."[41] Instead, these new biographies, she writes, would be characterized by a "lack of pose, humbug, solemnity."[42] This lowered formality and heightened artistry also meant that biographies became shorter. The masses of evidentiary documents (letters, diaries, newspapers) that had expanded Victorian biographies into multivolume works were largely excised, and the dependence upon documented facts as biographical scaffolding became far less prominent. The personality and inner life of the subject became far more important than the "series of exploits" that had structured biography in the nineteenth century, and, as a result, "in the first twenty years of the twentieth century, biographies must have lost half their weight."[43] Describing this newer, slimmer style of biography, Woolf admires the new biographer's implicit claim that "the man himself, the pith and essence of his character, shows itself to the observant eye in the tone of a voice, the turn of a head, some little phrase or anecdote picked up in passing,"[44] not as the result of archival work and close attention to the documented facts of his life. Indeed, the new biographer "does not cumber himself with a single fact about them. He waits till they have said or done something characteristic, and then he pounces on it with glee."[45]

Despite this claim for jubilance, Woolf would later revise her position on "facts" during her struggle to complete *Roger Fry*, the last of her explicit adventures in biography. In her other major essay on the genre, "The Art of Biography" (1938), she suggests that "the creative fact; the fertile fact; the fact that suggests and engenders"[46] is of greater importance than the mere accumulation of fact. She outlines what she sees as the trouble with biography itself: "It imposes conditions, and those conditions are that it must be based upon fact. And by fact in biography we mean facts that can be verified by other people besides the artist. If he invents facts as an artist invents them—facts that no one else can verify—and tries to combine them with facts of the other sort, they destroy each other."[47] Woolf's bitterness, here, about the conflict between art and biography can be traced back to her frustration with the composition of *Roger Fry*. After she completed *Orlando*, she felt that she had cast off the novel form, and she wanted to write more biographies (like, for example, *Flush*—a biography of Elizabeth Barrett Browning's dog—and the unwritten history of Newnham women) in the same style. When her friend Fry died, however, his family asked her to write his biography, and although she found the project to be extremely taxing, she didn't feel that it was possible to decline. Of all of her biographical work, *Roger Fry* most resembles a traditional biography, and "The Art of Biography" grapples with this sobering obligation to "facts." She qualifies her earlier assertion of the new biographical artistry by admitting that the biographer is "a craftsman, not an artist; and his work is not a work of art, but something betwixt and between."[48] Rather than concede that Woolf's earlier experiments in biography were naïve failures for their intermingling of fiction and fantasy, however, I maintain that the commissioned project (*Roger Fry*) demanded that Woolf adhere to documented evidence in the representation of her subject, while the project undertaken as a gift (*Orlando*) allowed Woolf to use her imagination as much as the archive. Citing Nicolson's *Some People*, Woolf suggests that "one can use many of the devices of fiction in dealing with real life," and this is precisely how she began to write *Orlando*.[49]

Part history, part fantasy, *Orlando* insists that fact and fiction must be nearly indecipherably entwined in the most compelling biographical work. Woolf's arguments in "The New Biography" directly inspired her decision to "revolutionise biography in a night" with *Orlando*. As she wrote in a diary entry, "I have never forgotten ... my vision of a fin rising on a wide blank sea. No biographer could possibly guess this important fact about my life in the summer of 1926: yet biographers pretend they know people."[50] For Woolf, the trouble with standard biographical practice is that biographers have no access to our innermost selves, our visions of fins. They have no record of our solitary reflections, our breaking epiphanies, our most intimate moments. No matter how carefully documented our lives, biography cannot do other than "guess" and "pretend," and so, in *Orlando*, Woolf chooses to exaggerate and highlight the acts of "guessing" and "pretending" that are too often rendered invisible in other biographies.

Throughout *Orlando*, Woolf invents fictional stories, situations, and statements—or, in other words, she insists upon guessing at and pretending she knows her subject—in order to demonstrate the power of the "creative fact" for modernist biographers. In an October 1927 letter, Woolf asked Sackville-West's permission to begin a project with "the kind of shimmer of reality which sometimes attaches to people, as the lustre on an oyster shell."[51] Comprised solely of neither fact nor fiction, *Orlando* would be "something betwixt and between": a modernist biography written by the artist-as-biographer. Instead of capitulating to that "simple formula of chronological sequence" so loathed by Symons, she imagines an entirely new life trajectory for her subject—one that need not even end. Although the biography does begin when Orlando is a young boy, the details of his birth and education are not given; although we first encounter Orlando as this young boy, he becomes a woman at the age of thirty; and, finally, although more than three hundred years have passed over the course of its more than three hundred pages, she has not yet died when the last page has been turned. Indeed, Woolf insists that the "true length of a person's life, whatever the *Dictionary of National Biography* may say, is always a matter of dispute":

> It cannot be denied that the most successful practitioners of the art of life, often unknown people by the way, somehow contrive to synchronise the sixty or seventy different times which beat simultaneously in every normal human system so that when eleven strikes, all the rest chime in unison, and the present is neither a violent disruption nor completely forgotten in the past. Of them we can justly say that they live precisely the sixty-eight or seventy-two years allotted them on the tombstone. Of the rest, some we know to be dead, though they walk among us; some are not yet born, though they go through the forms of life; others are hundreds of years old though they call themselves thirty-six.[52]

Although every "normal," "successful," often "unknown" individual contains "sixty or seventy different times which beat simultaneously," those who are not "normal"—including many of those who are "known," presumably through a trail of biographies—do not successfully synchronize these different times into a single unified self. In these cases, standard "life and times" biographies that fix individual lives into set allotments of historical time, such as the short lives contained in the *DNB*, are insufficient. Even the best biographies are unable to narrate fully the complexities of individual life, "since a biography is considered complete if it merely accounts for six or seven selves, whereas a person may well have as many thousand."[53] Modernist biographies, like so many modernist novels, highlight the individual, subjective experience of time in order to dissociate the multiple "lives" of private individuals from the unified "times" of public, historical record. If one of the projects of modernist biography is to represent more than "six or seven selves" in any given individual, then this taxonomy of people-in-time in *Orlando* indicates Woolf's refusal of the genre's insistence upon documented fact and reliance upon the standard chronology of "every normal human system." In *Orlando*, she demonstrates the power of fiction—even published, popular fiction!—to stretch our understandings of what constitutes the "normal" in biographical writing.

This may be, in part, simply the rejection of objectivity in favor of radical subjectivity that one expects from Woolf and other modernist writers, but this lesson, when delivered via the genre of biography, takes on new meaning. Formal choices about the representation of lives cannot be one-size-fits-all. If biography investigates, charts, records, and memorializes life, then the formal structure and generic conventions of biography are directly related to the types and ways of life that are understood as normal, or even possible, at any given time. The formal structure of biography teaches its readers about the possibilities—and impossibilities—of human life. In short, formal normativity protects and produces living normativity. Disrupting this form is not a merely literary decision; though playfully undertaken, this is not mere play. For Woolf, rupturing the generic conventions of biography is a means of unseating the keystone of normativity itself. I am suggesting that Woolf's questions are still our contemporary questions: How can one escape—or at least shift—the weight of standard time, standard expectations, standard lives?

Love Letters and Passion Projects

But why, we might ask, did Woolf's upending of biographical norms in general require that she write about Vita Sackville-West in particular? *Orlando* may well be a love letter, but, as Suzanne Raitt has argued, it is also "the story of one of the most public families, and one of the most notorious women, in the country."[54] Sackville-West was a provocative selection as the subject of this revolutionary biography for reasons far beyond her intimacy with Woolf. Writing about the nature of celebrity, cultural historian Leo Braudy suggests that "complex phenomena wear the reduced features of emblematic individualism,"[55] and, accordingly, writing an experimental biography of Sackville-West (and, as we will see, her family) meant entering debates about historiography, nationalism, and sexuality. As a woman notorious for her cross-dressing and bisexuality, Sackville-West was an unorthodox choice of subject for a genre that had been long monopolized by its long-deceased "great men," and, as a member of one of the oldest and most famous families in England, she provided Woolf with the opportunity to comment on issues of gendered inheritance and national heritage.

The national prominence (and, at times, notoriety) of Sackville-West and her family provided a guarantee that, as her status as both dedicatee and model for the book became more widely known, the public would be interested in reading—and, crucially, buying—an experimental biography. Although Sackville-West's life story is now better known than her literary works, which have been all but forgotten, she had been "a more popular and better-selling author" than Woolf throughout most of the 1920s.[56] In addition to several novels and books of poetry, she published biographies of Aphra Behn, Joan of Arc, and her own grandmother. Her history of her ancestral home, *Knole and the Sackvilles*, was extremely popular, and when *Orlando* was published, it was one of the first ways in which the book's subject became known: "Sales much better. Enthusiasm in the Birmingham Post [Mail]. Knole is discovered. They hint at you."[57] At the same time, however, *Orlando*'s growing popularity could also be attributed to the solipsism of wealth: according to a 1929 letter from Woolf to Sackville-West, public performances of *Orlando* were a hit because the descendants of every noble house in England assumed *Orlando* to be based, at least in part, on their own family histories and estates. Whether sales were driven by the news of Sackville-West's involvement or by the popular conception of *Orlando* as a fantastic history of a veiled aristocratic family, *Orlando* was enormously successful.

Sackville-West adored *Orlando*, which "made [her] cry with [its] passages about Knole," and charged Woolf with having "invented a new form of Narcissism,—I confess,—I am in love with Orlando—this is a complication I had not foreseen."[58] Her ability to fall "in love with Orlando" in part reflects the notorious ease with which she fell in love—or, at least, lust—with such a varied list of characters. In a July 1928 letter, Woolf teased her about the absence of her "loving heart": "For Promiscuous you are, and thats all there is to be said of you. Look in the Index to Orlando—after Pippin and see what comes next—Promiscuity *passim*."[59] She teased, yes, but she also took Sackville-West's affairs and unconventional marriage as an opportunity. Published the month before the *Well of Loneliness* trials, and composed in the shadow of Radclyffe Hall's persecution, *Orlando* deftly evaded charges of obscenity and libel, in large part due to its obviously fictional qualities.

Writing fantastically about Sackville-West's well-known "proclivities,"[60] as Woolf described her sexual affairs with women, allowed her to explore the possibilities of gender performance and lesbian desire in a way that straddled the line between fact and fantasy. Describing Orlando's change from male to female, for example, *Orlando*'s narrator wonders whether "it is the clothes that wear us and not we them" or whether "it was a change in Orlando herself that dictated her choice of a woman's dress and of a woman's sex":

> Perhaps in this she was only expressing rather more openly than usual—openness indeed was the soul of her nature—something that happens to most people without being thus plainly expressed. For here again, we come to a dilemma. Different though the sexes are, they intermix. In every human being a vacillation from one sex to the other takes place, and often it is only the clothes that keep the male or female likeness, while underneath the sex is the very opposite of what is above.[61]

This is, as Jay Prosser has argued, an "easy androgyny," and many critics have noted the ways in which Orlando's clothing, rather than Orlando's body, pronounce the novel's sudden gender change.[62] For Prosser, *Orlando* is "not about the sexed body at all but the cultural vicissitudes of gender," and Orlando moves freely through different gender presentations while Hall's Stephen Gordon "remains as trapped in her sexually inverted moment as she is in her body."[63] For this reason, Prosser finds *Orlando* more resonant with contemporary expressions of transgender and other forms of gender fluidity. In contrast, Elizabeth Freeman highlights the significance of Orlando's embodiment, arguing that "*Orlando*'s most interesting conceit . . . is that the protagonist him/herself experiences historical change as a set of directly corporeal and often sexual sensations."[64] The relation of Orlando's gender change to sexual desire is difficult to decipher. The text is quite adamant that Orlando begins as a man and becomes a woman, but the objects of Orlando's sexual desire are less clearly marked. At first sight, clothing prevents him from determining whether his first love is a man or a woman, and, without regard for gender, his crush develops so quickly that "when the boy, for alas, a boy it must be—no woman could skate with such speed and vigour—swept almost on tiptoe past him, Orlando was ready to tear his hair with vexation that the person was of his own sex, and thus all embraces were out of the question."[65] Whether embraces were in or out of the question, Orlando's desire for the androgynous skater motivated his "curiosity."[66] Later, after Orlando becomes a woman, her attraction to women does not wane:

> And as all Orlando's loves had been women, now, through the culpable laggardry of the human frame to adapt itself to convention, though she herself was a woman, it was still a woman she loved; and if the consciousness of being of the same sex had any effect at all, it was to quicken and deepen those feelings which she had had as a man.[67]

Orlando does eventually marry Shelmardine, but they are described as only "acting the parts of men and women."[68] Their marriage is anything but conventional, and the entire institution of marriage is described as nothing more than a nineteenth-century fad.

After her brief wedding ceremony, in which the word "Obey" is drowned out by "a clap of thunder," Orlando questions its relevance: "She was married, true; but if one's husband was always sailing around Cape Horn, was it marriage? If one liked him, was it marriage? If one liked other people, was it marriage? . . . She had her doubts."[69] DuPlessis considers this marriage to be part of a "strategy of overt conformity" in which "heterosexual romance and marriage are set aside precisely in being achieved," after which Orlando "is released into a space not only beyond narrative conventions but also beyond sexual norms."[70] Describing an intimate scene between the two androgynous lovers, *Orlando*'s narrator leaves "a great blank" on the page, careful to note that this "must be taken to indicate that the space is filled to repletion," and I suggest that this is Woolf's strategy throughout the book—a strategy that provides space for her subject's own "vision of a fin rising on a wide blank sea."[71] If, as Raitt claims, biographies "must always be associated with the establishment of community and with the definition of public and private—what can be disclosed and what must be held back," then *Orlando* bounces betwixt and between intimacy and publicity.[72] As Karyn Z. Sproles suggests, the biographies and letters of Woolf and Sackville-West "struggle to articulate their desire for one another and to resist the social pressures that work to repress women's desire altogether."[73] In Hope Mirrlees's phrase, they faced the problem of what to say and what to leave out.

Vita Sackville-West's Queer Inheritance

Alongside the private expression of desire figured in those blank seas, blank pages, and the as yet unwritten blankness of Orlando's life beyond the ending, Woolf questions the public, legal impact of gender and sexuality on issues of reputation and inheritance. In order to write *Orlando*, Woolf relied heavily on *Knole and the Sackvilles* (1922), Sackville-West's nostalgic history of the connection between her beloved family estate and the ancestors who lived there over the course of several centuries. It was her first gift to Woolf after they met in 1922. In her book, Sackville-West portrayed herself and her heritage to be irrevocably linked to the estate itself, and Woolf clearly understood this: in *Orlando*, Sackville-West *is* Knole as much as she is Orlando. Descriptions of Orlando's "perambulation of the house"—his restless strolls through its "long galleries," "the crypt where his ancestors lay," its "three hundred and sixty-five bedrooms" and "fifty-two staircases"—occur again and again, and, at times, the house seems to be as much the biography's subject as Sackville-West herself.[74] Indeed, Orlando, "who believed in no immortality" but who, nevertheless, does not die, "could not help feeling that her soul would come and go for ever with the reds on the panels and the greens on the sofa."[75] In both *Knole and the Sackvilles* and *Orlando*, the house stands in for her entire heritage. Sackville-West retains her ancestral history through the house itself, which is part of the reason why, in *Orlando*, Woolf begins her fantastic biography during the Elizabethan era, when Knole was first given to the family. Many of the stories in *Orlando* are adaptations of ancestral vignettes in *Knole and the Sackvilles*, and all of the photographs in *Orlando* were either taken from the Knole portrait gallery or staged at Knole, with Sackville-West's help, for inclusion in the volume. The names, stories, and images in *Orlando* are as well preserved as objects in an archive.

But *Orlando* is far more than a fictionalized family history—it is both passion project and passionate critique. As Hermione Lee relates, Woolf always considered Knole to be an intrinsic part of Sackville-West: it was her "first passion (she grew up there) and her greatest lost love (she could not inherit, as she was a woman)."[76] As Woolf was beginning the project, Sackville-West's father lay sick at Knole, and, in early 1928, he died. If she had been a man, Sackville-West would have been the next in line to inherit Knole, but as a woman, her "greatest lost love" passed into the hands of a cousin, and she was evicted. Heartbroken on her behalf and furious with this outcome, Woolf used *Orlando* to criticize the sexist conventions of

English inheritance law. Upon Orlando's return home after many years abroad, she finds that her rights to her family home are being contested:

> The chief charges against her were (1) that she was dead, and therefore could not hold any property whatsoever; (2) that she was a woman, which amounts to much the same thing; (3) that she was an English Duke who had married one Rosina Pepita, a dancer; and had had by her three sons, which sons now declaring that their father was deceased, claimed that all his property descended to them. . . . Thus it was in a highly ambiguous condition, uncertain whether she was alive or dead, man or woman, Duke or nonentity, that she posted down to her country seat.[77]

The law can read Orlando neither accurately nor justly—man or woman? dead or alive?—and it is not a stretch to understand this as a commentary on Sackville-West's situation. Her son, Nigel Nicolson—who had once described *Orlando* as a love letter—later (and less famously) called it "a memorial mass" for his grandfather's death and his mother's subsequent loss of Knole.[78] And Woolf's choice of genre in which to protest that loss of Knole is hardly a coincidence. In its integration of past into present, biography is a literary enactment of inheritance in which each generation works out its relation to its history, ancestry, and values. Sackville-West lost Knole during her lifetime, but Woolf gave it back to her in *Orlando*. Despite her inability to legally inherit the estate, her name continues to be intimately linked with Knole today. Indeed, the brief description of Knole on the website of the British National Trust once read: "History and grandeur in the heart of Kent. Birthplace of novelist and poet Vita Sackville-West."[79] For Woolf and Sackville-West, the intimate biography of *Orlando* is a demonstration of queer inheritance that is chosen rather than dictated. Sackville-West gave *Knole and the Sackvilles* to Woolf, and after she was denied inheritance in early 1928, Woolf reunited her with Knole, in both fantasy and the future national imaginary, later that year.

Toward an Unfinished Modernism

In *Orlando*, Woolf uses the generic conventions of biography in order to normalize what would otherwise be considered impossible: an absurdly long lifetime, a spontaneous change of sex, an illegal inheritance. If, for Woolf, other biographies were all too often as deadeningly reductive as "the wax figures now preserved in Westminster Abbey, that were carried in funeral processions through the street—effigies that have only a smooth superficial likeness to the body in the coffin," her own biographical passion project would avoid death entirely.[80] The structure of Orlando's biography would not be biology; indeed, it would not even be fully legible to most of its readers. Genre and sexuality are here inexorably entwined: in rejecting the form of a standard biography, Woolf rejects the standard form of a legible life. Instead, she offers an alternative model of a human lifetime that is bound by the limits of imagination and desire rather than by somatic facts. If queer feminist life stories fail to fit into normative forms of biography, then changing and disrupting these forms is an urgent pedagogical process. I suggest that Woolf's pedagogical process extends beyond the text itself: in giving the biography back to Sackville-West on the day that it ends, historical time is folded into living time, and Woolf indicates that such intimate biographical practices can—and perhaps should—make a difference in the unfinished life and legacy of their subjects. This is a vision of biography as provocative fantasy, as creative history, and as opportunity. Woolf positions herself as an advocate for the legitimacy of fiction as a powerfully valid way of engaging with, rather than escaping from, the world. In *Orlando*, Woolf isn't simply writing a "joke" biography of Sackville-West; she is modeling an alternative—feminist, modernist, queer—biographical structure that is not dependent upon normative social scripts. For Woolf, biography is both a form of historical preservation and a kind of extralegal inheritance claim—a plea for the affective and aesthetic recognition of those who are so often misrecognized and disinherited by the law. *Orlando*, given back to its veiled subject and explicit dedicatee, Vita Sackville-West, on the day of its publication, restores her literary, if not legal, position as the rightful heir of her ancestral home while simultaneously insisting that her ability to shape her own history is an incomplete, ongoing process.

In this way, *Orlando* asks us to rethink queer feminist modernism more generally as an unfinished project. If we take the gift of *Orlando* seriously, we realize that *Orlando* was actually designed to feel unfinished—and that, what's more, the possibility for its eventual completion requires its transfer from the hands of one woman into the hands of another. Rereading *Orlando* like this, beyond its ending, is to understand it as an unfinished portrait of the artist as a queer feminist modern(ist) subject. What's more, *Orlando* is both a prefiguration and near-mythologization of the work of the passion projects that would follow it. All the writers I have discussed in this book, from Troubridge and Warner to Barnes and Mirrlees to Anderson, Beach, and Toklas, lived their lives and wrote their stories in the shadow not only of the modernist men who would be remembered in their stead but of Woolf. The canonization of Virginia Woolf, in its comparatively stunning preservation and promulgation of her letters, diaries, drafts, and ephemera, is the alternate history haunting the passion projects of each of these other, unremembered women. But rather than position Woolf as the exception that proves the rule or the single success floating above a sea of failed minor writers, I argue that we must read her *with* these women. Her brilliance notwithstanding, the fact that she occupies a now inviolable place in the history of English literature was never guaranteed. Her status remains a beacon for the uphill climb of queer feminist passion projects then and now. In *Orlando*, beneath the clever, cutting satire and grand reparative gestures, we see a portrait of a woman who, for no other reason than that she is a Chloe who liked an Olivia in 1928, is at risk of losing everything she had. This is the life story of Vita Sackville-West, just as it is the life of Sylvia Beach or Alice B. Toklas or Margaret Anderson or any of the other artists and lovers of this era to whom history, and biography, have been so cruel. But in Woolf's passion project, she is something else, too—a patron saint of the trials and tribulations of those writers who would follow her. She is essentially incomplete, continuously evolving beyond the rules of earlier genres and generations, and her existence is dependent upon other women, then and now.

CODA

Biographical Criticism and the Passion Project Now

IN THE 2018 inaugural issue of *Feminist Modernist Studies*, Madelyn Detloff describes what she calls "the Sisyphe position": an affective state that recognizes the "difficult, unfortunately repetitive, seemingly unwinnable task before the queer feminist cultural worker who is faced with rolling a giant boulder (call it fascism, call it misogyny, racism, ablism, heterosexism, anti-intellectualism, militarism, xenophobia . . .) up a hill so that it does not careen down and crush the things one values."[1] Detloff's timely revision of Sisyphus is shot through with the peculiar admixture of despair and determination that has characterized so much cultural production since 2016's mirrored traumas of Trump and Brexit. Her Sisyphe is an angry, exasperated rebel forced to repeat variations of the same queer feminist cultural work from one generation to the next; her rock is "the sedimentation of unequal social dynamics moving under the force of cultural inertia."[2] On one level, this repetition is infuriating, as it is "neither outrageous nor unreasonable to insist that we get that rock over the hill so that we can devote ourselves to other work."[3] But on another level, this repetition—recovery, rearticulation, reinscription—is a fundamental part of queer feminist cultural work. If we now consider axiomatic the idea that gender and even sexuality are constituted by a kind of compulsory repetition without end, then social and cultural projects sparked by issues of gender and sexuality will also require ongoing effort. That it is necessary makes it no less exhausting, unfortunately, and this fatigue is palpable in so many recent speculations about the contemporary value of feminist scholarship within modernist studies.[4] But for Detloff, dedication to this repetitive work "is ongoing because justice is not an end to be achieved, but a mode of being, or more properly, a mode of doing life."[5] In this light, queer feminist modernism is an unfinished—perhaps unfinishable—project, and the biographical acts recovered in *The Passion Projects* constitute one method of rolling the rock up the hill again, and again, and again.

In this brief coda, I suggest that we have not stopped pushing the rock up the hill in this particular way, even if the "heyday of feminist literary recovery work" in academic scholarship peaked in the 1980s and 1990s.[6] As Jessica Berman observes in the same issue of *Feminist Modernist Studies*, this mode of scholarship, with its parallel investments in both marginalized texts and marginalized lives, is "unpopular—again—or still?—and is not likely to land many scholars top jobs."[7] But, as I have shown throughout this book, these kinds of projects—that is, these passion projects—have always been pursued despite, and in reaction to, their status as unlikely candidates for professional laurels. And if we look just slightly outside the frame of academic modernist studies toward more personal, intimate, and even amateur undertakings, we can easily see that, just as the passion projects detailed in this book were attempted long before the wave of scholarly recovery projects in the late twentieth century, our contemporary moment, now at least a generation after that wave, remains full of ongoing demonstrations—by writers and readers alike—of the value of queer feminist modernist lives and life stories.

In 2017, for example, the *Paris Review* published "Reappearing Women: A Conversation between Marie Darrieussecq and Kate Zambreno," shortly after the publication of both *Being Here Is Everything*, Darrieussecq's biography of the German Expressionist painter Paula Modersohn-Becker, and *Book of Mutter*, Zambreno's fragmented book about motherhood and feminist grief.[8] Darrieussecq admits that, initially, she "didn't want to write a biography, I wanted to write a novel, something completely different." But this initial reluctance to embrace the biographical was overridden by an ambivalent but unmistakable attachment to her subject:

> She was like a dead friend. It was not exactly a passion. I like fiction, I write novels. A biography is a bit more restrained—you have to tell what you know, so I didn't have to imagine. In the beginning, I thought I was going to do a novel, but I wanted to have this woman known, not my imagination of her. She was not a ghost, she was like a dead woman, and I wanted to honor her memory. When you love somebody, you want the other people you know to love her, too.[9]

What Darrieussecq shared with Modersohn-Becker, whom she calls only Paula because "it's hard to have a name when you're a woman," was something like transhistorical friendship—not passionate but intimate, and infused nevertheless with respect and even love. She did not intend to write a biography, but she felt compelled to do so in order "to have this woman known," and she even curated a museum exhibition of her paintings while working on the book. Yet even Darrieussecq's multimodal passion project contains historical opacity. In a discussion of the friendship of Modersohn-Becker and sculptor Clara Westhoff, Zambreno suggests that their story feels "unfinished" and that, even in *Being Here Is Everything*, which focuses on Modersohn-Becker, Westhoff was "a ghost in your text, fluttering in the margins."[10] Darrieussecq describes Westhoff's artistic life as "interrupted" by motherhood before being "completely erased" from most historical narratives, and her own book gestures toward their friendship as an unrecovered—perhaps even unrecoverable—story.

Zambreno's books, too, seem compelled toward the biographical, however much they move fluidly between genres. In *Heroines*, her book nominally about the "mad wives," the "women often marginalized in the modernist memory project," she compiles fragments of modernist history together with pieces of autobiographical narrative and snippets of theoretical commentary.[11] Even in the moments that most resemble a *kunstlerroman*, it is her readerly attention to the biographical—the recovered narratives and the destroyed or forgotten archives—that prompts her own literary experiments. She notes, for example, that she began to work on "a fictional notebook I call *Mad Wife* . . . when I first began reading the biographies."[12] And, crucially, her sense of herself as a critic begins to develop "during the time I [began] reading the biographies of the mad wives, stewing in my obsessions, feeling eerily like I was performing their lives."[13] This obsessive attachment to biography propels her toward what she remembers as her first act of criticism: a letter to *Poetry* magazine in response to a dismissive, sexist review of Djuna Barnes's posthumous poetry collection. Her criticism, she realizes with the publication of that letter, "always originates in *feeling*, in an angry protectiveness, especially towards my beloved women."[14] That wellspring of feeling is evidence that biography can *do* something: as a genre fundamentally interested in questions of inheritance, it can pass on, from one reader to the next, not only fact but affect. For Zambreno, biography is a tool, a weapon, a way of questioning the aesthetic judgment of someone who dared call Barnes a "minor writer." But it also carries a sense of responsibility that she takes very seriously: "I feel compelled to act as the literary executor of the dead and erased. I'm responsible for guarding their legacy."[15] Setting her work explicitly against the tendency of the "modernist memory project" to erase the archival reminders of her "heroines," she reaches back across time and links their life stories to her own: "What does it mean to be aware of one's own preservation? To preserve the self. I save myself, my days. This archive of the self. These women who haunt me, I want to save them too, to carry them forward with me."[16] Like Darrieussecq, Zambreno did not set out to write a biography, but her method of "carry[ing] them forward" required biographical criticism.

Zambreno's biographical writing takes up and transforms the unfinished aesthetic of queer feminist modernism. In both *Heroines* (which, like the more recent *Book of Mutter*, has been described as a "critical memoir") and the online writing (on her blog, *Frances Farmer Is My Sister*, which is now, ironically, inaccessible to the public but will eventually be archived by Duke University) that preceded it, Zambreno's preferred mode of preservation is the notebook.[17] The notebook, like the blog, is more of a textual archive than a coherent narrative. She traces her "apprenticeship" as a writer back to her "elaborate notebooking system," and her blog, too, "began as a cocky, ecstatic sprawl, weaving in and out of anecdotal passionate homages to women writers I adored, posting their fuck-me-fatale photos, to sacrilegious reflections on the Surrealists to a sort of aesthetics theory."[18] In print and online, Zambreno writes in these interwoven fragments; connections are implied but impermanent, left unfinished. Sometimes, of course, the online and analog notebooks she compiles act as "experimental incubators" for future work. But at other times, she insists, they "are just what they are—unfinished, fragmented, explorations into something. We don't wish to formalize them into books. We want them to remain as they are—RAW, our own material," with no need to "push towards 'finishing' towards 'polish' towards 'professionalism.'"[19] Making use of biographical scholarship without being scholarly itself, Zambreno's work—which she readily admits is "perhaps not 'serious' criticism, but intensely personal and emotional"[20]—is a cross-generational iteration of the passion projects explored in this book.

And these passion projects take other contemporary forms, too. Lisa Cohen's *All We Know: Three Lives* is a different kind of queer feminist guardianship. Working firmly within the triangular tradition of queer feminist life writing discussed in the third chapter of this book, she highlights the unfinished aesthetic of queer feminist modernism in the lives of Esther Murphy, Mercedes de Acosta, and Madge Garland—three names that had been almost entirely unknown within mainstream modernist studies. Though all three women were significant cultural figures in their time, their stories and archives have proven resistant to historical narrative. The challenge of writing about women who "each memorialized herself and colluded in her own invisibility" was part of what drove Cohen to take up the project:

> While each one published, each also produced a body of thought that was not and could not be worked out fully on paper. As a result, each has been seen as not quite part of history, when seen at all. Juxtaposing their lives was a way to illuminate work that has not been recognized as such: in Murphy's case, prolific conversation; in de Acosta's, the fervent, even shameful acts and feelings associated with being a fan and collector; in Garland's, a career in the ephemeral, often trivialized world of fashion.[21]

Cohen's chapter on Murphy is particularly relevant to the concerns of this book, as Murphy, a New York intellectual and dazzling conversationalist, failed to complete the major book project that dominated the last fifteen years of her life: a biography of Madame de Maintenon. But in each chapter, Cohen crafts a coherent historical narrative out of ephemeral scraps of intimate history. In this way, her triangulated prosopography provides a contemporary response to the narrator of Virginia Woolf's *A Room of One's Own*, who, "look[ing] about the shelves for books that were not there," anxiously scans the libraries for those feminist histories sure to be lost forever if left uncollected, unwritten, unpublished.[22] Cohen's *All We Know* has been almost universally praised by readers and critics; it is safe to say that Murphy, de Acosta, and Garland can now be found on the library's shelves. But the title of her book is deliberately ambivalent about the nature of this victory. "All we know," Cohen tells us, was one of Murphy's favorite ways to "begin a long disquisition" on virtually any subject, regardless of her actual expertise.[23] Pair it with a "for" and a shrug—"for all we know"—and it suggests the impossibility of separating fact from fiction; follow it with "for now" and an optimistic disposition—"all we know . . . for now"—and it implies a project to be passed into the hands of the next generation. The phrase thus works in multiple ways: it seems to signal historical triumph while simultaneously suggesting the incomplete, even unfinishable, nature of so many life stories. It is, in Cohen's view, "a declaration of comprehensiveness and incompletion."[24]

Some contemporary biographical novels focused on queer feminist modernist writers have also called attention to the inevitable incompleteness of the historical archive. In *The Book of Salt*, for example, Monique Truong returns to modernism's most iconic lesbian couple—Gertrude Stein and Alice B. Toklas—through the story of Bình, the Vietnamese cook who worked in their household. Her novel looks past the disinheritance of Toklas, discussed in this book, in order to ask what is inherited or stolen from a figure whose life was not preserved via the passionate attachments of a biographer, a collector, or a former lover. Whose stories are rendered invisible by the modernist archive compiled by Stein and Toklas? For Truong, this archive can only take us so far, and the fetishization of archival materials is a historical trap. In the novel, for example, when asked to steal one of Stein's manuscripts for an unnamed lover—"Choose something from the middle, you tell me. No one ever remembers what happens there."[25]—Bình is outraged to find his name in its pages:

> I did not give you my permission, Madame, to treat me in this way. I am here to feed you, not to serve as your fodder. I demand more money for such services, Madame. You pay me only for my time. My story, Madame, is mine. I alone am qualified to tell it.[26]

Truong herself has no such permission, of course, but as Bình narrates, "a gift or a theft depends on who is holding the pen."[27] *The Book of Salt* delivers a stinging critique of the racial (and classed) politics of high modernism that is both allied in principle with the queer feminist passion projects in this book and critical of their own exclusions. That the voice of this critique comes from inside the house of Stein and Toklas suggests that there are fates worse than being an exile of the modernist memory project alone.

And while it is precisely the precarious, even gestural nature of Truong's archival sources that provides her, too, with "fodder" for her biographical novel, her fictionalized account of a marginalized figure in this now famous household directs our attention to the archives we can never recover, the stories no one is fully qualified to tell. In David Eng's reading, *The Book of Salt* shifts our attention from "the problem of the real"—that is, the attempted recovery of actual historical figures—"to the politics of our lack of knowledge" about the relationship between the celebrated figures of high modernist Paris and the migrant colonial subjects on whom they depended.[28] This attention to absences and silences, the undecipherable and the unnameable, implicitly asks us to consider the "what-could-have-been in the what-can-be-known of historicism."[29] Sometimes all we know is all we are going to get, and sometimes all we know is wrong, or missing, or incomplete. But in such biographical fictions as Truong's, the heartrending inadequacy of "all we know" can be supplemented by an enveloping shadow sense of all we *might* have known (but, now, never will).

While Zambreno, Cohen, and Truong each feel a different kind of archival responsibility toward the life stories of their subjects, the late Jenny Diski's sense of biographical responsibility was born of a more intimate claim. Diski, who died of cancer in 2016, was a prolific writer of novels, stories, criticism, and creative nonfiction. She began writing what would become *In Gratitude*, the last of her books to be published in her lifetime, shortly after receiving a diagnosis of terminal lung cancer in 2014.[30] In the time between her diagnosis and death, she published most of the book as a series of essays for the *London Review of Books*, and the experience of reading those essays was, for me, nothing less than astonishing. Every byline was a calming revelation that she was, for now, still alive, her life unfinished and unfolding before us; every essay was a demonstration of the almost miraculous force of late work. For they contained two major subjects she had never written about before: the first, perhaps unsurprisingly, was the experience of living with a terminal disease, which she narrated in her characteristically acerbic and contrarian manner; the second, far less foreseeable, was the story of her life with Doris Lessing, who had taken her in at fifteen and provided her with a stable home and a model of how to be a fiercely feminist writer. The relationship between these two difficult, brilliant women was not uncomplicated, but while they lived in the same household together for only a few years, they remained in each other's lives for the next several decades. The abruptness of Diski's turn back toward this shared history after receiving her own diagnosis suggests that she knew Lessing had to be her final project—that since Lessing had died the year before, in 2013, it had to be written and shared before Diski died, too. The fact of their long friendship was hardly a secret, and it would surely have been entered into the literary-historical record in some way. But Diski refused to cede that control to future scholars; instead, knowing that, for women writers in particular, the biographical would be inextricable from aesthetic evaluation, she wrote her version of their story. In this way, she wrote not only "in gratitude" but also, as Lessing had so many years before, in self-defense. But with Lessing now dead (and thus defenseless), Diski's book was free to grapple with the seemingly unending knottiness of their relationship. What was the right word for who Lessing had been to her? And was she writing, finally, from an affective space of gratitude or ingratitude? For a writer as famous and laureled as Lessing, what was left for Diski alone to remember? What visions of fins were rising above the pages of their lives?

We, like Diski herself, cannot fully answer these questions. But the tension they gesture toward is, I think, related to Detloff's reconception of the Sisyphe position as a mode of living motivated by not only anger and exasperation but love. From the Sisyphe position, we return again and again to the queer feminist modernist past, pulled toward the biographical as an indispensable tool rather than a shameful vice. And, perhaps in part because these midcentury women (and their inheritors/recoverers in the latter half of the century) taught us not to be ashamed to find insight and hope in the lives of others, biographical criticism has become somewhat less of a lonely project. The history of passion projects in this book is, in many ways, a history of the failure of collaboration. Una Troubridge and Evguenia Souline could not see that their ultimately shared memorial task would have been more convincing, even unassailable, if they had compiled it together; Hope Mirrlees could not bring herself to share Jessie Stewart's vision of a biography that would benefit from both of their passions; the "residual Steins," in their urge to claim their ancestor's legacy, cheapened it by disrespecting Alice B. Toklas, the woman who knew her best. Even Sylvia Townsend Warner, author of perhaps the most hopeful of these passion projects, worked alone, relishing the isolation of her intimate archive.

But it is not a necessary precondition that these passion projects must be undertaken alone, that they must be born of solitude. Such biographical acts often happen in waves; the last two years alone have seen two very differently experimental books about Kathy Acker: Chris Kraus's *After Kathy Acker* (2017) and Olivia Laing's *Crudo* (2018). And as the encouragement that came to Margaret Anderson in letters from friends and the vibrant comments on Zambreno's blog suggest, sometimes even obscure biographical acts can be buoyed by the force of community. Indeed, the twenty-first-century rise of the Internet as a space of social and scholarly conversation has presented an opportunity to make new passion projects live through shared effort and pooled resources. Cambridge University Press's *The Orlando Project,* for example, takes its name and its inspiration from Woolf's novel. It is a dynamic, interactive, online "textbase" of critical and biographical material about women writers throughout history. With a focus on the work of "recovery," this growing project endeavors, through sheer force of accumulated evidence, to rewrite the history of English literature as, at least in part, a history of "women . . . writing about women writing." Similarly, the University of Virginia's *Collective Biographies of Women* began as a para-text to Allison Booth's 2004 scholarly monograph, *How to Make It as a Woman: Collective Biographical History from Victoria to the Present*. Since that time, it has become a collaboratively edited and annotated bibliography of biographies of women as well as a database of biographical information about as many as 8,600 women. What began as a sole-authored work of scholarship has become a sprawling, collective passion project. And sites like *The Heroine Collective* have emerged to chronicle—through interviews, biographical sketches, and critical content—the lives of women, past and present, who might appear at risk of being forgotten. These resources all place women's lives in relation to each other by rendering visible networks both old and new, expected and utterly surprising. And, moreover, they are able to do this by recognizing that such work is constitutively unfinished, sometimes even unfinishable. The Internet is by no means a stable archive; access to it is both enabled and put at risk by its essential immateriality. But these projects are animated by the optimistic notion that collective repetition of these thousands of biographical acts might yield something that lasts.

This coda is titled "Biographical Criticism and the Passion Project Now," and, in some ways, it is an ode to the long life of such criticism. But, at the same time, this book's focus on the critical, biographical acts of women is not incidental. In our histories of the field, we are often told that the rise of New Criticism banished the biographical from the scholarly mainstream. It is no coincidence that this period also saw the canonization of Eliot, Joyce, Pound, and the other male modernists who came to define their era at the cost of nearly all women writers, save Woolf and Stein. But to imagine that this process of canonization took place without recourse to the biographical, without scholarly interest in and even obsession with the legendary biographies of those men, is to rewrite literary history in a particularly damaging way. Indeed, as scholars have shown, the midcentury consolidation of modernism into an object of academic study took place primarily in male-dominated biographies, single-author studies, anthologies, and institutional archives.[31] This is how we received the major players, texts, and aesthetic principles of the field. New Criticism may have focused readers' attention on the words rather than the lives, but these foundational biographical acts helped cement which words were remembered. Because the field has been built on the backs of literary lives, the relative absence of biographical narratives of women's literary work and relationships has had a profound effect. Arguments about the value of biographical criticism from T. S. Eliot to Elena Ferrante are arguments worth having, but they must take place in the knowledge that, from New Criticism to New Formalism, the devalued genre of biography—in its many forms betwixt and between—has never abdicated its role in defining the field of literary and historical study. *The Passion Projects* is a work of recovery in solidarity with the long history of queer feminist modernist study, but it is also an argument that the act of stepping away from the biographical is the privilege of those who are already remembered, whose lives are already imprinted upon history. The passion projects in this book are records of women who fought against that forgetting, who sought to write the counterhistory of modernism while its official history was still being written. This book is an effort to tell a story with those writers at its center—to, in the words of Nathalie Léger that serve as my epigraph, "excavate a miniature model of modernity, reduced to its simplest, most complex form: a woman telling her story through that of another woman."

ABBREVIATIONS

EJCMA Elizabeth Jenks Clark Collection of Margaret Anderson. Yale Collection of American Literature, Beinecke Rare Book and Manuscript Library, Yale University. New Haven, Connecticut.

GSABTP Gertrude Stein and Alice B. Toklas Papers. Yale Collection of American Literature, Beinecke Rare Book and Manuscript Library, Yale University. New Haven, Connecticut.

GSC Gertrude Stein Collection in the Carleton Lake Collection. Harry Ransom Center, University of Texas at Austin.

HMP Hope Mirrlees Papers. Newnham College Archives, University of Cambridge.

JEHP Jane Ellen Harrison Papers. Newnham College Archives, University of Cambridge.

RHUTP Radclyffe Hall and Una Troubridge Papers. Harry Ransom Center, University of Texas at Austin.

SBP Sylvia Beach Papers. Manuscripts Division, Department of Rare Books and Special Collections, Princeton University Library.

STWA Sylvia Townsend Warner Archive. Dorset County Museum. Dorchester, England.

VBA Vera Brittain Archive. William Ready Division of Archives and Research Collections. McMaster University Library. Hamilton, Ontario, Canada.

NOTES

Introduction. Modernism's Unfinished Lives

1. Virginia Woolf, *A Room of One's Own* (1929; London: Harcourt, 2005), 78.
2. Ibid., 79.
3. Ibid., 80–81.
4. Jodie Medd, *Lesbian Scandal and the Culture of Modernism* (Cambridge: Cambridge University Press, 2012), 178.
5. Woolf, *A Room of One's Own*, 81.
6. Lillian Faderman, ed., *Chloe Plus Olivia: An Anthology of Lesbian Literature from the Seventeenth Century to the Present* (New York: Viking, 1994), viii; Nancy K. Miller, "A Feminist Friendship Archive," *Profession* (2011): 202. Drawing attention to the temporal gravity of the "vertical bonds" of family and generation that structure so many life stories, Miller considers friendship as a kind of "lateral bond," especially in memoirs "in which one tells about two and two become one" (199). She is especially interested in what she calls the "transpersonal" connections between people "to whom one is related by affinity (profession, passion, politics) but not (or not necessarily) by blood or marriage" (220–21), and she expands on these theories in *My Brilliant Friends: Our Lives in Feminism* (New York: Columbia University Press, 2019). Miller's theorization of the transpersonal has been taken up in Jean Mills, *Virginia Woolf, Jane Ellen Harrison, and the Spirit of Modernist Classicism* (Columbus: Ohio State University Press, 2014), 168–70.
7. Sharon Marcus, *Between Women: Friendship, Desire, and Marriage in Victorian England* (Princeton: Princeton University Press, 2007), 258.
8. Woolf, *A Room of One's Own*, 83, emphasis mine.
9. Academic scholarship has never been the sole (or even primary) mode of feminist and queer recovery work. Within independent publishing, for example, both Naiad Press and Virago Press were founded in 1973, while Persephone Books was founded in 1999 to publish neglected and out-of-print women's writing from the early to mid-twentieth century.
10. In refusing a careful distinction between the recovery of literature and biographical/cultural history, I remain indebted to earlier models of lesbian feminist historical work. See, for example, Shari Benstock, *Women of the Left Bank, 1900–1940* (Austin: University of Texas Press, 1986); Gillian Hanscombe and Virginia L. Smyers, *Writing for Their Lives: The Modernist Women, 1910–1940* (Boston: Northeastern University Press, 1987); Bonnie Kime Scott, ed., *The Gender of Modernism: A Critical Anthology* (Bloomington: Indiana University Press, 1990); and Andrea Weiss, *Paris Was a Woman: Portraits from the Left Bank* (San Francisco: Harper San Francisco, 1995).
11. Terry Castle, *The Apparitional Lesbian: Female Homosexuality and Modern Culture* (New York: Columbia University Press, 1993), 5. "One will search in vain," writes Castle, "for any unambiguously lesbian heroines in the annals of modern civilization: from Sappho to Greta Garbo, Queen Christina to Eleanor Roosevelt, virtually

every distinguished woman suspected of homosexuality has had her biography sanitized at one point or another in the interest of public safety."

12. Virginia Woolf, "Mr. Bennett and Mrs. Brown," *Collected Essays*, vol. 1 (London: Hogarth Press, 1966), 319; Willa Cather, *Not Under Forty* (1922; Lincoln: University of Nebraska Press, 1988), v. For critical accounts of the significance of 1922 in particular, see Michael North, *Reading 1922: A Return to the Scene of the Modern* (Oxford: Oxford University Press, 1999) and Kevin Jackson, *Constellation of Genius: 1922: Modernism Year One* (New York: Farrar, Straus and Giroux, 2012).

13. See, for example, Blanche Wiesen Cook, "'Women Alone Stir My Imagination': Lesbianism and the Cultural Tradition," *Signs* 4 (1979): 718–39; Bonnie Kime Scott, *Refiguring Modernism, Volume 1: Women of 1928* (Bloomington: Indiana University Press, 1996); Lillian Faderman, "Love between Women in 1928: Why Progressivism Is Not Always Progress," *Lodestar Quarterly* 13 (2005), http://lodestarquarterly.com/work/281/; Medd, *Lesbian Scandal and the Culture of Modernism*; Susan S. Lanser, "1928: Sapphic Modernity and the Sexuality of History," *Modernism/modernity Print Plus*, October 25, 2016, https://modernismmodernity.org/forums/posts/1928-sapphic-modernity-and-sexuality-history.

14. Laura Doan, *Fashioning Sapphism: The Origins of a Modern English Lesbian Culture* (New York: Columbia University Press, 2001), xii–xiii. For another important history of the trial and its aftermath, see Medd, *Lesbian Scandal and the Culture of Modernism*, esp. chap. 4.

15. Benjamin Kahan, "Queer Modernism," in *A Handbook of Modernism Studies*, ed. Jean-Michel Rabaté (Oxford: Wiley-Blackwell, 2013), 348.

16. Virginia Woolf, *Diary*, ed. Anne Olivier Bell (New York: Harcourt Brace Jovanovich, 1980), 3:262.

17. Vera Brittain, *Testament of Friendship: The Story of Winifred Holtby* (1940; New York: Wideview Books, 1981), 2.

18. See, for example, the cross-generational saga of our eventual inheritance of E. M. Forster's life story in Wendy Moffat, *A Great Unrecorded History: A New Life of E. M. Forster* (New York: Farrar, Straus and Giroux, 2010).

19. See, for example, Faderman, *Chloe Plus Olivia*; Carroll Smith-Rosenberg, "The Female World of Love and Ritual: Relations between Women in Nineteenth-Century America," *Signs* 1, no. 1 (1975): 1–29; and Marcus, *Between Women*.

20. Lawrence Rainey, *Institutions of Modernism: Literary Elites and Public Culture* (New Haven: Yale University Press, 1998), 8–9.

21. Charles Caramello, *Henry James, Gertrude Stein, and the Biographical Act* (Chapel Hill: University of North Carolina Press, 1996), ix–x. For another description of life writing as an "act," see Elizabeth Bruss, *Autobiographical Acts: The Changing Situation of a Literary Genre* (Baltimore: Johns Hopkins University Press, 1976).

22. Sean Latham and Gayle Rogers, *Modernism: Evolution of an Idea* (London: Bloomsbury, 2015), 70. Their account is soundly researched and utterly convincing, but it is also counterintuitive: despite the entanglement of modernism (as a movement) and New Criticism, they contend that it is nevertheless biographical criticism that would go on to play a large role in launching modernist studies (as a field).

23. Ibid., 72–73.

24. See Janet Beizer, *Thinking Through the Mothers: Reimagining Women's Biographies* (Ithaca: Cornell University Press, 2008), 14; Alison Booth, *How to Make It*

as a Woman: Collective Biographical History from Victoria to the Present (Chicago: University of Chicago Press, 2004), 3; and Ruth Hoberman, *Modernizing Lives: Experiments in English Biography, 1918–1939* (Carbondale: Southern Illinois University Press, 1987), especially chap. 5. For a related analysis of the impact of literary portraiture on queer modernism, see Jaime Hovey, *A Thousand Words: Portraiture, Style, and Queer Modernism* (Columbus: Ohio State University Press, 2006).

25. See, for example, the lesbian feminist criticism cited earlier; see also foundational criticism about writers of the Harlem Renaissance such as Thadious Davis, *Nella Larsen, Novelist of the Harlem Renaissance: A Woman's Life Unveiled* (Baton Rouge: Louisiana State University Press, 1994) and Arnold Rampersad, *The Life of Langston Hughes*, vols. 1 and 2 (Oxford: Oxford University Press, 1986, 1988), to take only two examples among many.

26. See, for example, the essays collected in A. Walton Litz, Louis Menand, and Lawrence Rainey, eds., *Modernism and the New Criticism*, vol. 7 of *Cambridge History of Literary Criticism*, ed. H. B. Nisbet and Claude Rawson (Cambridge: Cambridge University Press, 2000).

27. William S. McFeely, "Preface: Why Biography?" in *The Seductions of Biography*, ed. Mary Rhiel and David Suchoff (New York: Routledge, 1996), x. McFeely goes on to admit his ongoing wariness of the notion that biography is "distinct from other ways of trying to make sense, with words, of the world."

28. As we have seen, denigrating the biographical is a common critical stance, but this ongoing distaste can lead us into what Merve Emre, in the context of the scandal surrounding the 2016 doxing of Elena Ferrante, has described as a "misunderstanding of what kinds of claims the biographical allows one to make." See Merve Emre, "The Ferrante Paradox," *Public Books*, December 15, 2016, http://www.publicbooks.org/the-ferrante-paradox/. For an extended meditation on the kinds of "bad readers" drawn to the biographical among other genres deemed insufficiently theoretical, see Tyler Bradway, *Queer Experimental Literature: The Affective Politics of Bad Reading* (New York: Palgrave Macmillan, 2017) and Merve Emre, *Paraliterary: The Making of Bad Readers in Postwar America* (Chicago: University of Chicago Press, 2017).

29. See, for example, Maria DiBattista and Emily O. Wittman, eds., *Modernism and Autobiography* (Cambridge: Cambridge University Press, 2014); Gregory Castle, *Reading the Modernist Bildungsroman* (Gainesville: University Press of Florida, 2006); Jed Esty, *Unseasonable Youth: Modernism, Colonialism, and the Fiction of Development* (Oxford: Oxford University Press, 2012); Hovey, *A Thousand Words*; Georgia Johnston, *The Formation of 20th-Century Lesbian Autobiography* (New York: Palgrave Macmillan, 2007); Sean Latham, *The Art of Scandal: Modernism, Libel Law, and the Roman à Clef* (Oxford: Oxford University Press, 2009); Franco Moretti, *The Way of the World: The Bildungsroman in European Culture* (New York: Verso, 2000); and Wendy Steiner, *Exact Resemblance to Exact Resemblance: The Literary Portraiture of Gertrude Stein* (New Haven: Yale University Press, 1978).

30. Sylvia Townsend Warner to William Maxwell, April 13, 1970, in *The Element of Lavishness: Letters of Sylvia Townsend Warner and William Maxwell, 1938–1978*, ed. Michael Steinman (Washington, DC: Counterpoint, 2001), 211.

31. William Carlos Williams, *The Autobiography of William Carlos Williams* (New York: New Directions, 1967), 264–65.

32. Leo Bersani and Adam Phillips, *Intimacies* (Chicago: University of Chicago Press, 2008), 1.

33. For a compelling history on the transgenerational practice of collecting during the period, see Jeremy Braddock, *Collecting as Modernist Practice* (Baltimore: Johns Hopkins University Press, 2012).

34. Jacques Derrida, *Archive Fever*, trans. Eric Prenowitz (Chicago: University of Chicago Press, 1995), 18, 36.

35. Maryanne Dever, Sally Newman, and Ann Vickery, *The Intimate Archive: Journeys through Private Papers* (Canberra: National Library of Australia, 2009), 3. Scholarship using an inverted form of the phrase is both published and in development; see Melissa Autumn White, "Archives of Intimacy and Trauma: Queer Migrations Documents as Technologies of Affect," *Radical History Review* 120 (Fall 2014): 75–93 and Nadine Attewell, "Archives of Intimacy: Racial Mixing and Asian Lives in the Colonial Port City" (manuscript in progress).

36. Geraldine Pratt and Victoria Rosner, "Introduction: The Global and the Intimate," in *The Global and the Intimate: Feminism in Our Time*, ed. Pratt and Rosner (New York: Columbia University Press, 2012), 4. See also Jennifer Cooke, ed., *Scenes of Intimacy: Reading, Writing, and Theorizing Contemporary Literature* (London: Bloomsbury, 2013) and Diane P. Freedman, Olivia Frey, and Frances Murphy Zauhar, *The Intimate Critique: Autobiographical Literary Criticism* (Durham: Duke University Press, 1993).

37. J. Samaine Lockwood, *Archives of Desire: The Queer Historical Work of New England Regionalism* (Chapel Hill: University of North Carolina Press, 2015), 10, 155–64.

38. Lauren Berlant, "Intimacy: A Special Issue," in *Intimacy*, ed. Berlant (Chicago: University of Chicago Press, 2000), 3. See also Berlant, "Feminism and the Institutions of Intimacy," in *The Politics of Research*, ed. E. Ann Kaplan and George Levine (New Brunswick, NJ: Rutgers University Press, 1997), 143–61.

39. Judith Halberstam, *In a Queer Time and Place: Transgender Bodies, Subcultural Lives* (New York: New York University Press, 2005), 6; Annamarie Jagose, *Queer Theory: An Introduction* (New York: New York University Press, 1997), 99. For a clarifying assessment of this debate in the face of "queer liberalism," see David Eng, Judith Halberstam, and José Esteban Muñoz, "What's Queer about Queer Studies Now?" *Social Text* 23, nos. 3–4 (84–85) (2005): 1–17. See also Michael Warner, "Queer and Then?: The End of Queer Theory?" *Chronicle of Higher Education*, January 1, 2012, http://www.chronicle.com/article/QueerThen-/130161.

40. Lauren Berlant and Michael Warner, "What Can Queer Theory Teach Us about X?" *PMLA* 110, no. 3 (1995): 345.

41. Eve Kosofsky Sedgwick, *Tendencies* (Durham: Duke University Press, 1993), 8. See also Judith Butler's insistence on understanding queerness as necessarily contingent in "Critically Queer," *GLQ* 1, no. 1 (1993): 17–32.

42. Sedgwick, *Tendencies*, 8–9.

43. Valerie Rohy, *Impossible Women: Lesbian Figures and American Literature* (Ithaca: Cornell University Press, 2000), 9. For other examples of resistance to the indeterminacy of the word "queer," see Lynne Huffer, *Are the Lips a Grave? A Queer Feminist on the Ethics of Sex* (New York: Columbia University Press, 2013), 65–67;

and Patricia Morgne Cramer, "Woolf and Theories of Sexuality," in *Virginia Woolf in Context*, ed. Bryony Randall and Jane Goldman (Cambridge: Cambridge University Press, 2012), 129–46.

44. Adrienne Rich, "Compulsory Heterosexuality and Lesbian Existence," *Signs* 5, no. 4 (1980): 631–60.

45. See, for example, Benjamin Kahan, *Celibacies: American Modernism & Sexual Life* (Durham: Duke University Press, 2013). Kahan's theorization of "the expressive hypothesis" posits that queer theory's historically conditioned use of a "paranoid hermeneutic that 'reads through' censorship to recover sexual expression—in order to make sure that one's sexual identities, desires, and pleasures never fall victim to suppression—inadvertently reduces possible connotations into a single denotation" (5).

46. See, for example, Carolyn Dinshaw, *Getting Medieval: Sexualities and Communities, Pre- and Postmodern* (Durham: Duke University Press, 1999); Carolyn Dinshaw et al., "Theorizing Queer Temporalities: A Roundtable Discussion," *GLQ* 13, no. 2–3 (2007): 177–95; Elizabeth Freeman, *Time Binds: Queer Temporalities, Queer Histories* (Durham: Duke University Press, 2010); Halberstam, *In a Queer Time and Place*; and José Esteban Muñoz, *Cruising Utopia: The Then and There of Queer Futurity* (New York: New York University Press, 2009). See also Michael D. Snediker, *Queer Optimism: Lyric Personhood and Other Felicitous Persuasions* (Minneapolis: University of Minnesota Press, 2009).

47. See Heather Love, *Feeling Backward: Loss and the Possibilities of Queer History* (Cambridge, MA: Harvard University Press, 2007), esp. chap. 1. I engage with Love's argument in the next chapter of this book. See also David Halperin, *How to Do the History of Homosexuality* (Chicago: University of Chicago Press, 2002). Halperin acknowledges the pleasures and possibilities of identification as "a form of cognition," but he ultimately doubles down on the necessity for historical specificity and "an approach to the history of sexuality that foregrounds historical differences, that attempts to acknowledge the alterity of the past as well as the irreducible cultural and historical specificities of the present" (17).

48. See, for example, Kate Eichhorn, *The Archival Turn in Feminism: Outrage in Gender* (Philadelphia: Temple University Press, 2013), which focuses on the Riot Grrrl Collection of feminist zines that is now held in NYU's Fales Library and Special Collections, and Ann Cvetkovich, "Personal Effects: The Material Archive of Gertrude Stein and Alice B. Toklas's Domestic Life," *No More Potlucks* 25 (2013), http://nomorepotlucks.org/site/personal-effects-the-material-archive-of-gertrude-stein-and-alice-b-toklass-domestic-life-ann-cvetkovich/.

49. Daniel Marshall, Kevin P. Murphy, and Zeb Tortorici, eds., "Queering Archives: Historical Unravelings," *Radical History Review* 120 (Fall 2014): 1.

50. Ibid., 2.

51. Ann Cvetkovich, *An Archive of Feelings: Trauma, Sexuality, and Lesbian Public Cultures* (Durham: Duke University Press, 2003), 244. For a different kind of resistance to queer archival pathology, see Scott Herring, *The Hoarders: Material Deviance in Modern American Culture* (Chicago: University of Chicago Press, 2014). See also Valerie Rohy, "In the Queer Archive," *GLQ* 16, no. 3 (2010): 341–61.

52. For a useful discussion of the fantasy of the "primal scene of archival research" from the perspective of an archivist, see Gabrielle Dean, "Disciplinarity and Disorder,"

Archive Journal (May 2011), http://www.archivejournal.net/essays/disciplinarity-and-disorder/. Dean is the William Kurrelmeyer Curator of Rare Books and Manuscripts at Johns Hopkins University. For further resistance to the scholarly romanticization of "the archive," see "The Caswell Test," from Bridget Whearty, "Invisible in 'The Archive': Librarians, Archivists, and the Caswell Test," *English, General Literature, and Rhetoric Faculty Scholarship* (2018): 4, https://orb.binghamton.edu/english_fac/4. The Caswell Test demands that scholars recognize and cite the work of archivists and librarians alongside the work of other humanities scholars.

53. Linda Morra, *Unarrested Archives: Case Studies in Twentieth-Century Canadian Women's Authorship* (Toronto: University of Toronto Press, 2014), 10.

54. Kevin Ohi, *Dead Letters Sent: Queer Literary Transmission* (Minneapolis: University of Minnesota Press, 2015), 1–2.

55. Scott Herring, "Tillie Olsen, Unfinished (Slow Writing from the Seventies)," *Studies in American Fiction* 37, no. 1 (2010): 82, 84, 93.

56. Ibid., 96–97.

57. Ibid., 97.

58. James Ramsey Wallen, "What Is an Unfinished Work?" *New Literary History* 46, no. 1 (2015): 126.

59. Ibid., 128. Wallen here notes the frequency of "an ambivalent rhetoric of lack," which, he claims, is "a means of validating literary paradigms of wholeness and unity through the diminishment of texts seen as incomplete and/or fragmentary."

60. Judith Halberstam, *The Queer Art of Failure* (Durham: Duke University Press, 2011), 88.

61. Carolyn Dinshaw, *How Soon Is Now? Medieval Texts, Amateur Readers, and the Queerness of Time* (Durham: Duke University Press, 2012), 32.

62. Ibid., 30–31.

Chapter 1. Intimate Archives: The Preservation of Partnership

1. Virginia Woolf, "The Lives of the Obscure," in *The Essays of Virginia Woolf*, vol. 4, ed. Andrew McNeillie (London: Hogarth, 1994), 118.

2. Ibid., 118–19.

3. Carolyn Dinshaw, *Getting Medieval: Sexualities and Communities, Pre- and Postmodern* (Durham: Duke University Press, 1999), 34–35.

4. Heather Love, *Feeling Backward: Loss and the Politics of Queer History* (Cambridge, MA: Harvard University Press, 2007), 33.

5. Woolf, "The Lives of the Obscure," 119.

6. Jessica Berman, "*Three Guineas* and the Politics of Interruption," in *A Companion to Virginia Woolf*, ed. Berman (Hoboken, NJ: John Wiley & Sons, 2016), 203–16.

7. For Love's extended response to Dinshaw's meditation on the phrase, see *Feeling Backward*, 39–40.

8. Martha Vicinus, *Intimate Friends: Women Who Loved Women, 1778–1928* (Chicago: University of Chicago Press, 2004), xxiv.

9. Elizabeth Freeman, "Time Binds, or, Erotohistoriography," *Social Text* 23, no. 3–4 (84–85) (2005): 61.

10. Carolyn Dinshaw et al., "Theorizing Queer Temporalities: A Roundtable Discussion," *GLQ* 13, no. 2–3 (2007): 178.

11. Freeman, "Time Binds," 61.

12. José Esteban Muñoz, *Cruising Utopia: The Then and There of Queer Futurity* (New York: New York University Press, 2009), 1.

13. Vera Brittain, "Facing Facts," n.p., VBA. The full text of Brittain's review is also available in the second chapter of Brittain, *Radclyffe Hall: A Case of Obscenity?* (London: Femina Books, 1968), 47–49.

14. Shortly after the trial, she discussed her desire to write "a longish article called 'Who are the Feminists'—a reply to the oft repeated statement . . . that feminists come from the ranks of the inverted." Her argument, she goes on, was to be based on "an analysis of the anti-feminism of 'The Well of Loneliness' & 'Extraordinary Women' in contrast to the sexually normal sex qualities . . . of such leading feminists as Mary Wollstonecraft, Josephine Butler, & Olive Schreiner & Mrs. Pankhurst." See Vera Brittain to George Catlin, February 5, 1929, VBA. And in "Why Feminism Lives," a pamphlet issued by the Six Points Group, Brittain's rhetoric is similarly uncomfortable for contemporary feminist, lesbian, and queer readers. Declaring the "unpopularity" of the feminist movement unjust, she emphasizes the "charm and elegance of the average modern feminist," and she maintains that feminism, "a much maligned word, . . . has come to stand for many irrelevancies, such as dowdiness and physical abnormality." Feminism, in other words, was for Brittain too often misrepresented by what she saw as the "dowdiness" of spinsters and the "physical abnormality" of lesbians. See Vera Brittain, "Why Feminism Lives," VBA, n.p.

15. In the decades after Brittain's book, a number of additional studies of Hall and her work have been published. See, for example, Lovat Dickson, *Radclyffe Hall at the Well of Loneliness: A Sapphic Chronicle* (New York: Collins, 1975); Michael Baker, *Our Three Selves: A Life of Radclyffe Hall* (London: William Morrow, 1985); Rebecca O'Rourke, *Reflecting on* The Well of Loneliness (London: Routledge, 1989); Terry Castle, *Noel Coward and Radclyffe Hall: Kindred Spirits* (New York: Columbia University Press, 1996); Sally Cline, *Radclyffe Hall: A Woman Called John* (Woodstock, NY: Overlook Press, 1997); Diana Souhami, *The Trials of Radclyffe Hall* (New York: Doubleday, 1998); Laura Doan and Jay Prosser, eds., *Palatable Poison: Critical Perspectives on* The Well of Loneliness (New York: Columbia University Press, 2002); Richard Dellamora, *Radclyffe Hall: A Life in the Writing* (Philadelphia: University of Pennsylvania Press, 2011). Only one biography of Troubridge has been published: Richard Ormrod, *Una Troubridge: The Friend of Radclyffe Hall* (London: Jonathan Cape, 1984).

16. Brittain, *Radclyffe Hall*, 29–30.

17. Even in more contemporary scholarship, the friendship remains "a contested site, the subject of a kind of rivalry between those who claim it as an ideal friendship between two heterosexual women, and those who see it as a repressed or camouflaged lesbian relationship." See Diana Wallace, *Sisters and Rivals: The Theme of Female Rivalry in Novels by Women, 1914–1939* (London: Macmillan, 2000), 120. For other accounts of their relationship, see Catherine Clay, *British Women Writers, 1914–1945: Professional Work and Friendship* (Hampshire: Ashgate, 2006); Deborah Gorham, *Vera Brittain: A Feminist Life* (Oxford: Blackwell, 1996); Paul Berry and Mark

Bostridge, *Vera Brittain: A Life* (London: Chatto & Windus, 1995); Lillian Faderman, *Surpassing the Love of Men: Romantic Friendship and Love between Women from the Renaissance to the Present* (New York: William Morrow, 1981); Sheila Jeffreys, *The Spinster and Her Enemies: Feminism and Sexuality, 1880–1930* (London: Pandora, 1985); Pam Johnson, "'The Best Friend Whom Life Has Given Me': Does Winifred Holtby Have a Place in Lesbian History?" in *Not a Passing Phase: Reclaiming Lesbians in History, 1840–1985* (London: The Woman's Press, 1989); and Jean E. Kennard, *Vera Brittain and Winifred Holtby: A Working Partnership* (Hanover, NH: University Press of New England, 1989).

18. James Milne, "A Literary Log," *The Scotsman*, December 14, 1939. Milne's characterization of *Testament of Friendship* as "almost an autobiography" highlights the similar generic confusion of Gertrude Stein's *The Autobiography of Alice B. Toklas*, which was first published in 1933, the same year as Brittain's *Testament of Youth*. See Vera Brittain, *Testament of Friendship: The Story of Winifred Holtby* (1940; New York: Wideview Books, 1981); Gertrude Stein, *The Autobiography of Alice B. Toklas* (1933; New York: Vintage, 1990); and Vera Brittain, *Testament of Youth: An Autobiographical Study of the Years 1900–1925* (1933; London: Virago Press, 2009).

19. "Biography and Reminiscences by Four Women Writers," *Nottingham Guardian*, January 18, 1940.

20. Qtd. in Berry and Bostridge, *Vera Brittain*, 337–38.

21. Monica Dickens, "Sentenced-to-Die Woman Novelist Wrote Best-seller," *Sunday Chronicle & Sunday Review*, December 31, 1939, n.p.

22. Ibid.

23. Brittain, *Radclyffe Hall*, 45.

24. Again citing Ruth and Naomi, Brittain's prologue contrasts the reception of female friendship with the "glory and acclamation" heaped upon friendships between men: "the friendships of women, in spite of Ruth and Naomi, have usually been not merely unsung, but mocked, belittled, and falsely interpreted. I hope that Winifred's story may . . . show its readers that loyalty and affection between women is a noble relationship which, far from impoverishing, actually enhances the love of a girl for her lover, of a wife for her husband, of a mother for her children." See Brittain, *Testament of Friendship*, 2.

25. Brittain, *Radclyffe Hall*, 45.

26. Lady Una Vincenzo Troubridge, *The Life and Death of Radclyffe Hall* (London: Hammond, Hammond, 1961), 5.

27. Ibid., 81–82.

28. Una Troubridge, Day Books, February 16, 1931, RHUTP. In the same entry, she declares that she has "very little sympathy indeed with the woman invert of independent means who resorts to camouflage."

29. Qtd. in Cline, *Radclyffe Hall*, 377.

30. Troubridge, *The Life and Death of Radclyffe Hall*, 5.

31. Ibid.

32. Radclyffe Hall to Evguenia Souline, July 31, 1934, in *Your John: The Love Letters of Radclyffe Hall*, ed. Joanne Glasgow (New York: New York University Press, 1997), 33.

33. Qtd. in Cline, *Radclyffe Hall*, 369.

34. Evguenia Souline to Una Troubridge, July 29, 1950, RHUTP. In personal correspondence, both Troubridge and Souline refer to Hall as "John," the name Hall used with close friends, and they use she/her pronouns.

35. Una Troubridge to Evguenia Souline, August 4, 1950, RHUTP.

36. Ibid.

37. Ibid.

38. In *The Life and Death of Radclyffe Hall*, Troubridge claimed that Hall's reason for wanting this manuscript destroyed was "simple": "she had, during the closing years of her life, been very deeply hurt by someone and when she knew that her days were numbered she had forgiven both the injury and the person concerned. But she felt that into the writing of that book she had almost unconsciously allowed the intrusion of a measure of her personal suffering and natural resentment and, as she said when she told me to destroy it: 'It isn't forgiveness if one leaves a record that might be recognized and give pain'" (171).

39. Troubridge, *The Life and Death of Radclyffe Hall*, 72.

40. Ibid., 69–70.

41. Ibid., 73.

42. Ibid., 77.

43. Ibid., 75.

44. Ibid., 72, 81. According to Troubridge, she devised the titles for *Adam's Breed*, *The Well of Loneliness*, *The Master of the House*, and *The Sixth Beatitude*.

45. Ibid., 47.

46. Richard Ormrod, *Una Troubridge: The Friend of Radclyffe Hall* (London: Jonathan Cape, 1984), 309.

47. Souhami, *Trials of Radclyffe Hall*, 398–99. According to Souhami, a reader for Macmillan "damned the book," and her lawyer told her that it "libeled Evguenia."

48. Qtd. in ibid., 416.

49. Qtd. in Cline, *Radclyffe Hall*, 378. See also Souhami, *Trials of Radclyffe Hall*, 413–15.

50. Radclyffe Hall to Evguenia Souline, November 10, 1935, in *Your John*, ed. Glasgow, 141. In 1938, Hall and Souline even discussed the possibility of Souline assisting with her literary work: "You are mistaken if you think that Una would have opposed your working as my secretary—she might have at first, but not for a long time past. Only of course you would have had to let her help you a bit to get into the work, and this I suppose you would not have liked. But, my God, what a comfort & help it would have been to me, especially with my troublesome eyes these days!" See Hall to Souline, June 23, 1938, in *Your John*, ed. Glasgow, 181.

51. Sylvia Townsend Warner to William Maxwell, April 13, 1970, in *The Element of Lavishness: Letters of Sylvia Townsend Warner and William Maxwell, 1938–1978*, ed. Michael Steinman (Washington, DC: Counterpoint, 2001), 211.

52. Claire Harman, *Sylvia Townsend Warner: A Biography* (London: Chatto & Windus, 1989), 300–301.

53. Sylvia Townsend Warner, *The Diaries of Sylvia Townsend Warner*, ed. Claire Harman (London: Chatto & Windus, 1994), 331.

54. Warner to Maxwell, July 12, 1970, in *The Element of Lavishness*, ed. Steinman, 212.

55. Warner to Maxwell, October 9, 1970, in *The Element of Lavishness*, ed. Steinman, 213.

56. Maxwell to Warner, November 1970, in *The Element of Lavishness*, ed. Steinman, 214.

57. Warner to Maxwell, July 22, 1967, in *The Element of Lavishness*, ed. Steinman, 179. Warner's disclaimer that she began the White biography as a "dare" carries tonal echoes of Virginia Woolf's early insistence that she began *Orlando: A Biography* (1928; London: Harcourt, 1956) as a "joke."

58. For the dangers residing in the optimistic belief in this kind of queer-community-to-come, and the possible consequences of Warner's own investment, despite its less conventional traffic across generations of queers, in "preserving the familiar familial narrativity" of what he calls "reproductive futurism," see Lee Edelman, *No Future: Queer Theory and the Death Drive* (Durham: Duke University Press, 2004), 2, 9.

59. G. Thomas Couser, *Vulnerable Subjects: Ethics and Life Writing* (Ithaca: Cornell University Press, 2003), xii.

60. Although *The Flint Anchor*, Warner's last novel, was published in 1954, and she became increasingly preoccupied with these biographical and archival projects, she did not entirely abstain from writing fiction during this period. She continued to publish occasional short stories in the *New Yorker*, and *Kingdoms of Elfin*, a collection of fantasy stories, was published a year before her death.

61. For recent critical accounts of lateness, see Edward W. Said, *On Late Style: Music and Literature against the Grain* (New York: Vintage, 2006); Jane Gallop, *The Deaths of the Author: Reading and Writing in Time* (Durham: Duke University Press, 2011); and Gordon McMullan and Sam Smiles, eds., *Late Style and Its Discontents: Essays in Art, Literature, and Music* (London: Oxford University Press, 2016).

62. Said, *On Late Style*, 6.

63. Carolyn G. Heilbrun, "Virginia Woolf in Her Fifties," *Twentieth Century Literature* 27, no. 1 (1981): 19.

64. Ibid.

65. For a welcome exception to this common oversight, see Janet Montefiore, "Sylvia Townsend Warner and the Biographer's 'Moral Sense,'" *Journal of the Sylvia Townsend Warner Society* (2003): 15–30. For an overview of criticism on Warner published through 2013, see Janet Montefiore, "Sylvia Townsend Warner Scholarship, 1978-2013: An Annotated Bibliography with Introduction," *Literature Compass* 11, no. 12 (2014): 786–811. See also Maud Ellmann, "Sylvia Townsend Warner," *Oxford Handbooks Online* (May 2016): DOI 10.1093/oxfordhb/9780199935338.013.31.

66. Ann Cvetkovich, "Drawing the Archive in Alison Bechdel's *Fun Home*," *Women's Studies Quarterly* 36, no. 1 & 2 (2008): 114.

67. Ibid.

68. Warner to Maxwell, August 1, 1966, in *The Element of Lavishness*, ed. Steinman, 165; qtd. in Harman, *Sylvia Townsend Warner*, 257.

69. Elizabeth Freeman, "Introduction," *GLQ* 13, no. 2–3 (2007): 165.

70. Cvetkovich, "Drawing the Archive," 126.

71. Harman, *Sylvia Townsend Warner*, 279.

72. Ibid.

73. Warner to Maxwell, March 31, 1962, in *The Element of Lavishness*, ed. Steinman, 116–17.

74. Warner, *Diaries*, 290.

75. Ibid., 293.

76. Warner to Maxwell, June 9, 1964, in *The Element of Lavishness*, ed. Steinman, 141. Later in this letter, she confesses that she has decided to take on the task of writing White's biography, but she stresses that she wants to keep writing short stories, too, in order to "restore myself with some tractable fiction after warring with the truth."

77. Ibid.

78. Warner to Garnett, June 8, 1964, in *Sylvia and David: The Townsend Warner/Garnett Letters*, ed. Richard Garnett (London: Sinclair-Stevenson, 1994), 73.

79. Like Cvetkovich describing the desires of Bechdel's father, I hesitate to use the word "pedophilia" since it "carries connotations that presume its criminality or immorality," but I, too, use it here in order to challenge those assumptions and judgments ("Drawing the Archive," 113).

80. Warner to Garnett, October 26, 1966, in Sylvia Townsend Warner and David Garnett, "Conversing on Their Tomb: The Correspondence of Sylvia Townsend Warner and David Garnett. Transcribed by Richard Garnett," unpublished typescript, 174–75, STWA.

81. Garnett to Warner, June 9, 1965, in *Sylvia and David*, ed. Garnett, 84.

82. Warner to Garnett, September 25, 1965, in "Conversing on Their Tomb," 135.

83. Warner to Garnett, October 23, 1967, in *Sylvia and David*, ed. Garnett, 126–27.

84. Ibid.

85. Warner to Maxwell, August 1, 1966, in *The Element of Lavishness*, ed. Steinman, 165.

86. Valentine Ackland, *For Sylvia: An Honest Account* (London: Chatto & Windus, 1985), 29.

87. Ibid., 31. She goes on to explain that anonymity is "fairly easy to assume, even in a Modern State. Fill in a typical Government Form, for instance, leaving blanks for the Christian Names(s) Surname and National Registration Number. Thus: *Sex*: F. *Age*: 42. *Nationality*: British. *Height*: 5 ft. 11 inches. *Colour of Hair*: Brown. *Colour of Eyes*: Grey. *Special Peculiarities*: None. *Place of Birth*: London. *Married or Single*: . . . Here, though the answer would not endanger anonymity, we stop. The answer to this question, and to any others the Form sets out, will no doubt be supplied in the course of this work."

88. Val Warner and Michael Schmidt, "Sylvia Townsend Warner in Conversation," *PN Review* 23, 8, no. 3 (1981): 37.

89. This recording has been preserved. It is housed in the STWA.

90. Ann Cvetkovich, *An Archive of Feelings: Trauma, Sexuality, and Lesbian Public Cultures* (Durham: Duke University Press, 2003), 244.

91. Carolyn Steedman, *Dust: The Archive and Cultural History* (New Brunswick, NJ: Rutgers University Press, 2002), 150–51.

92. Warner to Garnett, January 23, 1965, in *Sylvia and David*, ed. Garnett, 78.

93. Ibid.

94. The originals, along with a copy of the typescript, are now stored in the STWA. For a detailed account of the current location of Warner's letters, see Peter Tolhurst, "Sylvia Townsend Warner's Letters: Where Are They Now?" *Journal of the Sylvia Townsend Warner Society* (2017): 65–76.

95. Susanna Pinney, "Editor's Note," in Sylvia Townsend Warner and Valentine Ackland, *I'll Stand by You: The Letters of Sylvia Townsend Warner and Valentine Ackland: With Narrative by Sylvia Townsend Warner*, ed. Susanna Pinney (London: Pimlico, 1998), vii.

96. Janet Gurkin Altman, *Epistolarity: Approaches to a Form* (Columbus: Ohio State University Press, 1982), 89.

97. For references to their "marriage," see Warner and Ackland, *I'll Stand by You*, 80, 97; to their "wedded love," see 78, 97; to themselves as "wives," see 41, 55, 77; to themselves as "lesbians," see 162.

98. Warner to Ackland, June 5, 1964, STWA.

99. Lauren Berlant, *The Female Complaint: The Unfinished Business of Sentimentality in American Culture* (Durham: Duke University Press, 2008), 168–72.

100. In the long early period of their love, everything was charged with eroticism, and the letters are forthright about this: Warner muses on the "bi-sexuality" of buffalos (41–42); Ackland "fingers" the skill of Warner's poetry "with exactly the same excitement [she] felt from touching the lovely hinges of [Warner's] body" (39); Warner lustily describes the ways in which Ackland "bite[s] and bully[s]" her during afternoons in bed.

101. Warner to Maxwell, September 27, 1971, in *The Element of Lavishness*, ed. Steinman, 224–25.

102. Warner and Ackland, *I'll Stand by You*, 163.

103. Pinney, "Editor's Note," vii.

104. Alice B. Toklas, *Staying on Alone: The Letters of Alice B. Toklas*, ed. Edward Burns (New York: Liveright, 1973).

105. Berlant, *The Female Complaint*, ix.

106. Muñoz, *Cruising Utopia*, 1.

107. For an in-depth theorization of the "semi-private," see Ellen Rooney, "A Semi-Private Room," *differences: A Journal of Feminist Cultural Studies* 13, no. 1 (Spring 2002): 128–56.

108. Berlant, *The Female Complaint*, viii. In her ensuing theorization of the "intimate public" of U.S. women's culture in the nineteenth and twentieth centuries, Berlant describes the first mass-cultural intimate public sphere as a heavily commodified, sentimental, and "juxtapolitical" space in which the affective attachments of its participants provide recognition and allow for identification. While I am deeply indebted to Berlant's thinking about affect, pedagogy, and the importance of alternative life narratives, I am trying here to imagine the possibilities and effects of smaller, less hegemonic intimate publics.

109. Warner had been planning to review it for the *New Yorker*, but although she submitted a copy to the magazine in 1962 and an editor made several substantial changes to the typescript, "The American Museum" was never published. It was later donated—along with several stories, including "The Beggar's Wedding" and "Total Loss"—by William Maxwell to the STWA.

110. Sylvia Townsend Warner, "The American Museum," unpublished typescript, 2, STWA.

111. Ibid., 16–17. As she continues, she further empathizes with the difficult position of the curators: "When a new departure engages the popular goodwill, as the

American Museum has done so signally, every one wants to make it a present; and that present, alas, of the nature that is called personal—a mug with a transfer portrait of Lincoln on it, a tole tray that came into the family with an American great aunt. I speak from my own guilty heart; for did I not, after my first visit, decide that a finishing touch to the Deer Park Parlour would be my copy of the 1776 Philadelphia de la Rochefoucauld, and almost have it packed, before it occurred to me how much easier it is to give than to refuse?"

112. Ibid., 4.

113. Ibid., 2. Rather than construct a new building for the museum, the founders (an Englishman and an American) purchased Claverton Manor, a "handsome and dignified" house on the outskirts of Bath. The building was made of Bath stone.

114. Ibid., 5.

115. Ibid.

116. Ibid., 12.

117. Ibid., 13.

118. Personal conversation and correspondence with Krissdottir, June 2010 and August 2018.

119. Warner to Maxwell, August 1, 1966, in *The Element of Lavishness*, ed. Steinman, 165.

Chapter 2. Abandoned Lives: Impossible Projects and Archival Remains

1. Judith Halberstam, *The Queer Art of Failure* (Durham: Duke University Press, 2011).

2. Ibid., 2–3.

3. Sigmund Freud, "Mourning and Melancholia," in *The Freud Reader*, ed. Peter Gay, 584–89 (1917; New York: W. W. Norton, 1989), 586.

4. Michael D. Snediker, *Queer Optimism: Lyric Personhood and Other Felicitous Persuasions* (Minneapolis: University of Minnesota Press, 2009). In Snediker's account, queer optimism is not "promissory," not holding out hope for some better future; instead, it is "immanently rather than future oriented" (2–3). As I have demonstrated, Warner's archival optimism is oriented away from the present and toward the future dismissed by much recent writing within queer theory, but—thinking back to Pinney's tears as she typed, for example—it is also in the present.

5. Djuna Barnes, "Obituary," *transition* 11 (February 1928): 19.

6. Irene Gammel, *Baroness Elsa: Gender, Dada, and Everyday Modernity* (Cambridge, MA: MIT Press, 2002), 7. In a letter to Barnes, the Baroness herself declared that she was not "made for suicide—unless it could be done gaily—victoriously—with flourish I think that is death in battle or tournament." Barnes chose to publish this letter in *transition*. See Elsa von Freytag-Loringhoven, "Selections from the Letters of Elsa Baroness von Freytag-Loringhoven," *transition* 11 (February 1928): 27.

7. For an expansive reconsideration of Barnes's late style, see Scott Herring, "Djuna Barnes and the Geriatric Avant-Garde," *PMLA* 130, no. 1 (2015): 69–91.

8. See Jane Heap, "Dada," *Little Review* 8, no. 2 (Spring 1922): 46 and Robert Hughes, "Days of Antic Weirdness: A Look Back at Dadaism's Brief, Outrageous

Assault on the New York Scene," *Time* 149, no. 4 (January 27, 1997): 70–71. For a more scholarly discussion of her place in the history of New York Dada, see Gammel, *Baroness Elsa*, 4–5, and the chapter devoted to the Baroness in Francis M. Naumann, *New York Dada, 1915-23* (New York: Abrams, 1994), 168–75.

9. Barnes, "Obituary," 19.

10. Gammel, *Baroness Elsa*, 10.

11. Djuna Barnes, *Collected Poems, With Notes toward the Memoirs*, ed. Phillip Herring and Osías Stutman (Madison: University of Wisconsin Press, 2005), 254.

12. Margaret Anderson, *My Thirty Years' War: An Autobiography* (New York: Covici, Friede, 1930), 177.

13. Ibid., 194, 179.

14. Ibid., 178. A description of a very similar outfit is given in Matthew Josephson, *Life among the Surrealists: A Memoir* (New York: Holt, Rinehart and Winston, 1962), 75.

15. Anderson, *My Thirty Years' War*, 194.

16. Ibid., 211. At the end of this "exhibit," she announced that "shaving one's head is like having a new love experience." For Williams's recollection of their brief, tempestuous relationship, see Williams, *The Autobiography of William Carlos Williams* (New York: New Directions, 1967), 163–69.

17. Freytag-Loringhoven, "Selections from the Letters," 26.

18. George Biddle, *An American Artist's Story* (New York: Little, Brown, 1939), 138.

19. Djuna Barnes, "Farewell Paris," in *Collected Poems, With Notes toward the Memoirs*, ed. Phillip Herring and Osías Stutman (Madison: University of Wisconsin Press, 2005), 254.

20. Djuna Barnes, "Preface," signed typescript, dated December 7, 1924, Djuna Barnes Papers, Special Collections, University of Maryland Libraries, College Park.

21. Freytag-Loringhoven, "Selections from the Letters," 26.

22. Paul I. Hjartarson and Douglas O. Spettigue, introduction to *Baroness Elsa*, by Elsa von Freytag-Loringhoven, ed. Hjartarson and Spettigue (Ontario: Oberon Press, 1992), 13. Describing this "confessional" style, the editors of her autobiography note that the Baroness "presents herself as honest to the point of self-destruction; she cannot dissemble to save her life."

23. It is important to note that Barnes was far from the only supporter of the Baroness's short literary career. In one of Ford Madox Ford's memoirs, for example, he describes the way that Ernest Hemingway, who had briefly been the assistant editor of Ford's *transatlantic review*, maneuvered to publish the Baroness: "Mr. Hemingway . . . assisted me by trying to insert as a serial the complete works of Baroness von Freytag Loringhofen [*sic*]. I generally turned round in time to take them out of the contents table. But when I paid my month's visit to New York he took charge, and accomplished his purpose at the expense of cutting a short story of Mrs. H. G. Wells down to forty lines—and the London Letter of an esteemed correspondent down to three." See Ford, *It Was the Nightingale*, ed. John Coyle (1933; Manchester: Carcanet, 2007), 309.

24. Freytag-Loringhoven, "Selections from the Letters," 25.

25. For further description of Eliot's involvement with the proposed biography, see Andrew Field, *Djuna: The Life and Times of Djuna Barnes* (New York: G. P. Putnam's Sons, 1983), 215 and Phillip Herring, *Djuna: The Life and Work of Djuna Barnes* (New York: Viking, 1995), 232.

26. Djuna Barnes, *Nightwood* (1937; New York: New Directions, 1961), 13; Gammel, *Baroness Elsa*, 192–94.

27. Lynn Devore, "The Backgrounds of *Nightwood*: Robin, Felix, and Nora," *Journal of Modern Literature* 10, no. 1 (1983): 71–90. Devore also details the ways in which *Nightwood*'s Felix Volkbein is derived from the Baroness's former husband, Felix Paul Greve, who later became known as the Canadian novelist Frederick Philip Grove. Curiously, Devore's biographical assessment of the novel does not mention Barnes's former lover, Thelma Wood, who is widely considered to be the other major influence on *Nightwood*'s Robin Vote.

28. Barnes, *Nightwood*, 55.

29. Ibid., 55–56.

30. Freytag-Loringhoven, "Selections from the Letters," 27.

31. Hank O'Neal, *"Life Is Painful, Nasty & Short . . . In My Case It Has Only Been Painful & Nasty": Djuna Barnes, 1978–1981* (New York: Paragon House, 1990), 57.

32. Herring, "Djuna Barnes and the Geriatric Avant-Garde," 76–79.

33. Ibid., 76.

34. O'Neal, *"Life Is Painful, Nasty & Short,"* 58.

35. Ibid., 58–59.

36. For more about this most recent project, see Tanya E. Clement, "BaronessElsa: An Autobiographical Manifesto," in *Making Canada New: Editing, Modernism, and New Media*, ed. Dean Irvine, Vanessa Lent, and Bart A. Vautour (Toronto: University of Toronto Press, 2017), 139–60.

37. Similar accounts can be found elsewhere, too. See, for example, Carolyn Dinshaw's account of Hope Emily Allen's unending editorship of *The Book of Margery Kempe* in *How Soon Is Now?: Medieval Texts, Amateur Readers, and the Queerness of Time* (Durham: Duke University Press, 2012); and, as I discuss in the coda to this book, Lisa Cohen's description of Esther Murphy's unfinished biography of Madame de Maintenon, the secret second wife of Louis XIV, in *All We Know: Three Lives* (New York: Farrar, Straus & Giroux, 2012).

38. It, too, is preserved in the HMP.

39. See, for example, Mary Beard, *The Invention of Jane Harrison* (Cambridge, MA: Harvard University Press, 2000), especially "Pandora's Box," her chapter on the relationship between Harrison and Mirrlees; Julia Briggs, "Hope Mirrlees and Continental Modernism," in *Gender in Modernism: New Geographies, Complex Intersections*, ed. Bonnie Kime Scott (Chicago: University of Illinois Press, 2007), 261–70; Julia Briggs, "'Modernism's Lost Hope': Virginia Woolf, Hope Mirrlees, and the Printing of *Paris*," in *Reading Virginia Woolf* (Edinburgh: Edinburgh University Press, 2006), 80–95; John Connor, "Hope Mirrlees and the Archive of Modernism," *Journal of Modern Literature* 37, no. 2 (2014): 177–82; Nancy Gish, "Modifying Modernism: Hope Mirrlees and 'The Really New Work of Art,'" in *Newsletter of the T. S. Eliot Society*, no. 74–75 (2011): 1–2; Sandeep Parmar's edition of Hope Mirrlees, *Collected Poems* (Manchester: Carcanet, 2011); and Michael Stanwick, *Hope-in-the-Mist: The Extraordinary Career & Mysterious Life of Hope Mirrlees* (Upper Montclair, NJ: Temporary Culture, 2009). In 2005, Cold Spring Press republished Mirrlees's last novel with a foreword by Neil Gaiman, whose advocacy of Mirrlees has resulted in a renewal of her popularity among fantasy enthusiasts.

Still, very little attention has been paid to the biographical work undertaken in her late career.

40. Herring, "Djuna Barnes and the Geriatric Avant-Garde," 71. While Mirrlees never mentioned Barnes in correspondence, she compared herself to Woolf throughout her life. In a letter to her mother, Mirrlees familiarly complained about her supposed difficulties in front of a camera: "Rockett sent me the last *Vogue*, with Virginia in it. Oh dear! Why don't I take better? I look such a scrubby little bounder compared to her." Hope Mirrlees to Emily Mirrlees, May 19, 1924, HMP, Series 2, Box 1, Folder 3.

41. Anthony Powell, *To Keep the Ball Rolling: The Memoirs of Anthony Powell* (Chicago: University of Chicago Press, 1983), 306.

42. Hope Mirrlees, "The Religion of Women," *The Nation & Athenaeum* 41, no. 8 (May 28, 1927): 259. A typescript of this essay is available in the HMP, and the essay is now available in Sandeep Parmar's edition of Mirrlees's *Collected Poems*.

43. Ibid., 260. She explains that "the reason they look sad is that the ears of their body are always hearing the sound of:—'Time's wingèd chariot hurrying near,' the chariot that leaves in its wake a cloud of dust, which is the past. And here the spirit comes in and takes a share of the sadness; for though it is the body that hears the chariot, it is the spirit that sees the dust. If, as Mrs. Woolf says, George Eliot is the great mouthpiece of woman's sensibility, it is not without significance that she has based her ethics on an emotion towards the past" (259).

44. Ibid., 259.

45. In a timely anticipation of this project, John Connor has suggested, in his own dissertation chapter on Mirrlees, that "a queer reading of Mirrlees is, perhaps paradoxically, better sustained by the life-writing she undertook after Harrison's death than by what she wrote while Harrison was alive" (67). See John Connor, "Midcentury Romance: Modernist Afterlives of the Historical Novel" (PhD diss., University of Pennsylvania, 2010).

46. JEHP, Series 4, Box 3, Folder 1. In several loose pages at the end of one of the notebooks she used to prepare her biography of Harrison, Mirrlees reflected upon this "disapproval" (which, in its first version, she had characterized as "resentment"): "Phenomenon of our intolerance of our own faults in others perhaps mystical—it really is a projection of ourself that we are hating. . . . Long before Freud, she had observed that fathers fell in love with their daughters & sisters with their brothers."

47. JEHP, Series 4, Box 3, Folder 2.

48. Annabel Robinson, *The Life and Work of Jane Ellen Harrison* (Oxford: Oxford University Press, 2002), 236.

49. JEHP, Series 4, Box 3, Folder 1.

50. Mary Beard, *The Invention of Jane Harrison* (Cambridge, MA: Harvard University Press, 2000), 154.

51. Gertrude Stein, *The Autobiography of Alice B. Toklas* (1933; New York: Vintage, 1990), 145. In this description, "Miss Harrison and Miss Stein did not particularly interest each other," which is likely why Stein reversed the usual hierarchy of the Harrison-Mirrlees relationship, making Harrison, rather than Mirrlees, the "pet enthusiasm."

52. Dora de Houghton Carrington, *Carrington: Letters and Extracts from Her Diaries*, ed. David Garnett (London: Jonathan Cape, 1970), 258.

53. Virginia Woolf to Jacques Raverat, February 5, 1925, in *The Letters of Virginia Woolf*, vol. 3, ed. Nigel Nicolson and Joanne Trautmann (New York: Harcourt Brace Jovanovich, 1975), 164.

54. Woolf to Clive Bell, September 24, 1919, in *Letters*, 2:391.

55. Woolf to Lady Cecil, September 1, 1925, in *Letters*, 3:200.

56. Woolf to Molly MacCarthy, April 22, 1923, in *Letters*, 3:30. As mentioned in the text, since the published edition of these letters appeared while Mirrlees was still alive, it omits the phrase "who have a Sapphic flat somewhere." Woolf later described this Parisian meeting in a letter to Jacques Raverat on July 30, 1923: "On my way back from Spain I stayed a week in Paris and there met Hope Mirrlees and Jane Harrison. This gallant old lady, very white, hoary, and sublime in a lace mantilla, took my fancy greatly; partly for her superb high thinking agnostic ways, partly for her appearance. 'Alas,' she said, 'you and your sister and perhaps Lytton Strachey are the only ones of the younger generation I can respect. You alone carry on the traditions of our day.' This referred to the miserable defection of Fredegond [Shove] (mass; confession; absolution, and the rest of it)" (*Letters*, 3:58).

57. Woolf to Hope Mirrlees, April 17, 1928, in *Letters*, 3:484.

58. Victoria de Bunsen to Hope Mirrlees, April 16, 1928, JEHP, Series 4, Box 1, Folder 3. In Harrison's own *Reminiscences of a Student's Life*, published by the Woolfs' Hogarth Press in 1925, she refers to Mirrlees as her "ghostly daughter, dearer than any child after the flesh" (90).

59. Agnes Conway to Hope Mirrlees, April 15, 1928, JEHP, Series 4, Box 1, Folder 3.

60. Mabel Robinson to Hope Mirrlees, April 22, 1928, JEHP, Series 4, Box 1, Folder 3.

61. Alys Russell to Hope Mirrlees, April 16, 1928, JEHP, Series 4, Box 1, Folder 3.

62. Brother Mirrlees to Hope Mirrlees, May 9, 1928, JEHP, Series 4, Box 1, Folder 3.

63. According to Michael Stanwick (*Hope-in-the-Mist*), Mirrlees stipulated in her will that her first novel, *Madeleine*, should not be reproduced until at least fifty years after her death, and Mirrlees annotated and hand-corrected any potentially blasphemous unpublished writing after her conversion.

64. Mirrlees, JEHP, Series 4, Box 3, Folder 1.

65. Beard, *The Invention of Jane Harrison*, 157.

66. Qtd. in ibid.

67. Mirrlees to Jessie Stewart, May 10, 1932, JEHP, Series 4, Box 1, Folder 6.

68. Mirrlees to Stewart, December 29, 1932, JEHP, Series 4, Box 1, Folder 6.

69. Carolyn Heilbrun, introduction to Vera Brittain, *Testament of Friendship: The Story of Winifred Holtby* (1940; New York: Wideview Books, 1981), xxviii.

70. Mirrlees to Stewart, no date [1943?], HMP, Series 1, Box 1, Folder 6.

71. Harrison, *Reminiscences of a Student's Life*, 90.

72. Beard, *The Invention of Jane Harrison*, 155.

73. Hope Mirrlees, "Outline of Life," JEHP, Series 4, Box 3, Folder 2.

74. Ibid.

75. Agnes Horsfield to Jessie Stewart, March 24, 1943, JEHP, Series 4, Box 1, Folder 6.

76. John Johnson to Stewart, May 6, 1954, JEHP, Series 4, Box 2, Folder 1. Johnson was Stewart's agent, and he included Woolf's comments, which had been addressed to him, in his letter to Stewart.

77. D. S. MacColl to Mirrlees, May 20, 1944, HMP, Series 1, Box 1, Folder 6.

78. Stewart to Mirrlees (draft), May 5, 1946, JEHP, Series 4, Box 3, Folder 2.

79. Mirrlees to Stewart, September 27, 1959, JEHP, Series 2, Box 1, Folder 2.

80. This is part of the official description of Mirrlees's draft biography on the website of the Newnham College Archives.

81. David Kazanjian, "Scenes of Speculation," *Social Text* 33, no. 4 (125) (2015): 80–81. In this essay, Kazanjian makes an impassioned defense of "overreading," a charge that "typically means that the overeager has attributed a meaning to a text that would have been impossible for the context in which the text was written or for the people who wrote the text" (80). While Kazanjian is here addressing the archives of the nineteenth-century black Atlantic, overreading is an accusation often leveled against queer readings of both literature and history, too. And his call for "overreading archived quotidiana for the scenes of speculation it so often entails, scenes too often eclipsed by the single-minded pursuit of answers to the questions of who did what, where, and when," is echoed in the methodology subtending this chapter.

82. See Carroll Smith-Rosenberg, "The Female World of Love and Ritual: Relations between Women in Nineteenth-Century America," *Signs* 1, no. 1 (1975): 1–29 and Sharon Marcus, *Between Women: Friendship, Desire, and Marriage in Victorian England* (Princeton: Princeton University Press, 2007), especially her response to Smith-Rosenberg on 30–31.

83. Mirrlees, JEHP, Series 4, Box 3, Folder 1.

84. Ibid.

85. In one of the most striking recent uses of the term, Rita Felski closes her introduction to *Uses of Literature* by asking us to consider a reading strategy that would allow for mature, rather than childish or sentimental, affective attachment to the texts we read: "Is it possible to discuss the value of literature without falling into truisms and platitudes, sentimentality and *Schwärmerei*?" See Felski, *Uses of Literature* (Oxford: Blackwell, 2008), 22.

86. JEHP, Series 4, Box 3, Folder 1. According to Caroline B. Mitchell (née Dutton), Jane once told her that "her [unreadable: perhaps 'G.P.'?] was so violent that when Miss Beale told her that her people wanted to take her away [from Cheltenham], Jane fainted dead away."

87. Ibid.

88. Ibid.

89. JEHP, Series 4, Box 3, Folder 2.

90. Hope Mirrlees, *A Fly in Amber: Being an Extravagant Biography of the Romantic Antiquary, Sir Robert Bruce Cotton* (London: Faber and Faber, 1962), 77.

91. Ibid., 88.

92. The second volume of the biography is titled "The Lost Pearl," and it contains a foreword in which Mirrlees explains its structure. I quote at length: "The shape of this book requires an apology. Although it is a continuation of *A Fly in Amber* (of which the subtitle is: *Being an extravagant biography of the romantic antiquary, Sir Robert Bruce Cotton*) the first half does not mention Cotton, but is entirely concerned with

Lord Harry Howard and his family. He is the anti-hero (as he was also of *A Fly in Amber*). He is, therefore, a very important character in both books, and his double function was to help Cotton to find the Pearl, and also to lose it. Lord Harry is one of history's villains, and also Cotton's bad angel. Villains are no longer painted all black. To paint them thus is against both theology and psychology. And to know something of Lord Harry's childhood and years of poverty and struggle, though it will not remove his blackness, it well may modify it." Mirrlees seems to have prepared this quite extensively for publication, as there is an opening typescript page of instructions to "the publishers" and the note that "An index is being prepared." HMP, Series 7, Box 2, Folder 1.

93. Mirrlees, JEHP, Series 4, Box 1, Folder 3. In a later revision of this passage, she put an asterisk next to this line, adding, at the bottom of the page, that she "wrote this before [she] became a Catholic."

94. Mirrlees, *A Fly in Amber*, 92. Mirrlees goes on to compare the relative skill of antiquaries and poets, and finds that antiquaries "alone among mortals can restore the past and preserve the present, *tangibly*—and it is touch that matters most" (92–93).

95. Ibid., 146.

96. Ibid.

97. Ibid., 24–25.

98. Mirrlees, JEHP, Series 4, Box 1, Folder 3. "Virginia" likely refers to Virginia Woolf; "Dörpfeld" refers to Wilhelm Dörpfeld, a German architect and archaeologist. This passage appears in several loose pages at the end of one of her notebooks.

99. Virginia Woolf, "The Art of Biography," in *Collected Essays* (London: Hogarth, 1967), 4:228.

100. Mirrlees, *A Fly in Amber*, 62.

101. For example, Mirrlees demonstrates the historical difference in the word "curious": "If someone had asked Cotton why he loved his gem-like manuscripts, his answer would probably have been, 'Because I am a curious man.' But he would not have meant by this, 'Because I am a queer person.' He would have been using 'curious' in what has now become an obsolete sense. . . . The *N.E.D.* gives as the obsolete meanings of curiosity *carefulness, scrupulousness, accuracy, ingenuity, undue niceness*, or *subtlety*" (*A Fly in Amber*, 71). And, early in the book, she jokes about the indecipherable etymology of "auncious": "No etymologist, it is true, with the exception of Humpty Dumpty, would venture to explain *auncious*, but it certainly looks like a variety of *ancient*, and *old-established* is clear enough" (17).

102. Ibid., 58.

103. Cotton had organized his library according to the placement of a particular book or manuscript in the room where it was stored. For example, a bust of a Caesar was mounted upon the top of each bookshelf in his library, so the call number of each book referred first to the particular Caesar, then to the shelf number, and then to the volume. The British Library has preserved this classification system.

104. Mirrlees, *A Fly in Amber*, 56–57.

105. Ibid., 57.

106. In many cases, Cotton's records are the only reason we know about the existence of some manuscripts that, by the twentieth and twenty-first centuries, can no longer be found.

Chapter 3. Modernists Explain Things to Me: Collecting as Queer Feminist Response

1. The *Little Review* ran from 1914 to 1929, though the editorial history is slightly more complicated. Anderson founded the *Little Review* in Chicago in 1914, and Heap joined her as coeditor in 1916. Together, they moved the publication to New York in 1917. In 1923, Heap took over as sole editor, but they collaborated on the *Little Review*'s final issue in 1929.

2. Margaret Anderson, *My Thirty Years' War* (New York: Horizon Press, 1969), 271.

3. *Little Review* 12, no. 2 (May 1929). Despite the cover's trumpeting of "the foremost men in the arts," the issue also included responses from a number of prominent women writers, including Djuna Barnes, H.D., Emma Goldman, Dorothy Richardson, Edith Sitwell, and Gertrude Stein.

4. Anderson, *My Thirty Years' War*, 271. In her memoir, Anderson notes that she wished they had added another question: "Do you know what has been the motivating force behind every act of your life?"

5. Qtd. in ibid., 272.

6. Ibid.

7. Jessa Crispin, *The Dead Ladies Project: Exiles, Expats & Ex-Countries* (Chicago: University of Chicago Press, 2015), 86.

8. Sarah Blackwood, "Editing as Carework: The Gendered Labor of Public Intellectuals," *Avidly*, June 6, 2014, http://avidly.lareviewofbooks.org/2014/06/06/editing-as-carework-the-gendered-labor-of-public-intellectuals/.

9. Ibid.

10. Ibid. Lurking in the background of Blackwood's essay are both her coeditorship, with Sarah Mesle, of *Avidly*, and her status as a tenure-stream academic: "It will be difficult to articulate the editorial labor I put into *Avidly* within the structure of the standardized tenure file, which is interested mainly in my voice, heard singly and forcefully within the strictures of liberal individualist understandings of authorship."

11. Jayne E. Marek, *Women Editing Modernism: "Little" Magazines & Literary History* (Lexington: University Press of Kentucky, 1995), 9.

12. Crispin, *Dead Ladies Project*, 86.

13. Kate Zambreno, *Heroines* (Cambridge, MA: Semiotext(e), 2012), 13.

14. Sean Latham and Gayle Rogers, *Modernism: Evolution of an Idea* (London: Bloomsbury, 2015), 71–72.

15. Jeremy Braddock, *Collecting as Modernist Practice* (Baltimore: Johns Hopkins University Press, 2012), 3.

16. Ibid., 2.

17. Qtd. in Hugh Ford, *Published in Paris: American and British Writers, Printers, and Publishers in Paris, 1920–1939* (New York: Macmillan, 1975), 3. Recalling the repetition of lesbian-feminist triangles discussed earlier in this chapter, Ford's book contains a foreword written by journalist Janet Flanner, titled "Three Amateur Publishers," about Beach, Gertrude Stein, and Nancy Cunard.

18. Sylvia Beach, *Shakespeare and Company* (1959; Lincoln: University of Nebraska Press, 1991), 77–83, 115, 215–16.

19. SBP, Box 81, Folder 2.

20. Beckett's *L'innommable* was first published in French in 1953. The first English translation was published by Grove Press in 1958.

21. SBP, Box 81, Folder 4.

22. Beach, *Shakespeare and Company*, 220.

23. Cyril Connolly, "A Rendezvous for Writers," *Mercure* (1959): 162, as qtd. in Noel Riley Fitch, *Sylvia Beach and the Lost Generation: A History of Literary Paris in the Twenties & Thirties* (New York: W. W. Norton, 1983), 412.

24. Ellen Gruber Garvey, *Writing with Scissors: American Scrapbooks from the Civil War to the Harlem Renaissance* (Oxford: Oxford University Press, 2013), 4, 10.

25. James Laughlin, "Introduction to the New Edition," in Sylvia Beach, *Shakespeare and Company* (Lincoln: University of Nebraska Press, 1991), xxi. It is both grammatically unsurprising and nevertheless telling that Laughlin assumes that Beach's memories might be about "him or it" but never "her."

26. Sylvia Beach to Harriet Weaver, January 23, 1957, in *The Letters of Sylvia Beach*, ed. Keri Walsh (New York: Columbia University Press, 2010), 254.

27. Ibid., 255.

28. Sylvia Beach to Harriet Weaver, January 13, 1956, in *The Letters of Sylvia Beach*, ed. Walsh, 251.

29. The rest of her papers and memorabilia are now held in Princeton University's Firestone Library—in her home state of New Jersey.

30. See Fitch, *Sylvia Beach and the Lost Generation*, 413, for an account of Beach's central role in this popular and critically acclaimed exhibit.

31. Qtd. in ibid., 408.

32. Beach, *Shakespeare and Company*, 12.

33. Ibid.

34. Ibid., 206.

35. Ibid., 113.

36. Ibid., 112.

37. Ann Cvetkovich, *An Archive of Feelings: Trauma, Sexuality, and Lesbian Public Cultures* (Durham: Duke University Press, 2003), 244.

38. This line appears on some of the book's covers. In M. F. K. Fisher's foreword to the 1984 edition of *The Alice B. Toklas Cookbook*, she attributes the phrase to the *Columbia Encyclopedia*. See Fisher, foreword to Alice B. Toklas, *The Alice B. Toklas Cookbook* (1954; New York: Harper Perennial, 2010), ix.

39. Toklas, *Alice B. Toklas Cookbook*, 259. She notes that "euphoria and brilliant storms of laughter; ecstatic reveries and extensions of one's personality on several simultaneous planes are to be complacently expected."

40. See Simon Michael Bessie, "A Happy Publisher's Note to the 1984 Edition," in Toklas, *Alice B. Toklas Cookbook*, vii.

41. See Toklas, *Alice B. Toklas Cookbook*; Alice B. Toklas, *Aromas and Flavors of Past and Present: A Book of Exquisite Cooking* (1958; New York: Lyons, 1996); Alice B. Toklas, *What Is Remembered* (New York: Holt, Rinehart and Winston, 1963).

42. In a letter from her literary agent, he describes the origin of her title: "I read to John Schaffner your remarks about the title. You said: 'An English friend says call it The Autobiography of Alice B. Toklas by Alice B. Toklas but it is not an autobiography but what is remembered.' When I read this to John, he said: 'Call it What

Is Remembered'. I think his idea (taken from yours) is nice." See Robert Lescher to Alice B. Toklas, June 22, 1961, GSC, Box 278, Folder 9. See also Linda Simon, *The Biography of Alice B. Toklas* (Lincoln: University of Nebraska Press, 1977), 305.

43. Toklas, *What Is Remembered*, 173.

44. Donald Gallup, "The Gertrude Stein Collection," *Yale University Library Gazette* 22, no. 2 (1947): 23.

45. Carl Van Vechten to Alice B. Toklas, March 9, 1947, GSABTP, Box 138, Folder 3223.

46. Copies of Stein's will have been preserved in the GSC, Box 279, Folder 4.

47. Ibid.

48. Carl Van Vechten to Alice B. Toklas, March 9, 1947, GSABTP, Box 138, Folder 3223.

49. Ibid.

50. Edgar Allan Poe to Alice B. Toklas, February 15, 1961, GSC, Box 279, Folder 4. In a bizarre example of queer temporality, the court-appointed estate lawyer's name was Edgar Allan Poe: the poet's great-nephew. Buried in the Stein and Toklas Papers at both the Beinecke and the Ransom Center, there are a great many letters in which Edgar Allan Poe—and he used his full name every time, *of course*—writes in a disapproving tone to Toklas about the dissipation of the Stein estate.

51. Donald Gallup to Alice B. Toklas, December 7, 1962, GSC, Box 278, Folder 1.

52. Gallup, "The Gertrude Stein Collection," 32, 30.

53. Poe, as the lawyer for the estate, was in favor of selling some of the paintings "while they are bringing such exceedingly high prices. I do not believe these prices will continue." He also suggested that, since the insurance would benefit the Stein children, "they should pay for [it]." Since they, of course, refused to do this, he provided yet another option, in which some of the artwork could be "temporarily lent to a public museum where they would be insured at governmental expense." Edgar Allan Poe to Alice B. Toklas, February 1, 1961, GSC, Box 279, Folder 4.

54. See Lee Edelman, *No Future: Queer Theory and the Death Drive* (Durham: Duke University Press, 2004).

55. See Simon, *Biography of Alice B. Toklas*, 307–10. For other versions of this story, see Janet Malcolm, *Two Lives: Gertrude and Alice* (New Haven: Yale University Press, 2007), 199–205 and Alice T. Friedman, "Queer Old Things," *Places Journal* (February 2015), https://placesjournal.org/article/queer-old-things/.

56. Friedman, "Queer Old Things."

57. Kevin Ohi, *Dead Letters Sent: Queer Literary Transmission* (Minneapolis: University of Minnesota Press, 2015), 1.

58. Qtd. in Friedman, "Queer Old Things."

59. GSABTP, Box 8, Folder 98. Toklas also recounted her memory of the absent pictures in several letters.

60. Anna Linzie, *The True Story of Alice B. Toklas: A Study of Three Autobiographies* (Iowa City: University of Iowa Press, 2006), 112.

61. Ibid., 114.

62. EJCMA, Box 12, Folder 239.

63. Janet Flanner, "Memory Is All," *New Yorker*, December 15, 1975, 149.

64. Ibid., 153.

65. Ibid.

66. In the first chapter of *The Unknowable Gurdjieff*, Anderson describes the book as "a sort of primer" rather than "a study, a portrait, a treatise, a manual or a document." Just as she was more interested in the "conversation" than the biographical details of her friends and colleagues in *My Thirty Years' War*, her focus in *The Unknowable Gurdjieff* is on his teachings: "I have little interest in the facts that people seem to want most . . . where was he born? what were his circumstances? his education? his training? what legends grow up about him? was he the preceptor of the Dalai Lama? etc., etc., etc. . . . What matters is the knowledge."

67. Edmund Wilson, *Axel's Castle: A Study of the Imaginative Literature of 1870–1930* (1931; New York: Farrar, Straus and Giroux, 2004), 3. Wilson's grouping of Yeats, Joyce, Eliot, Stein, Proust, and Valéry, now so familiar to us, was then a bold suggestion: "It is not usually recognized that writers such as W. B. Yeats, James Joyce, T. S. Eliot, Gertrude Stein, Marcel Proust, and Paul Valéry represent the culmination of a self-conscious and very important literary movement; and even when we have become aware that these writers have something in common, that they belong to a common school, we are likely to be rather vague as to what its distinguishing features are" (3).

68. Anderson, *My Thirty Years' War*, 3.

69. Alfred Kazin, "A Life Led as a Work of Art," *New York Times*, August 16, 1970, http://www.nytimes.com/1970/08/16/archives/a-life-led-as-a-work-of-art-anderson.html.

70. Elizabeth Francis, *The Secret Treachery of Words: Feminism & Modernism in America* (Minneapolis: University of Minnesota Press, 2002), 40.

71. Ibid.

72. Kazin, "A Life Led as a Work of Art."

73. This quotation is an excerpt from a draft of a letter to Kazin that Anderson included in a letter she wrote to Coburn Britton. See Anderson to Britton, August 16, 1970, EJCMA, Box 1, Folder 12.

74. Margaret Anderson to Coburn Britton, January 23, 1970, EJCMA, Box 1, Folder 10.

75. Anderson, *My Thirty Years' War*, 35.

76. Carolyn Dinshaw, *How Soon Is Now? Medieval Texts, Amateur Readers, and the Queerness of Time* (Durham: Duke University Press, 2012), 6.

77. Marjorie Garber, *Academic Instincts* (Princeton: Princeton University Press, 2001), 5.

78. EJCMA, Box 1, Folder 10. Similarly, in a letter to Solita Solano (December 29, 1964), she described her frustrating correspondence with an academic historian: "I'm trying to make him understand what a farce History is—a purely subjective reaction to events; and when the historian is a person who can't 'see,' observe or interpret a propos, nothing but farce is left." EJCMA, Box 2, Folder 24.

79. EJCMA, Box 1, Folder 10.

80. Margaret Anderson to Michael Currer-Briggs, March 28, 1973, EJCMA, Box 14, Folder 253.

81. Margaret Anderson to Michael Currer-Briggs, August 16, [1973?], EJCMA, Box 14, Folder 256.

82. Ibid.

83. Margaret Anderson to Coburn Britton, January 23, 1970, EJCMA, Box 1, Folder 10.

84. Margaret Anderson to Michael Currer-Briggs, March 28, 1973, EJCMA, Box 14, Folder 253.

85. Margaret Anderson to Coburn Britton, June 10, 1971, EJCMA, Box 1, Folder 11. As Mathilda M. Hills notes in her "Editor's Postscript" to Anderson's *Forbidden Fires* (Tallahassee, FL: Naiad, 1996), Anderson's peculiarly precise practices as a correspondent continued throughout her life. In letters to Solita Solano and Elizabeth Jenks Clark, for example, she would type only on the right side of the page in the expectation that they would reply directly on the other side.

86. Margaret Anderson to Elizabeth Jenks Clark, June 12, (1973?), EJCMA, Box 1, Folder 18.

87. EJCMA, Box 12, Folder 235.

88. Ibid. Anderson avers that her copies "are *not* faked. They are exact copies, comma by comma. . . . It had never occurred to me in those days that one could make money by selling the actual letters of famous writers and artists. Nor does it occur to me today that anyone could doubt my word."

89. Ibid.

90. Ibid.

91. Ibid.

92. Ibid.

93. Sara Ahmed, *Willful Subjects* (Durham: Duke University Press, 2014), 152–53. In this book, she compiles a "willfulness archive," and she describes how it can be "empowering to find that [feminist killjoy] scene elsewhere, in other words, not only to have your own memories handy but to be reached by the hands of others. I have been collecting 'feminist killjoy' scenes. I consider this part of the work of becoming a killjoy: *collection*" (152–53).

94. Rebecca Solnit, *Men Explain Things to Me* (Chicago: Haymarket Books, 2014), 4–5.

95. For an extensive summary and helpful debunking of the prevailing mythology of Pound as a kind of editorial puppet master, see Marek, *Women Editing Modernism*, 167–92. According to Marek, "Pound has been credited with some important accomplishments that actually belong in whole or in part to women, including the editorial procedures of some magazines" (167).

96. EJCMA, Box 12, Folder 235. The three lines quoted here are from Stevens's "Two Letters," first published in 1954.

97. Ibid.

98. Ibid.

99. See, for example, Laura Doan, *Fashioning Sapphism: The Origins of a Modern English Lesbian Culture* (New York: Columbia University Press, 2001); Jodie Medd, *Lesbian Scandal and the Culture of Modernism* (Cambridge: Cambridge University Press, 2012); and Elizabeth English, *Lesbian Modernism: Censorship, Sexuality and Genre Fiction* (Edinburgh: Edinburgh University Press, 2015).

100. EJCMA, Box 12, Folder 235.

101. "Two Letters," first published less than a year before Stevens's death in 1955, was eventually republished in *Opus Posthumous*, ed. Milton J. Bates (1957; New York:

Knopf, 1989). The lines come from the first part of the poem, "A Letter From," which continues on, "As if we were all seated together again / And one of us spoke and all of us believed / What we heard and the light, though little, was enough" (132–33).

102. EJCMA, Box 12, Folder 236.

103. David Kazanjian, "Scenes of Speculation," *Social Text* 33, no. 4 (125) (2015): 80–81.

104. Margaret Anderson to Elizabeth Jenks Clark and Solita Solano, December 1964, EJCMA, Box 2, Folder 22.

105. Margaret Anderson to Elizabeth Jenks Clark and Solita Solano, August 9, 1965, EJCMA, Box 2, Folder 32. When she eventually receives Ford's book, *Published in Paris*, in 1973, she describes it as "conventional, deadly dull—no personality. . . . It will be liked and will probably sell." See Margaret Anderson to Elizabeth Jenks Clark and Solita Solano, January 8, 1973, EJCMA, Box 5, Folder 70.

106. Margaret Anderson to Elizabeth Jenks Clark and Solita Solano, February 8, 1973, EJCMA, Box 5, Folder 70.

107. EJCMA, Box 13, Folder 241. She goes on to note that "the only way I could hope for publication would be to become a publisher myself and create a new *Little Review*, especially for this story."

108. Anderson, *My Thirty Years' War*, 3.

109. Margaret Anderson to Elizabeth Jenks Clark and Solita Solano, February 9, 1973, EJCMA, Box 5, Folder 70.

110. EJCMA, Box 12, Folder 235.

111. In a letter to Clark, for example, she notes that it would be "impossible to invite anyone in" to her living quarters. "The whole floor is covered with boxes of Papers—where could I put them, until I've desproyed [*sic*] hundreds? To arrange the room, put in order and ask you into it, would take me at least 3 days, I imagine." Margaret Anderson to Elizabeth Jenks Clark, December 30, 1972, EJCMA, Box 1, Folder 18.

Chapter 4. The Sense of Unending: Revisiting Virginia Woolf's Orlando: A Biography

1. Rachel Blau DuPlessis, *Writing beyond the Ending: Narrative Strategies of Twentieth-Century Women Writers* (Bloomington: Indiana University Press, 1985), x.

2. Ibid., xi.

3. Ibid., 56.

4. Ibid., 62, 64.

5. Virginia Woolf, *Orlando: A Biography* (1928; London: Harcourt, 1956), 302, 304–5.

6. For a more detailed description of this story, see Hermione Lee, *Virginia Woolf* (1996; New York: Vintage, 1999), 478–79. For a more extensive discussion of Woolf's gifts, see Kathryn Simpson, *Gifts, Markets and Economics of Desire in Virginia Woolf* (New York: Palgrave Macmillan, 2008).

7. Vita Sackville-West to Virginia Woolf, October 9, 1928, in *The Letters of Virginia Woolf*, vol. 3, ed. Nigel Nicolson and Joanne Trautmann (New York: Harcourt Brace Jovanovich, 1975), 287.

8. Sackville-West to Woolf, October 11, 1928, in *The Letters of Virginia Woolf*, vol. 3, ed. Nicolson and Trautmann, 289.

9. Nigel Nicolson, *Portrait of a Marriage* (New York: Atheneum, 1973), 202–3.

10. Carolyn Dinshaw et al., "Theorizing Queer Temporalities: A Roundtable Discussion," *GLQ* 13, no. 2–3 (2007): 178. For one of the founding texts of queer temporality studies, see also Dinshaw, *Getting Medieval: Sexualities and Communities, Pre- and Postmodern* (Durham: Duke University Press, 1999).

11. Elizabeth Freeman, "Introduction," *GLQ* 13, no. 2–3 (2007): 163.

12. Terry Eagleton, "Buried in the Life: Thomas Hardy and the Limits of Biographies," *Harper's Magazine* 315, no. 1890 (November 2007): 89.

13. Juliette Atkinson, *Victorian Biography Reconsidered: A Study of Nineteenth-Century "Hidden" Lives* (Oxford: Oxford University Press, 2010), 12. For further attention to the continuity between Leslie Stephen's and Woolf's biographical theory, see Laura Marcus, *Auto/Biographical Discourses: Theory, Criticism, Practice* (Manchester: Manchester University Press, 1994), 98.

14. A. O. J. Cockshut, *Truth to Life: The Art of Biography in the Nineteenth Century* (London: Collins, 1974), 16.

15. David Amigoni, *Victorian Biography* (New York: St. Martin's Press, 1993), 14. Nicolson, he notes, praises the pedagogical potential of nineteenth-century biographical projects like the *DNB* and the English Men of Letters series.

16. Virginia Woolf, "The New Biography," in *Collected Essays* (London: Hogarth, 1967), 4:231, 229.

17. Sidney Lee, *Principles of Biography* (Cambridge: Cambridge University Press, 1911), 9. Lee was Leslie Stephen's successor as the editor of the *Dictionary of National Biography*. This volume is a revised version of the Leslie Stephen lecture he delivered at Cambridge in 1911.

18. Qtd. in Ira Bruce Nadel, *Biography: Fiction, Fact and Form* (New York: St. Martin's Press, 1984), 15.

19. For a reassessment of the importance of auto/biographical writing within modernist literature, see Max Saunders, *Self Impression: Life-Writing, Autobiographiction and the Forms of Modern Literature* (Oxford: Oxford University Press, 2010).

20. E. M. Forster, *Goldsworthy Lowes Dickinson and Related Writings*, vol. 13 of *The Abinger Edition of E. M. Forster*, ed. Oliver Stallybrass (1934; London: Edward Arnold, 1973), 121.

21. Woolf, "The Art of Biography," 226.

22. A. J. A. Symons, *Essays and Biographies*, ed. Julian Symons (London: Cassell, 1969), 2.

23. Qtd. in Dinshaw et al., "Theorizing Queer Temporalities," 181–82.

24. Woolf, *Orlando*, 98.

25. Woolf to Sackville-West, October 9, 1927, in *The Letters of Virginia Woolf*, vol. 3, ed. Nicolson and Trautmann, 429.

26. Virginia Woolf, *Diary*, vol. 3, ed. Anne Olivier Bell (New York: Harcourt Brace, 1980), 198.

27. Ibid., 157, 185.

28. Woolf, *Orlando*, 139.

29. Sigmund Freud, *Leonardo da Vinci and a Memory of His Childhood*, ed. James Strachey, trans. Alan Tyson (1910; New York: W. W. Norton, 1961), 16. But Woolf was clearly critical of Freud, too. As DuPlessis notes, *Orlando* mocks several

significant Freudian theories, especially that of the "arrested development" of homosexual desire (*Writing beyond the Ending*, 63–65).

30. Woolf, *Orlando*, 139.

31. Ibid., 268.

32. Ibid., 269.

33. We can read one of Woolf's most famous visions of her father's relationship to this work in *To the Lighthouse*, in which Mr. Ramsey, who fears that he will never reach the letter R, is partially a figure for Stephen.

34. H. C. G. Matthew, *Leslie Stephen and the* New Dictionary of National Biography (Cambridge: Cambridge University Press, 1995), 13.

35. Virginia Woolf, "Men and Women," in *Books and Portraits*, ed. Mary Lyon (New York: Harcourt Brace Jovanovich, 1977), 28.

36. Virginia Woolf, "A Sketch of the Past," in *Moments of Being: Unpublished Autobiographical Writings*, ed. Jeanne Schulkind (New York: Harcourt Brace Jovanovich, 1976), 126.

37. Ruth Hoberman, *Modernizing Lives: Experiments in English Biography, 1918–1939* (Carbondale: Southern Illinois University Press, 1987), 134. Woolf's description of this generational debate is taken from *Three Guineas*.

38. Ellen Hawkes, "Woolf's Magical Garden of Women," in *New Feminist Essays on Virginia Woolf*, ed. Jane Marcus (Lincoln: University of Nebraska Press, 1981), 43.

39. Woolf, *Diary*, 3:203.

40. Virginia Woolf, "The New Biography," in *Collected Essays* (London: Hogarth, 1967), 4:231.

41. Ibid.

42. Ibid., 232–33.

43. Ibid., 231.

44. Ibid., 232.

45. Ibid., 233.

46. Woolf, "The Art of Biography," 228.

47. Ibid.

48. Ibid., 227.

49. Woolf, "The New Biography," 233.

50. Woolf, *Diary*, 3:153.

51. Woolf to Sackville-West, October 9, 1927, in *Letters*, 3:428–29.

52. Woolf, *Orlando*, 305–6.

53. Ibid., 306.

54. Suzanne Raitt, *Vita and Virginia: The Work and Friendship of V. Sackville-West and Virginia Woolf* (Oxford: Clarendon Press, 1993), 25.

55. Leo Braudy, *The Frenzy of Renown: Fame and Its History* (1986; New York: Vintage, 1997), 601.

56. Lee, *Virginia Woolf*, 481.

57. Woolf to Sackville-West, October 12, 1928, in *Letters*, 3:544.

58. Sackville-West to Woolf, October 11, 1928, in *Letters*, 3:289.

59. Woolf to Sackville-West, July 25, 1928, in *Letters*, 3:514.

60. In a diary entry written on December 14, 1922, shortly after she met Vita for the first time, Woolf described her in terms of her well-known "proclivities": "She is a

pronounced Sapphist, & may . . . have an eye on me, old as I am. Nature might have sharpened her faculties. Snob as I am, I trace her passions 500 years back, & they become romantic to me, like old yellow wine." See Louise DeSalvo and Mitchell A. Leaska, eds., *The Letters of Vita Sackville-West to Virginia Woolf* (New York: William Morrow, 1985), 23.

61. Woolf, *Orlando*, 188–89.

62. Jay Prosser, *Second Skins: The Body Narratives of Transsexuality* (New York: Columbia University Press, 1998), 168. See also Carroll Smith-Rosenberg, *Disorderly Conduct: Visions of Gender in Victorian America* (1985; Oxford: Oxford University Press, 1986); Esther Newton, "The Mythic Mannish Lesbian: Radclyffe Hall and the New Woman" *Signs* 9, no. 4 (1984): 557–75; and Jessica Berman, "Is the Trans in Transnational the Trans in Transgender?" *Modernism/modernity* 24, no. 2 (2017): 217–44.

63. Prosser, *Second Skins*, 168–69.

64. Elizabeth Freeman, *Time Binds: Queer Temporalities, Queer Histories* (Durham: Duke University Press, 2010), 107.

65. Woolf, *Orlando*, 38.

66. Ibid.

67. Ibid., 161.

68. Ibid., 179.

69. Ibid., 262–64.

70. DuPlessis, *Writing beyond the Ending*, 63.

71. Woolf, *Orlando*, 253–54. This strategy, in which blankness hails or becomes legible to a select group of readers, is a significant aspect of the complicated gift economy at work between Woolf and Sackville-West.

72. Raitt, *Vita and Virginia*, 25.

73. Karyn Z. Sproles, *Desiring Women: The Partnership of Virginia Woolf and Vita Sackville-West* (Toronto: University of Toronto Press, 2006), 5.

74. Woolf, *Orlando*, 316, 70, 112.

75. Ibid., 317.

76. Lee, *Virginia Woolf*, 481.

77. Woolf, *Orlando*, 168.

78. Nicolson, *Portrait of a Marriage*, 208.

79. The current site features a much more robust narrative about Knole that includes a separate section about Vita and her association with Woolf. See https://www.nationaltrust.org.uk/knole and https://www.nationaltrust.org.uk/knole/features/vita-sackville-west-and-knole. For a more recent account of the house and its history, see Robert Sackville, *Inheritance: The Story of Knole and the Sackvilles* (London: Walker Books, 2010).

80. Woolf, "The Art of Biography," 229.

Coda. Biographical Criticism and the Passion Project Now

1. Madelyn Detloff, "Strong-armed Sisyphe: Feminist Queer Modernism Again . . . Again," *Feminist Modernist Studies* 1, no. 1–2 (2018): 36.

2. Ibid., 37.

3. Ibid.

4. See, for example, the contributions of editor Cassandra Laity and contributor Jessica Berman within the same issue of *Feminist Modernist Studies*. See also Pamela Caughie, "Lessons Learned," *Literature Compass: The Future of Women in Modernism* 10, no. 1 (2013): 1–7; Anne E. Fernald, "Women's Fiction, New Modernist Studies, and Feminism," *Modern Fiction Studies* 59, no. 2 (2013): 229–40; and Urmila Seshagiri, "Mind the Gap! Modernism and Feminist Praxis," *Modernism/modernity Print Plus Forum* 2, no. 2 (2017), https://modernismmodernity.org/forums/modernism-and-feminist-praxis.

5. Detloff, "Strong-armed Sisyphe," 40. For a differently situated argument about the creative possibilities inherent in feminist (and feminine) repetition, see Jennifer Fleissner, *Women, Compulsion, Modernity: The Moment of American Naturalism* (Chicago: University of Chicago Press, 2004).

6. Jessica Berman, "Practicing Transnational Feminist Recovery Today," *Feminist Modernist Studies* 1, no. 1–2 (2018): 9.

7. Ibid.

8. "Reappearing Women: A Conversation between Marie Darrieussecq and Kate Zambreno," *Paris Review*, October 23, 2017, https://www.theparisreview.org/blog/2017/10/23/reappearing-women-a-conversation-between-marie-darrieussecq-and-kate-zambreno.

9. Ibid.

10. Ibid.

11. Kate Zambreno, *Heroines* (Cambridge, MA: Semiotext(e), 2012), 13.

12. Ibid., 48.

13. Ibid., 138.

14. Ibid., 138–39.

15. Ibid., 110.

16. Ibid., 284.

17. For a detailed discussion of the relationship between Zambreno's book and her blog, see Melanie Micir and Aarthi Vadde, "Obliterature: Toward an Amateur Criticism," *Modernism/modernity* 25, no. 3 (2018): 517–49.

18. Zambreno, *Heroines*, 273, 280.

19. Ibid., 283.

20. Ibid., 279.

21. Lisa Cohen, *All We Know: Three Lives* (New York: Farrar, Straus & Giroux, 2012), 5.

22. Virginia Woolf, *A Room of One's Own* (1929; London: Harcourt, 2005), 45, 88.

23. Cohen, *All We Know*, 11.

24. Ibid.

25. Monique Truong, *The Book of Salt* (Boston: Mariner, 2003), 208.

26. Ibid., 215.

27. Ibid.

28. David L. Eng, "The End(s) of Race," *PMLA* 123, no. 5 (2008): 1484.

29. David L. Eng, *The Feeling of Kinship: Queer Liberalism and the Radicalization of Intimacy* (Durham: Duke University Press, 2010), 65.

30. See Jenny Diski, *In Gratitude* (London: Bloomsbury, 2016).

31. See Sean Latham and Gayle Rogers, *Modernism: Evolution of an Idea* (London: Bloomsbury, 2015), esp. chap. 2.

BIBLIOGRAPHY

Ackland, Valentine. *For Sylvia: An Honest Account*. London: Chatto & Windus, 1985.
Ahmed, Sara. *Willful Subjects*. Durham: Duke University Press, 2014.
Altman, Janet Gurkin. *Epistolarity: Approaches to a Form*. Columbus: Ohio State University Press, 1982.
Amigoni, David. *Victorian Biography*. New York: St. Martin's Press, 1993.
Anderson, Margaret. *Forbidden Fires*. Edited by Mathilda M. Hills. Tallahassee, FL: Naiad, 1996.
——. *My Thirty Years' War: An Autobiography*. New York: Covici, Friede, 1930.
Atkinson, Juliette. *Victorian Biography Reconsidered: A Study of Nineteenth-Century "Hidden" Lives*. Oxford: Oxford University Press, 2010.
Baker, Michael. *Our Three Selves: A Life of Radclyffe Hall*. London: William Morrow, 1985.
Barnes, Djuna. *Collected Poems, With Notes toward the Memoirs*. Edited by Phillip Herring and Osías Stutman. Madison: University of Wisconsin Press, 2005.
——. *Nightwood*. New York: New Directions, 1961. First published 1937 by Harcourt, Brace (New York).
——. "Obituary." *transition* 11 (February 1928): 19.
Beach, Sylvia. *Shakespeare and Company*. Lincoln: University of Nebraska Press, 1991. First published 1959 by Harcourt, Brace (New York).
Beard, Mary. *The Invention of Jane Harrison*. Cambridge, MA: Harvard University Press, 2000.
Beizer, Janet. *Thinking Through the Mothers: Reimagining Women's Biographies*. Ithaca: Cornell University Press, 2008.
Benjamin, Walter. *Illuminations*. Edited by Hannah Arendt. Translated by Harry Zohn. New York: Schocken Books, 1968.
Benstock, Shari. *Women of the Left Bank, 1900–1940*. Austin: University of Texas Press, 1986.
Berlant, Lauren. *The Female Complaint: The Unfinished Business of Sentimentality in American Culture*. Durham: Duke University Press, 2008.
——. "Intimacy: A Special Issue." In *Intimacy*, edited by Lauren Berlant, 1–8. Chicago: University of Chicago Press, 2000.
Berlant, Lauren, and Michael Warner. "What Does Queer Theory Teach Us about X?" *PMLA* 110, no. 3 (1995): 343–49.
Berman, Jessica. "Is the Trans in Transnational the Trans in Transgender?" *Modernism/modernity* 24, no. 2 (2017): 217–44.
——. "Practicing Transnational Feminist Recovery Today." *Feminist Modernist Studies* 1, no. 1–2 (2018): 9–21.
——. "*Three Guineas* and the Politics of Interruption." In *A Companion to Virginia Woolf*, edited by Jessica Berman, 203–16. Hoboken, NJ: John Wiley & Sons, 2016.
Berry, Paul, and Mark Bostridge. *Vera Brittain: A Life*. London: Chatto & Windus, 1995.

Bersani, Leo, and Adam Phillips. *Intimacies*. Chicago: University of Chicago Press, 2008.
Best, Stephen, and Sharon Marcus. "Surface Reading: An Introduction." *Representations* 109, no. 1 (2010): 1–21.
Biddle, George. *An American Artist's Story*. New York: Little, Brown, 1939.
"Biography and Reminiscences by Four Women Writers." *Nottingham Guardian*. January 18, 1940.
Bishop, Alan. Introduction to *Chronicle of Friendship: Diary of the Thirties, 1932–1939*, by Vera Brittain, 11–26. Edited by Alan Bishop. London: Victor Gollancz, 1986.
Blackwood, Sarah. "Editing as Carework: The Gendered Labor of Public Intellectuals." *Avidly*. June 6, 2014. http://avidly.lareviewofbooks.org/2014/06/06/editing-as-carework-the-gendered-labor-of-public-intellectuals/.
Booth, Alison. *How to Make It as a Woman: Collective Biographical History from Victoria to the Present*. Chicago: University of Chicago Press, 2004.
Braddock, Jeremy. *Collecting as Modernist Practice*. Baltimore: Johns Hopkins University Press, 2012.
Bradway, Tyler. *Queer Experimental Literature: The Affective Politics of Bad Reading*. New York: Palgrave Macmillan, 2017.
Braudy, Leo. *The Frenzy of Renown: Fame and Its History*. New York: Vintage, 1997. First published 1986 by Oxford University Press.
Briggs, Julia. "Hope Mirrlees and Continental Modernism." In *Gender in Modernism: New Geographies, Complex Intersections*, edited by Bonnie Kime Scott, 261–70. Chicago: University of Illinois Press, 2007.
———. *Reading Virginia Woolf*. Edinburgh: Edinburgh University Press, 2006.
Brittain, Vera. *Chronicle of Friendship: Diary of the Thirties, 1932–1939*. Edited by Alan Bishop. London: Victor Gollancz, 1986.
———. *Radclyffe Hall: A Case of Obscenity?* London: Femina Books, 1968.
———. "Review of *The Well of Loneliness*." *Time and Tide*. August 10, 1928.
———. *Testament of Friendship: The Story of Winifred Holtby*. New York: Wideview Books, 1981. First published 1940 by Macmillan (London).
———. *Testament of Youth: An Autobiographical Study of the Years 1900–1925*. London: Virago Press, 2009. First published 1933 by Victor Gollancz (London).
Bruss, Elizabeth. *Autobiographical Acts: The Changing Situation of a Literary Genre*. Baltimore: Johns Hopkins University Press, 1976.
Butler, Judith. "Critically Queer." *GLQ* 1, no. 1 (1993): 17–32.
Caine, Barbara. *English Feminism, 1780–1980*. Oxford: Oxford University Press, 1997.
Caramello, Charles. *Henry James, Gertrude Stein, and the Biographical Act*. Chapel Hill: University of North Carolina Press, 1996.
Carrington, Dora de Houghton. *Carrington: Letters and Extracts from Her Diaries*. Edited by David Garnett. London: Jonathan Cape, 1970.
Castle, Gregory. *Reading the Modernist Bildungsroman*. Gainesville: University Press of Florida, 2006.
Castle, Terry. *The Apparitional Lesbian: Female Homosexuality and Modern Culture*. New York: Columbia University Press, 1993.
———. *Noel Coward and Radclyffe Hall: Kindred Spirits*. New York: Columbia University Press, 1996.

Cather, Willa. *Not Under Forty*. Lincoln: University of Nebraska Press, 1988. First published 1922 by A. A. Knopf (New York).
Caughie, Pamela. "Lessons Learned." *Literature Compass: The Future of Women in Modernism* 10, no. 1 (2013): 1–7.
Clay, Catherine. *British Women Writers, 1914–1945: Professional Work and Friendship*. Hampshire: Ashgate, 2006.
Clement, Tanya E. "BaronessElsa: An Autobiographical Manifesto." In *Making Canada New: Editing, Modernism, and New Media*, edited by Dean Irvine, Vanessa Lent, and Bart A. Vautour, 139–60. Toronto: University of Toronto Press, 2017.
Cline, Sally. *Radclyffe Hall: A Woman Called John*. Woodstock, NY: Overlook Press, 1997.
Cockshut, A. O. J. *Truth to Life: The Art of Biography in the Nineteenth Century*. London: Collins, 1974.
Cohen, Lisa. *All We Know: Three Lives*. New York: Farrar, Straus & Giroux, 2012.
Connor, John. "Hope Mirrlees and the Archive of Modernism." *Journal of Modern Literature* 37, no. 2 (2014): 177–82.
———. "Mid-century Romance: Modernist Afterlives of the Historical Novel." PhD diss., University of Pennsylvania, 2010.
Cook, Blanche Wiesen. "'Women Alone Stir My Imagination': Lesbianism and the Cultural Tradition." *Signs* 4 (1979): 718–39.
Cooke, Jennifer, ed. *Scenes of Intimacy: Reading, Writing, and Theorizing Contemporary Literature*. London: Bloomsbury, 2013.
Couser, G. Thomas. *Vulnerable Subjects: Ethics and Life Writing*. Ithaca: Cornell University Press, 2003.
Coviello, Peter. "World Enough: Sex and Time in Recent Queer Studies." *GLQ* 13, no. 2–3 (2007): 387–401.
Cowley, Malcolm. *Exile's Return: A Literary Odyssey of the 1920s*. 1951. New York: Penguin, 1994.
Cramer, Patricia Morgne. "Woolf and Theories of Sexuality." In *Virginia Woolf in Context*, edited by Bryony Randall and Jane Goldman, 129–46. Cambridge: Cambridge University Press, 2012.
Crispin, Jessa. *The Dead Ladies Project: Exiles, Expats & Ex-Countries*. Chicago: University of Chicago Press, 2015.
Cvetkovich, Ann. *An Archive of Feelings: Trauma, Sexuality, and Lesbian Public Cultures*. Durham: Duke University Press, 2003.
———. "Drawing the Archive in Alison Bechdel's *Fun Home*." *Women's Studies Quarterly* 36, no. 1 & 2 (2008): 111–28.
———. "Personal Effects: The Material Archive of Gertrude Stein and Alice B. Toklas's Domestic Life." *No More Potlucks* 25 (2013). http://nomorepotlucks.org/site/personal-effects-the-material-archive-of-gertrude-stein-and-alice-b-toklass-domestic-life-ann-cvetkovich/.
Daugherty, Beth Rigel, ed. "'You see you kind of belong to us, and what you do matters enormously': Letters from Readers to Virginia Woolf." *Woolf Studies Annual* 12 (2006): 2–229.
Davis, Thadious. *Nella Larsen, Novelist of the Harlem Renaissance: A Woman's Life Unveiled*. Baton Rouge: Louisiana State University Press, 1994.

Dean, Gabrielle. "Disciplinarity and Disorder." *Archive Journal* (May 2011). http://www.archivejournal.net/essays/disciplinarity-and-disorder/.
Dellamora, Richard. *Radclyffe Hall: A Life in the Writing*. Philadelphia: University of Pennsylvania Press, 2011.
Derrida, Jacques. *Archive Fever*. Translated by Eric Prenowitz. Chicago: University of Chicago Press, 1995.
DeSalvo, Louise, and Mitchell A. Leaska, eds. *The Letters of Vita Sackville-West to Virginia Woolf*. New York: William Morrow, 1985.
Detloff, Madelyn. "Strong-armed Sisyphe: Feminist Queer Modernism Again . . . Again." *Feminist Modernist Studies* 1, no. 1–2 (2018): 36–43.
Dever, Maryanne, Sally Newman, and Ann Vickery. *The Intimate Archive: Journeys through Private Papers*. Canberra: National Library of Australia, 2009.
DeVore, Lynn. "The Backgrounds of *Nightwood*: Robin, Felix, and Nora." *Journal of Modern Literature* 10, no. 1 (1983): 71–90.
DeVoto, Bernard. "The Skeptical Biographer." *Harper's Magazine* 166 (1933): 181–92.
DiBattista, Maria, and Emily O. Wittman, eds. *Modernism and Autobiography*. Cambridge: Cambridge University Press, 2014.
Dickens, Monica. "Sentenced-to-Die Woman Novelist Wrote Best-seller." *Sunday Chronicle & Sunday Review*. December 31, 1939.
Dickson, Lovat. *Radclyffe Hall at the* Well of Loneliness*: A Sapphic Chronicle*. New York: Collins, 1975.
Dinshaw, Carolyn. *Getting Medieval: Sexualities and Communities, Pre- and Postmodern*. Durham: Duke University Press, 1999.
——. *How Soon Is Now?: Medieval Texts, Amateur Readers, and the Queerness of Time*. Durham: Duke University Press, 2012.
Dinshaw, Carolyn, Lee Edelman, Roderick A. Ferguson, Carla Freccero, Elizabeth Freeman, Judith Halberstam, Annamarie Jagose, Christopher Nealon, and Nguyen Tan Hoang. "Theorizing Queer Temporalities: A Roundtable Discussion." *GLQ* 13, no. 2–3 (2007): 177–95.
Diski, Jenny. *In Gratitude*. London: Bloomsbury, 2016.
Doan, Laura. *Fashioning Sapphism: The Origins of a Modern English Lesbian Culture*. New York: Columbia University Press, 2001.
Doan, Laura, and Jane Garrity. Introduction to *Sapphic Modernities: Sexuality, Women, and National Culture*, edited by Laura Doan and Jane Garrity, 1–13. New York: Palgrave Macmillan, 2006.
Doan, Laura, and Jay Prosser, eds. *Palatable Poison: Critical Perspectives on* The Well of Loneliness. New York: Columbia University Press, 2002.
DuPlessis, Rachel Blau. *Writing beyond the Ending: Narrative Strategies of Twentieth-Century Women Writers*. Bloomington: Indiana University Press, 1985.
Eagleton, Terry. "Buried in the Life: Thomas Hardy and the Limits of Biographies." *Harper's Magazine* 315, no. 1890 (2007): 89–91.
Edel, Leon. *Literary Biography*. Toronto: Toronto University Press, 1957.
——. *Writing Lives: Principia Biographica*. New York: W. W. Norton, 1984.
Edelman, Lee. *No Future: Queer Theory and the Death Drive*. Durham: Duke University Press, 2004.
Eichhorn, Kate. *The Archival Turn in Feminism: Outrage in Gender*. Philadelphia: Temple University Press, 2013.

Emre, Merve. "The Ferrante Paradox." *Public Books*. December 15, 2016. http://www.publicbooks.org/the-ferrante-paradox/.

———. *Paraliterary: The Making of Bad Readers in Postwar America*. Chicago: University of Chicago Press, 2017.

Eng, David. "The End(s) of Race." *PMLA* 123, no. 5 (2008): 1479–93.

———. *The Feeling of Kinship: Queer Liberalism and the Radicalization of Intimacy*. Durham: Duke University Press, 2010.

Eng, David, Judith Halberstam, and José Esteban Muñoz. "What's Queer about Queer Studies Now?" *Social Text* 23, no. 3–4 (84–85) (2005): 1–17.

English, Elizabeth. *Lesbian Modernism: Censorship, Sexuality and Genre Fiction*. Edinburgh: Edinburgh University Press, 2015.

Ervine, St. John. "My Box of Books." *Daily Express* (Manchester). September 19, 1929.

Esty, Jed. *Unseasonable Youth: Modernism, Colonialism, and the Fiction of Development*. Oxford: Oxford University Press, 2012.

Faderman, Lillian, ed. *Chloe Plus Olivia: An Anthology of Lesbian Literature from the Seventeenth Century to the Present*. New York: Viking, 1994.

———. "Love between Women in 1928: Why Progressivism Is Not Always Progress." *Lodestar Quarterly* 13 (2005). http://lodestarquarterly.com/work/281/.

———. *Surpassing the Love of Men: Romantic Friendship and Love between Women from the Renaissance to the Present*. New York: William Morrow, 1981.

Faderman, Lillian, and Brigitte Eriksson, eds. *Lesbians in Germany, 1890s–1920s*. Tallahassee, FL: Naiad, 1990.

Felski, Rita. "After Suspicion." *Profession* (2009): 28–35.

———. *Uses of Literature*. Oxford: Blackwell, 2008.

Fernald, Anne E. "Women's Fiction, New Modernist Studies, and Feminism." *Modern Fiction Studies* 59, no. 2 (2013): 229–40.

Field, Andrew. *Djuna: The Life and Times of Djuna Barnes*. New York: G. P. Putnam's Sons, 1983.

Fitch, Noel Riley. *Sylvia Beach and the Lost Generation: A History of Literary Paris in the Twenties & Thirties*. New York: W. W. Norton, 1983.

Flanner, Janet. "Memory Is All." *New Yorker*. December 15, 1975. 141–54.

Fleissner, Jennifer. *Women, Compulsion, Modernity: The Moment of American Naturalism*. Chicago: University of Chicago Press, 2004.

Ford, Ford Madox. *It Was the Nightingale*. Edited by John Coyle. Manchester: Carcanet, 2007. First published 1933 by J. B. Lippincott (Philadelphia and London).

———. *Joseph Conrad: A Personal Remembrance*. Boston: Little, Brown, 1924.

Ford, Hugh. *Published in Paris: American and British Writers, Printers, and Publishers in Paris, 1920–1939*. New York: Macmillan, 1975.

Forster, E. M. *Goldsworthy Lowes Dickinson and Related Writings*. Vol. 13 of *The Abinger Edition of E. M. Forster*, edited by Oliver Stallybrass. London: Edward Arnold, 1973. First published 1934.

Francis, Elizabeth. *The Secret Treachery of Words: Feminism & Modernism in America*. Minneapolis: University of Minnesota Press, 2002.

Freccero, Carla. *Queer/Early/Modern*. Durham: Duke University Press, 2006.

Freedman, Diane P., Olivia Frey, and Frances Murphy Zauhar. *The Intimate Critique: Autobiographical Literary Criticism*. Durham: Duke University Press, 1993.

Freeman, Elizabeth. "Introduction." *GLQ* 13, no. 2–3 (2007): 159–76.

Freeman, Elizabeth. "Packing History, Count(er)ing Generations." *New Literary History* 31 (2000): 727–44.
———. "Time Binds, or, Erotohistoriography." *Social Text* 23, no. 3–4 (84–85) (2005): 57–68.
———. *Time Binds: Queer Temporalities, Queer Histories*. Durham: Duke University Press, 2010.
Freud, Sigmund. *Leonardo da Vinci and a Memory of His Childhood*. 1910. Edited by James Strachey. Translated by Alan Tyson. New York: W. W. Norton, 1961. Reprinted with an introduction by Peter Gay, 1989.
———. "Mourning and Melancholia." 1917. In *The Freud Reader*, edited by Peter Gay, 584–89. New York: W. W. Norton, 1989. Paperback reissue 1995.
Freytag-Loringhoven, Elsa von. "Selections from the Letters of Elsa Baroness von Freytag-Loringhoven." *transition* 11 (February 1928): 20–30.
Friedman, Alice T. "Queer Old Things." *Places Journal* (February 2015). https://placesjournal.org/article/queer-old-things/.
Gallop, Jane. *The Deaths of the Author: Reading and Writing in Time*. Durham: Duke University Press, 2011.
Gallup, Donald. "The Gertrude Stein Collection." *Yale University Library Gazette* 22, no. 2 (October 1947): 21–32.
Gammel, Irene. *Baroness Elsa: Gender, Dada, and Everyday Modernity*. Cambridge, MA: MIT Press, 2002.
Garber, Marjorie. *Academic Instincts*. Princeton: Princeton University Press, 2001.
Garvey, Ellen Gruber. *Writing with Scissors: American Scrapbooks from the Civil War to the Harlem Renaissance*. Oxford: Oxford University Press, 2013.
Gish, Nancy. "Modifying Modernism: Hope Mirrlees and 'The Really New Work of Art.'" *Newsletter of the T. S. Eliot Society*, no. 74–75 (2011): 1–2.
Glasgow, Joanne, ed. *Your John: The Love Letters of Radclyffe Hall*. New York: New York University Press, 1997.
Gorham, Deborah. *Vera Brittain: A Feminist Life*. Oxford: Blackwell, 1996.
Halberstam, Judith. *In a Queer Time and Place: Transgender Bodies, Subcultural Lives*. New York: New York University Press, 2005.
———. *The Queer Art of Failure*. Durham: Duke University Press, 2011.
Halperin, David. *How to Do the History of Homosexuality*. Chicago: University of Chicago Press, 2002.
Hanscombe, Gillian, and Virginia L. Smyers. *Writing for Their Lives: The Modernist Women 1910–1940*. Boston: Northeastern University Press, 1987.
Harman, Claire. *Sylvia Townsend Warner: A Biography*. London: Chatto & Windus, 1989.
Harrison, Jane Ellen. *Reminiscences of a Student's Life*. London: Hogarth Press, 1925.
Hawkes, Ellen. "Woolf's Magical Garden of Women." In *New Feminist Essays on Virginia Woolf*, edited by Jane Marcus, 31–60. Lincoln: University of Nebraska Press, 1981.
Heap, Jane. "Dada." *Little Review* 8, no. 2 (Spring 1922): 46.
Heilbrun, Carolyn G. Introduction to *Testament of Friendship: The Story of Winifred Holtby*, by Vera Brittain, xv–xxxii. New York: Wideview Books, 1981.
———. "Virginia Woolf in Her Fifties." *Twentieth Century Literature* 27, no. 1 (1981): 16–33.

———. *Writing a Woman's Life*. New York: W. W. Norton, 1988.
Herring, Phillip. *Djuna: The Life and Work of Djuna Barnes*. New York: Viking, 1995.
Herring, Scott. "Djuna Barnes and the Geriatric Avant-Garde." *PMLA* 130, no. 1 (2015): 69–91.
———. *The Hoarders: Material Deviance in Modern American Culture*. Chicago: University of Chicago Press, 2014.
———. "Tillie Olsen, Unfinished (Slow Writing from the Seventies)." *Studies in American Fiction* 37, no. 1 (2010): 81–99.
Hjartarson, Paul I., and Douglas O. Spettigue. Introduction to *Baroness Elsa*, by Elsa von Freytag-Loringhoven, 9–40. Edited by Paul I. Hjartarson and Douglas O. Spettigue. Ontario: Oberon Press, 1992.
Hoberman, Ruth. *Modernizing Lives: Experiments in English Biography, 1918–1939*. Carbondale: Southern Illinois University Press, 1987.
Holden, Katherine. *The Shadow of Marriage: Singleness in England, 1914–1960*. Manchester: Manchester University Press, 2007.
Hovey, Jaime. *A Thousand Words: Portraiture, Style, and Queer Modernism*. Columbus: Ohio State University Press, 2006.
Huffer, Lynne. *Are the Lips a Grave?: A Queer Feminist on the Ethics of Sex*. New York: Columbia University Press, 2013.
Hughes, Robert. "Days of Antic Weirdness: A Look Back at Dadaism's Brief, Outrageous Assault on the New York Scene." *Time* 149, no. 4 (January 27, 1997): 70–71.
Jackson, Kevin. *Constellation of Genius: 1922: Modernism Year One*. New York: Farrar, Straus and Giroux, 2012.
Jagose, Annamarie. "Feminism's Queer Theory." *Feminism & Psychology* 19, no. 2 (2009): 157–74.
———. *Queer Theory: An Introduction*. New York: New York University Press, 1997.
Jameson, Fredric. *The Political Unconscious: Narrative as a Socially Symbolic Act*. Ithaca: Cornell University Press, 1982.
Jeffreys, Sheila. *The Spinster and Her Enemies: Feminism and Sexuality, 1880–1930*. London: Pandora, 1985.
Johnson, Pam. "'The Best Friend Whom Life Has Given Me': Does Winifred Holtby Have a Place in Lesbian History?" In *Not a Passing Phase: Reclaiming Lesbians in History, 1840–1985*. London: The Woman's Press, 1989.
Johnston, Georgia. *The Formation of 20th-Century Lesbian Autobiography*. New York: Palgrave Macmillan, 2007.
Josephson, Matthew. *Life among the Surrealists: A Memoir*. New York: Holt, Rinehart and Winston, 1962.
Kahan, Benjamin. *Celibacies: American Modernism and Sexual Life*. Durham: Duke University Press, 2013.
———. "Queer Modernism." In *A Handbook of Modernism Studies*, edited by Jean-Michel Rabaté, 347–61. Oxford: Wiley-Blackwell, 2013.
———. "'The Viper's Traffic-Knot': Celibacy and Queerness in the 'Late' Marianne Moore." *GLQ: A Journal of Lesbian and Gay Studies* 14, no. 4 (2008): 509–35.
Kazanjian, David. "Scenes of Speculation." *Social Text* 33, no. 4 (125) (2015): 77–84.
Kazin, Alfred. "A Life Led as a Work of Art." *New York Times*. August 16, 1970. http://www.nytimes.com/1970/08/16/archives/a-life-led-as-a-work-of-art-anderson.html.

Kelleher, Paul. "If Love Were All: Reading Sedgwick Sentimentally." In *Regarding Sedgwick: Essays on Queer Culture and Critical Theory*, edited by Stephen M. Barber and David L. Clark, 143–64. New York: Routledge, 2002.

Kennard, Jean E. *Vera Brittain and Winifred Holtby: A Working Partnership*. Hanover, NH: University Press of New England, 1989.

Kern, Stephen. *The Culture of Time and Space, 1880–1918*. Cambridge, MA: Harvard University Press, 1983. Paperback reissue 2003.

Kraus, Chris. *After Kathy Acker: A Literary Biography*. Cambridge, MA: Semiotext(e), 2017.

Kumin, Maxine. "A Friendship Remembered." In *To Make a Prairie: Essays on Poets, Poetry, and Country Living*, 83–93. Ann Arbor: University of Michigan Press, 1979.

Laing, Olivia. *Crudo*. New York: W. W. Norton, 2018.

Lanser, Susan S. "Mapping Sapphic Modernity." In *Comparatively Queer: Crossing Time, Crossing Cultures*, edited by Jarrod Hayes, Margaret Higonnet, and William Spurlin, 69–89. London: Palgrave Macmillan, 2010.

———. "1928: Sapphic Modernity and the Sexuality of History." *Modernism/modernity Print Plus*. October 25, 2016. https://modernismmodernity.org/forums/posts/1928-sapphic-modernity-and-sexuality-history.

———. "Novel (Lesbian) Subjects: The Sexual History of Form." *Novel: A Forum on Fiction* 42, no. 3 (2009): 497–503.

Latham, Sean. *The Art of Scandal: Modernism, Libel Law, and the Roman à Clef*. Oxford: Oxford University Press, 2009.

Latham, Sean, and Gayle Rogers. *Modernism: Evolution of an Idea*. London: Bloomsbury, 2015.

Latour, Bruno. "Why Has Critique Run Out of Steam? From Matters of Fact to Matters of Concern." *Critical Inquiry* 30, no. 2 (2004): 227–50.

Laughlin, James. "Introduction to the New Edition." In *Shakespeare and Company*, by Sylvia Beach, xv–xxii. Lincoln: University of Nebraska Press, 1991.

Lee, Hermione. *Virginia Woolf*. New York: Vintage, 1999. First published 1996 by Chatto & Windus (London).

Lee, Sidney. *Principles of Biography*. Cambridge: Cambridge University Press, 1911.

Leger, Nathalie. *Suite for Barbara Loden*. Translated by Natasha Lehrer and Cécile Menon. St. Louis: Dorothy, a publishing project, 2016.

Levine, Caroline. *Forms: Whole, Rhythm, Hierarchy, Network*. Princeton: Princeton University Press, 2015.

Levinson, Marjorie. "What Is New Formalism?" *PMLA* 122, no. 2 (2007): 558–69.

Linzie, Anna. *The True Story of Alice B. Toklas: A Study of Three Autobiographies*. Iowa City: University of Iowa Press, 2006.

Litz, A. Walton, Louis Menand, and Lawrence Rainey, eds. *Modernism and the New Criticism*. Vol. 7 of *Cambridge History of Literary Criticism*, edited by H. B. Nisbet and Claude Rawson. Cambridge: Cambridge University Press, 2000.

Lockwood, J. Samaine. *Archives of Desire: The Queer Historical Work of New England Regionalism*. Chapel Hill: University of North Carolina Press, 2015.

Love, Heather. *Feeling Backward: Loss and the Politics of Queer History*. Cambridge, MA: Harvard University Press, 2007.

———. "Gyn/Apology: Sarah Orne Jewett's Spinster Aesthetics." *ESQ: A Journal of the American Renaissance* 55, no. 3 (2009): 305–34.

Malcolm, Janet. *Two Lives: Gertrude and Alice*. New Haven: Yale University Press, 2007.

Marcus, Laura. *Auto/Biographical Discourses: Theory, Criticism, Practice*. Manchester: Manchester University Press, 1994.

Marcus, Sharon. *Between Women: Friendship, Desire, and Marriage in Victorian England*. Princeton: Princeton University Press, 2007.

Marek, Jayne E. *Women Editing Modernism: "Little" Magazines & Literary History*. Lexington: University Press of Kentucky, 1995.

Marshall, Daniel, Kevin P. Murphy, and Zeb Tortorici, eds. "Queering Archives: Historical Unravelings." *Radical History Review* 120 (Fall 2014): 1–11.

Matthew, H. C. G. *Leslie Stephen and the New Dictionary of National Biography*. Cambridge: Cambridge University Press, 1995.

McFeely, William S. "Preface: Why Biography?" In *The Seductions of Biography*, edited by Mary Rhiel and David Suchoff, ix–xiii. New York: Routledge, 1996.

McIntire, Gabrielle. *Modernism, Memory, and Desire: T. S. Eliot and Virginia Woolf*. Cambridge: Cambridge University Press, 2008.

McMullan, Gordon, and Sam Smiles, eds. *Late Style and Its Discontents: Essays in Art, Literature, and Music*. London: Oxford University Press, 2016.

Medd, Jodie. *Lesbian Scandal and the Culture of Modernism*. Cambridge: Cambridge University Press, 2012.

Micir, Melanie, and Aarthi Vadde. "Obliterature: Toward an Amateur Criticism." *Modernism/modernity* 25, no. 3 (2018): 517–49.

Miller, D. A. *The Novel and the Police*. Berkeley: University of California Press, 1988.

Miller, Nancy K. "A Feminist Friendship Archive." *Profession* (2011): 198–224.

———. "Getting Transpersonal: The Cost of an Academic Life." *Prose Studies* 31, no. 3 (2009): 166–80.

Mills, Jean. *Virginia Woolf, Jane Ellen Harrison, and the Spirit of Modernist Classicism*. Columbus: Ohio State University Press, 2014.

Milne, James. "A Literary Log." *The Scotsman*. December 14, 1939.

Mirrlees, Hope. *Collected Poems*. Edited by Sandeep Parmar. Manchester: Carcanet, 2011.

———. *A Fly in Amber: Being an Extravagant Biography of the Romantic Antiquary, Sir Robert Bruce Cotton*. London: Faber and Faber, 1962.

———. "The Religion of Women." *The Nation & Athenaeum* 41, no. 8 (May 28, 1927): 259–60.

Moffat, Wendy. *A Great Unrecorded History: A New Life of E. M. Forster*. New York: Farrar, Straus and Giroux, 2010.

Montefiore, Janet. "Sylvia Townsend Warner and the Biographer's 'Moral Sense.'" *Journal of the Sylvia Townsend Warner Society* (2003): 15–30.

———. "Sylvia Townsend Warner Scholarship, 1978–2013: An Annotated Bibliography with Introduction." *Literature Compass* 11, no. 12 (2014): 786–811.

Moretti, Franco. *The Way of the World: The Bildungsroman in European Culture*. New York: Verso, 2000.

Morra, Linda. *Unarrested Archives: Case Studies in Twentieth-Century Canadian Women's Authorship*. Toronto: University of Toronto Press, 2014.

Mulford, Wendy. *This Narrow Place: Sylvia Townsend Warner and Valentine Ackland: Life, Letters and Politics, 1930–1951*. London: Pandora Press, 1988.

Muñoz, José Esteban. *Cruising Utopia: The Then and There of Queer Futurity*. New York: New York University Press, 2009.

——. "Ephemera as Evidence: Introductory Notes to Queer Acts." *Women & Performance: A Journal of Feminist Theory* 8, no. 2 (1996): 5–16.

Nadel, Ira Bruce. *Biography: Fiction, Fact and Form*. New York: St. Martin's Press, 1984.

Naumann, Francis M. *New York Dada, 1915–23*. New York: Abrams, 1994.

Newton, Esther. "The Mythic Mannish Lesbian: Radclyffe Hall and the New Woman." *Signs* 9, no. 4 (1984): 557–75.

Nicolson, Harold. *The Development of English Biography*. 1927. Reprint, London: Hogarth Press, 1968.

Nicolson, Nigel. *Portrait of a Marriage*. New York: Atheneum, 1973.

North, Michael. *Reading 1922: A Return to the Scene of the Modern*. Oxford: Oxford University Press, 1999.

Ohi, Kevin. *Dead Letters Sent: Queer Literary Transmission*. Minneapolis: University of Minnesota Press, 2015.

O'Neal, Hank. *"Life Is Painful, Nasty & Short . . . In My Case It Has Only Been Painful & Nasty": Djuna Barnes, 1978–1981*. New York: Paragon House, 1990.

Oram, Alison. "Repressed and Thwarted, or Bearer of the New World? The Spinster in Inter-War Feminist Discourses." *Women's History Review* 1, no. 3 (1992): 413–34.

Ormrod, Richard. *Una Troubridge: The Friend of Radclyffe Hall*. London: Jonathan Cape, 1984.

O'Rourke, Rebecca. *Reflecting on* The Well of Loneliness. London: Routledge, 1989.

Parmar, Sandeep. "Introduction." In Hope Mirrlees, *Collected Poems*, ix–xlvii. Manchester: Carcanet, 2011.

Pinney, Susanna. "Editor's Note." In *I'll Stand by You: The Letters of Sylvia Townsend Warner and Valentine Ackland: With Narrative by Sylvia Townsend Warner*, edited by Susanna Pinney. London: Pimlico, 1998.

Powell, Anthony. *To Keep the Ball Rolling: The Memoirs of Anthony Powell*. Chicago: University of Chicago Press, 1983.

Pratt, Geraldine, and Victoria Rosner. "Introduction: The Global and the Intimate." In *The Global and the Intimate: Feminism in Our Time*, edited by Geraldine Pratt and Victoria Rosner, 1–27. New York: Columbia University Press, 2012.

Prosser, Jay. *Second Skins: The Body Narratives of Transsexuality*. New York: Columbia University Press, 1998.

Rainey, Lawrence. *Institutions of Modernism: Literary Elites and Public Culture*. New Haven: Yale University Press, 1998.

Raitt, Suzanne. *Vita and Virginia: The Work and Friendship of V. Sackville-West and Virginia Woolf*. Oxford: Clarendon Press, 1993.

Rampersad, Arnold. *The Life of Langston Hughes*. Vol. 1. Oxford: Oxford University Press, 1986. Vol. 2. Oxford: Oxford University Press, 1988.

"Reappearing Women: A Conversation between Marie Darrieussecq and Kate Zambreno." *Paris Review*. October 23, 2017. https://www.theparisreview.org/blog

/2017/10/23/reappearing-women-a-conversation-between-marie-darrieussecq-and-kate-zambreno/.
Rich, Adrienne. "Compulsory Heterosexuality and Lesbian Existence." *Signs* 5, no. 4 (1980): 631–60.
Robinson, Annabel. *The Life and Work of Jane Ellen Harrison.* Oxford: Oxford University Press, 2002.
Rohy, Valerie: *Impossible Women: Lesbian Figures and American Literature.* Ithaca: Cornell University Press, 2000.
———. "In the Queer Archive." *GLQ* 16, no. 3 (2010): 341–61.
Roiphe, Katie. *Uncommon Arrangements.* New York: Dial Press, 2007.
Rooney, Ellen. "A Semi-Private Room." *differences: A Journal of Feminist Cultural Studies* 13, no. 1 (Spring 2002): 128–56.
Sackville, Robert. *Inheritance: The Story of Knole and the Sackvilles.* London: Walker Books, 2010.
Said, Edward W. *On Late Style: Music and Literature against the Grain.* New York: Vintage, 2006.
Saunders, Max. *Self Impression: Life-Writing, Autobiographiction and the Forms of Modern Literature.* Oxford: Oxford University Press, 2010.
Scott, Bonnie Kime, ed. *Gender in Modernism: New Geographies, Complex Intersections.* Chicago: University of Illinois Press, 2007.
———, ed. *The Gender of Modernism: A Critical Anthology.* Bloomington: Indiana University Press, 1990.
———. *Refiguring Modernism, Volume I: Women of 1928.* Bloomington: Indiana University Press, 1996.
Sedgwick, Eve Kosofsky. "Paranoid Reading and Reparative Reading, or, You're So Paranoid, You Probably Think This Essay Is about You." In *Touching Feeling: Affect, Pedagogy, Performativity,* 123–51. Durham: Duke University Press, 2003.
———. *Tendencies.* Durham: Duke University Press, 1993.
Seshagiri, Urmila. "Mind the Gap! Modernism and Feminist Praxis." *Modernism/modernity Print Plus Forum* 2, no. 2 (2017). https://modernismmodernity.org/forums/modernism-and-feminist-praxis.
Shaw, Marion. *The Clear Stream: A Life of Winifred Holtby.* London: Virago Press, 1999.
Silver, Brenda R. *Virginia Woolf Icon.* Chicago: University of Chicago Press, 1999.
Simon, Linda. *The Biography of Alice B. Toklas.* Lincoln: University of Nebraska Press, 1977.
Simpson, Kathryn. *Gifts, Markets and Economics of Desire in Virginia Woolf.* New York: Palgrave Macmillan, 2008.
Smith, Sidonie. "Narrating Lives." *Profession* (2011): 19–42.
Smith-Rosenberg, Carroll. *Disorderly Conduct: Visions of Gender in Victorian America.* Oxford: Oxford University Press, 1986. First published 1985 by A. A. Knopf (New York).
———. "The Female World of Love and Ritual: Relations between Women in Nineteenth-Century America." *Signs* 1, no. 1 (1975): 1–29.
Snediker, Michael D. *Queer Optimism: Lyric Personhood and Other Felicitous Persuasions.* Minneapolis: University of Minnesota Press, 2009.

Solnit, Rebecca. *Men Explain Things to Me*. Chicago: Haymarket Books, 2014.
Souhami, Diana. *The Trials of Radclyffe Hall*. New York: Doubleday, 1998.
Sproles, Karyn Z. *Desiring Women: The Partnership of Virginia Woolf and Vita Sackville-West*. Toronto: University of Toronto Press, 2006.
Stanley, Liz. "The Epistolarium: On Theorizing Letters and Correspondences." *Auto/Biography* 12, no. 3 (2004): 201–35.
———. "Romantic Friendship? Some Issues in Researching Lesbian History and Biography." *Women's History Review* 1, no. 2 (1992): 193–216.
Stanwick, Michael. *Hope-in-the-Mist: The Extraordinary Career & Mysterious Life of Hope Mirrlees*. Upper Montclair, NJ: Temporary Culture, 2009.
Steedman, Carolyn. *Dust: The Archive and Cultural History*. New Brunswick, NJ: Rutgers University Press, 2002.
Stein, Gertrude. *The Autobiography of Alice B. Toklas*. New York: Vintage, 1990. First published 1933 by Harcourt, Brace (New York).
Steiner, Wendy. *Exact Resemblance to Exact Resemblance: The Literary Portraiture of Gertrude Stein*. New Haven: Yale University Press, 1978.
Stevens, Wallace. *Opus Posthumous*. Edited by Milton J. Bates. New York: Knopf, 1989.
Stewart, Jessie. *Jane Ellen Harrison: A Portrait from Letters*. London: Merlin Press, 1959.
Symons, A. J. A. *Essays and Biographies*. Edited by Julian Symons. London: Cassell, 1969.
Toklas, Alice B. *The Alice B. Toklas Cookbook*. New York: Harper Perennial, 2010. First published 1954 by Michael Joseph (London).
———. *Aromas and Flavors of Past and Present: A Book of Exquisite Cooking*. New York: Lyons, 1996. First published 1958 by Harper & Brothers (New York).
———. *Staying on Alone: The Letters of Alice B. Toklas*. Edited by Edward Burns. New York: Liveright, 1973.
———. *What Is Remembered*. New York: Holt, Rinehart and Winston, 1963.
Tolhurst, Peter. "Sylvia Townsend Warner's Letters: Where Are They Now?" *Journal of the Sylvia Townsend Warner Society* (2017): 65–76.
Traub, Valerie. "The Present Future of Lesbian Historiography." In *A Companion to Lesbian, Gay, Bisexual, Transgender, and Queer Studies*, edited by George Garrity and Molly McGarry, 124–45. Oxford: Blackwell, 2007.
Troubridge, Lady Una Vincenzo. *The Life and Death of Radclyffe Hall*. London: Hammond, Hammond, 1961.
Truong, Monique. *The Book of Salt*. Boston: Mariner, 2003.
Vicinus, Martha. *Independent Women: Work and Community for Single Women, 1850–1920*. Chicago: University of Chicago Press, 1985.
———. *Intimate Friends: Women Who Loved Women, 1778–1928*. Chicago: University of Chicago Press, 2004.
Wallace, Diana. *Sisters and Rivals: The Theme of Female Rivalry in Novels by Women, 1914–1939*. London: Macmillan, 2000.
Wallen, James Ramsey. "What Is an Unfinished Work?" *New Literary History* 46, no. 1 (2015): 125–42.
Walsh, Keri, ed. *The Letters of Sylvia Beach*. New York: Columbia University Press, 2010.

Warner, Michael. *Publics and Counterpublics*. New York: Zone Books, 2002.

———. "Queer and Then?: The End of Queer Theory?" *Chronicle of Higher Education*. January 1, 2012. http://www.chronicle.com/article/QueerThen-/130161.

Warner, Sylvia Townsend. *The Diaries of Sylvia Townsend Warner*. Edited by Claire Harman. London: Chatto & Windus, 1994.

———. *Letters*. Edited by William Maxwell. New York: Viking, 1982.

———. *T. H. White*. New York: Viking, 1967.

Warner, Sylvia Townsend, and Valentine Ackland. *I'll Stand by You: The Letters of Sylvia Townsend Warner and Valentine Ackland: With Narrative by Sylvia Townsend Warner*. Edited by Susanna Pinney. London: Pimlico, 1998.

Warner, Sylvia Townsend, and David Garnett. *Sylvia and David: The Townsend Warner/Garnett Letters*. Edited by Richard Garnett. London: Sinclair-Stevenson, 1994.

Warner, Sylvia Townsend, and William Maxwell. *The Element of Lavishness: Letters of Sylvia Townsend Warner and William Maxwell, 1938–1978*. Edited by Michael Steinman. Washington, DC: Counterpoint, 2001.

Warner, Val, and Michael Schmidt. "Sylvia Townsend Warner in Conversation." *PN Review* 23, 8, no. 3 (1981): 35–37.

Weiss, Andrea. *Paris Was a Woman: Portraits from the Left Bank*. San Francisco: Harper San Francisco, 1995.

Whearty, Bridget. "Invisible in 'The Archive': Librarians, Archivists, and the Caswell Test." *English, General Literature, and Rhetoric Faculty Scholarship* (2018): 4. https://orb.binghamton.edu/english_fac/4.

White, Melissa Autumn. "Archives of Intimacy and Trauma: Queer Migrations Documents as Technologies of Affect." *Radical History Review* 120 (2014): 75–93.

Williams, William Carlos. *The Autobiography of William Carlos Williams*. New York: New Directions, 1967.

Wilson, Edmund. *Axel's Castle: A Study of the Imaginative Literature of 1870–1930*. New York: Farrar, Straus & Giroux, 2004. First published 1931 by C. Scribner's Sons (New York and London).

Woolf, Virginia. "The Art of Biography." In Vol. 4 of *Collected Essays*, 221–28. London: Hogarth, 1967.

———. *Diary*. Edited by Anne Olivier Bell. 5 vols. Vols. 2–5, assisted by Andrew McNeillie. New York: Harcourt Brace Jovanovich, 1977–82. Vol. 5, London: Hogarth, 1984.

———. *Flush: A Biography*. Toronto: Oxford University Press, 1947. First published 1933 by Hogarth (London).

———. *The Letters of Virginia Woolf*. Edited by Nigel Nicolson and Joanne Trautmann. 6 vols. New York: Harcourt Brace Jovanovich, 1975–82.

———. "The Lives of the Obscure." In Vol. 4 of *The Essays of Virginia Woolf*, edited by Andrew McNeillie, 118–45. London: Hogarth, 1994.

———. "Men and Women." In *Books and Portraits*, edited by Mary Lyon, 28–30. New York: Harcourt Brace Jovanovich, 1977.

———. "Mr. Bennett and Mrs. Brown." In Vol. 1 of *Collected Essays*, 319–37. London: Hogarth, 1966.

———. "The New Biography." In Vol. 4 of *Collected Essays*, 229–35. London: Hogarth, 1967.

Woolf, Virginia. *Orlando: A Biography*. London: Harcourt, 1956. First published 1928 by Hogarth (London).

———. *A Room of One's Own*. London: Harcourt, 2005. First published 1929 by Hogarth (London).

———. "A Sketch of the Past." In *Moments of Being: Unpublished Autobiographical Writings*, edited by Jeanne Schulkind, 61–138. New York: Harcourt Brace Jovanovich, 1976.

Young-Bruehl, Elisabeth. *Subject to Biography: Psychoanalysis, Feminism, and Writing Women's Lives*. Cambridge, MA: Harvard University Press, 1998.

Zambreno, Kate. *Heroines*. Cambridge, MA: Semiotext(e), 2012.

INDEX

Page numbers in italics refer to figures.

Abbott, Berenice, 55, 103
absence: death as narrative absence, 84; emotional "archives of feeling" and, 13; and marginalization, 136–37; and neglect of women's biographies, 139; queer archives and, 12–13; silence and absence in history, 51–52; and "unfinishedness," 12–13, 84
Acker, Kathy, 138
Ackland, Valentine, 20; archival collection, 10; autobiographical writing of, 41; as biographer of Warner, 16, 41–42; and cooperative archival project with Warner, 41–42; death of, 20, 32, 34; and future orientation, 42; intimacy with Warner, 45, 81; Mulford biography of, 43; relationship with E. W. White, 45; Warner and epistolary archives of, 32–33; Warner's archival project, 16, 20
activism: biographical acts as, 3–4, 6–7, 17–18, 60, 88, 128, 133–34, 139–40
After Kathy Acker (Kraus), 138
aging: and archival impulse, 36–38; and decline in productivity, 61; "late style" and, 34–35; Mirrlees and "the cult of the past," 61–62; and temporality, 61; Warner and, 24–25, 36–38; Woolf and, 35
Ahmed, Sara, 101
The Alice B. Toklas Cookbook (Toklas), 89
All We Know (Cohen), 134–35
aloneness, 33, 45–46, 138
Altman, Janet, 43–44
amateurism, 9, 12, 14–15, 97, 132, 134
"The American Museum" (Warner), 47–48
Amigoni, David, 115
Anderson, Margaret, 4, 16–17; as central figure in modernism, 79, 106–8, 109; and collection, compilation, and annotation, 98–99; Collection (unpublished project), 98–103, *105*, 106, *107*, 108–9; and "conversation" as value, 97, 99, 100–101; critical reception of *My Thirty Years' War*, 96–97; and curation, 17, 97, 98–99, 106; on dilettantes, 97–98; as doubly-marginalized, 96; as editor, 77–79, 80, 82–84, 95, 96, 97, 109; as experimental writer, 97; and feminist critiques of patriarchy, 106–8; and future orientation, 101, 109; intimacy with Heap, 102, 103; list of men who fail as conversationalists, 100–101, 102; literary reputation of, 80, 81, 96–98, 102; and logic of collection and annotation, 106; obscenity trial of Joyce's *Ulysses*, 79; pictured, *104*, *105*; and resistance to publication of "book," 98; sexual identity of, 96; on Toklas after Stein's death, 94; and *Ulysses* obscenity trial, 79
Anderson, Margaret:: *The Fiery Fountains*, 95; *Forbidden Fires*, 95, 108; *My Thirty Years' War*, 53, 81, 95, 96, 98, 108, 113; *The Strange Necessity*, 95; *The Unknowable Gurdjieff*, 95
Anderson, Sherwood, 77, 95–96, 100
androgyny, 58, 125–26
anecdotal theory of failure, 52
anecdotes, 16–17, 81–82, 85–86, 96, 98, 120, 134; and Beach's compositional process, 85; and curation, 85–86; memoirs and, 81; Zambreno's blog and, 134
anonymity, 42, 153n87
archives: and anachronistic mode of thinking, 45–46; archival desire, 18; archiving as compositional process, 46; and archivists, 147–48n52; as biographical acts, 8–9; and the Caswell Test, 148n52; Cotton and preservation of literary history, 76; destruction of documents, 28–29, 63, 66, 76, 100; epistolary collections, 20 (*see also*

archives (*continued*)
under specific individuals); as existential act, 92; as expression of biographical impulse, 9; as feminist act, 88; and future orientation, 19–21, 32–34, 45–47, 49; institutional collecting and, 81–82; Internet and digital, 138–39; modernism and, 81–82, 88; passion projects as intimate, 15; as sites of queer pedagogy, 13; as "tin box" for posterity, 32–34, 46, 49; as "unfinished work," 9–10, 52, 88, 108–9. *See also* collection; curation

"archives of feeling" (Cvetkovich), 13, 16, 42, 88

Aromas and Flavors of Past and Present (Toklas), 89

A Room of One's Own (Woolf), 1–2, 4–5, 135

"The Art of Biography" (Woolf), 121

Atkinson, Juliette, 114–15

Auden, W. H., 8

audience: contemporary audience as judgmental or hostile, 39–40; future reader as imagined, 17, 30, 37, 42, 45–46, 101; imagined for passion projects, 15, 17; "intimate public" as, 46; letters and the epistolary pact, 43; for passion projects, 15; as public *vs.* private or intimate, 41–42; readers as impossible or unimaginable, 25; as supportive community, 138

autobiography: of Baroness con Freytag-Loringhoven, 16, 57, 59; biography as cover for, 6–7; generational, 95; honesty and, 156n22; in modernist studies, 8; *Testament of Friendship* as "almost an," 22; Toklas and resistance to, 89, 91, 94, 163n42; Warner and resistance to, 42; Zambreno's use of, 133

The Autobiography of Alice B. Toklas (Stein), 63, 88–89, 93–94

Axel's Castle (Wilson), 95

Barnes, Djuna, 3, 78; archival collection of, 10; and archival control, 16; Beach on, 88; and "failed" biographical acts, 50–51, 59–60; and future orientation, 56; and lateness, 58; as literary executor for Freytag-Loringhoven, 52, 57; and unfinishedness, 16; Zambreno's criticism and, 133

@Baroness Elsa project (Clement), 59

Beach, Sylvia, 4, 16–17; and anecdotal mode, 85–86; and archival consciousness, 86–87; as archivist and cataloger, 86; as chronicler of modernism, 85, 88; and collection of women modernists, 88; compositional process, 85–86; intimacy with Monnier, 83–84, 86, 87–88; memoir writing as process of curation, 85–86; and publication of Joyce's *Ulysses*, 80, 82, 86, 87

Beard, Mary, 60–61, 63, 66, 68, 70, 75–76

Bechdel, Alison, 36

Beinecke Library, 10. *See also* Yale Collection of American Literature

Being Here is Everything (Darrieussecq), 132–33

Bell, Vanessa, 110

Berlant, Lauren, 11, 44, 45, 46, 154n108

Berman, Jessica, 19, 132

Bersani, Leo, 9

Between the Acts (Woolf), 110

Biddle, George, 54–55

biographical acts: as activism, 3–4, 6–7, 17–18, 60, 88, 128, 133–34, 139–40; collection and curation as, 65–66; digital communication and, 138; elision or omission, 66; and future orientation, 7, 9–10, 15–16, 40, 115; as intentionally private, 25; intimacy and scholarly reproduction, 47; as literary enactment of inheritance, 128; and narrative control, 4, 16, 28–32, 49, 137, 140; on-line collections of women's, 138–39; as passion projects, 15; as pedagogical, 46, 115; and recovery of history, 3–4; "reproductive time" and the biographical form, 114; and resistance to marginalization, 3–4; and responsibility to the biographical subject, 20, 69, 74–75, 83–84, 133–34; and "schwärmerei," 72; and subjectivity of the biographer, 22, 26, 66, 123; and witness to sexuality, 36–37

biographical consciousness, 73

biographical criticism, 7–8, 134, 138–40, 144n22

biographical fiction, 111–12, 117, 119–23, 134–35
biographical impulses, 4, 6, 9
biography, as genre: and avoidance of sex or sexuality, 118; and biographical criticism, 139–40; as counterhistory or counternarrative, 7; as cover for autobiography, 6; and critical analysis, 5–6; as devalued, 139–40; as experimental, 15, 85, 111, 113, 116–17, 123, 138; fictionalized biographies or biographical fiction, 111–12, 117, 119–22; and focus on events or "exploits," 115–16, 118–19, 120; and future orientation, 7, 9–10, 15–17, 40, 42, 115; and generic confusion, 150n18; as minimized or devalued, 8, 139–40; modernism and, 3–4, 7–8, 120; and modernist studies, 7–8; modernist women and, 3–4; as objective and factual, 22, 26, 66, 123; and objectivity, 22–23, 115, 120–21, 123; passion projects, 3, 15; as pedagogical, 115, 123; and public/private audiences, 126; "reproductive time" and the biographical form, 114–15; and sanitized or "apparitional" subjects, 3; sexuality and sympathy with subject of, 39; as subjective art, 115–16; as subject of research, 5–6; and the unknowable, 122; Victorian, 8, 114–15, 119–20. *See also* biographical acts; memoirs
Blackwood, Sarah, 79
Book of Mutter (Zambreno), 132
The Book of Salt (Truong), 136–37
Bookslut.com, 80
Braddock, Jeremy, 17, 82
Braudy, Leo, 124braudy
Briggs, Julia, 60–61
Brittain, Vera, 21, 67; as biographer of Holtby, 22–23; critical reception of *Testament of Friendship*, 23; and feminism, 149n14; and friendships between women, 5, 23–24; *Radclyffe Hall: A Case of Obscenity*, 21–22; and subjectivity in biographical acts, 22–24; *Testament of Friendship*, 22–24; *Testament of Youth*, 21
Britton, Coburn, 97
Butcher, Henry, 71
Butts, Mary, 88

canonizing of life narratives, 16–17
Caramello, Charles, 6
Carrington, Dora, 63
Caruso, Dorothy, 102–3
Cather, Willa, 4
censorship: and erasure of queer subjects, 3; as protection of the reader, 106; and role of biographer, 38. *See also* obscenity trials
Champcommunal, Elspeth, 103, 104–6
Chartres Biron, Henry, 1
Clark, Elizabeth Jenks, 99, 103
Clement, Tanya E., 59
coding or coded language, 40–41
Cohen, Lisa, 4, 17, 81, 134–35, 137
collage: collection and annotation as, 103
Collecting as Modernist Practice (Braddock), 17, 82
collection: and archives of feeling, 88; as biographical act, 16–17; as feminist act, 88, 101; as modernist act, 82, 88, 113; as prewriting or deferred writing process, 45; as queer practice, 88 (*see also* curation)
Collection (Anderson's unpublished project), 98–103, *105*, 106, *107*, 108–9; manuscript page from, *107*
Collective Biographies of Women (University of Virginia, online resource), 138–39
Connor, John, 60–61, 158n45
control of narrative, 28–32
Cornford, Francis, 71
correspondence: Altman's "epistolary pact," 43–44; archival preservation of, 16, 32–33, 43, 49, 66–67, 89–90; and "competing" archival collections, 20, 30–32; destruction of, 28–30, 99–100; and epistolary form, 43–44; "love letters," 43–44, 67, 113, 123, 126, 128; mourning and continued relationship through, 25, 33; ownership of, 31–32. *See also specific individuals*
Cotton, Robert Bruce, Sir, 60, 65, 73–76
The Counterplot (Mirrlees), 63
Couser, G. Thomas, 34
Cowley, Malcolm, 95–96
Crane, Hart, 100
Crispin, Jessa, 79, 80, 96
Crudo (Laing), 138

curation: amateur, 97; Anderson and, 17, 97–99, 106; and anecdotal narrative, 85–86; and annotation, 66; and archives of feeling, 88; Beach and, 86–87; competing efforts at, 66; contrasted with editing, 79–80; and control, 75–76; as creative composition, 85–86, 106; Darrieussecq and, 132–33, 134; and destruction of documents, 28–29, 63, 66, 76, 100; devalued as "service work," 79–80; of future experience, 48–49; of intimate archives as intentional, 10, 15, 19–20, 39 (*see also* silence); Mirrlees and the Harrison Papers, 10, 65–66, 70, 75; as modernist act, 15; museums and, 47–48; *Shakespeare and Company* and, 85; Warner and, 47–49

Currer-Briggs, Michael, 98

Cvetkovich, Ann, 13, 16, 36–37, 42, 88

Darrieussecq, Marie, 132–33, 134

Darwin, Gwen, 71

de Acosta, Mercedes, 134–35

death: archival impulse and response to, 32–33; and deferred publication, 30, 59 (*see also* posthumous publication of work); suicide and "unfinishedness," 84, 110; in Woolf's *Orlando*, 122–23, 128–29. *See also* aging; grief and mourning

de Bunsen, Victoria, 62–63, 71

Derrida, Jacques, 10

Detloff, Madelyn, 131, 138

The Development of English Biography (Nicolson), 115

Dever, Maryanne, 10

DeVore, Lynn, 58

Dictionary of National Biography (DNB), 119

Dinshaw, Carolyn, 12, 14, 18, 20, 97, 114

disinheritance. *See* inheritance

Diski, Jenny, 4, 17, 137

Doan, Laura, 4

Dorset County Museum, Dorset, England, 10

Dreiser, Theodore, 100

DuPlessis, Rachel Blau, 110–12

Eagleton, Terry, 114–15

Edelman, Lee, 92, 114

editing, as gendered service work, 79–81

Eliot, T. S., 10, 23, 50, 57–58, 61, 73, 139

Ellmann, Richard, 7

Eminent Victorians (Strachey), 8

end of life: and biographical acts, 138. *See also* aging; lateness

Eng, David, 136

Epistolarity: Approaches to a Form (Altman), 43–44

"ethos of incompletion" (Herring), 13–14

Exile's Return (Crowley), 95–96

Faderman, Lillian, 2, 5, 24, 34

failure, failed biographical projects: Barnes and, 16, 52; collaboration and, 138; as intentional subversive choice, 14, 16, 94; intimate archives as failed biographical acts, 16; and melancholia, 51–52; Mirrlees and, 16, 60, 65; narrative of failure as avoided or neglected, 65; queerness and, 12, 14, 16, 51; trauma and, 50, 51; unfinishedness and, 14; value and meaning of, 50–51; Woolf's genre experimentation and, 121

feminism: and end of life "lateness," 35; and image of modern women, 4–5; lesbianism as threat to, 21–22, 149n14; and literary or historical recovery, 88, 113, 116, 131–32, 139–40, 143n9; queer feminism as Sisyphean project, 131, 138

Feminist Modernist Studies (journal), 131, 132

Ferrante, Elena, 139

The Fiery Fountains, 95

The Fiery Fountains (Anderson), 95

Fitzgerald, F. Scott, 101

Flanner, Janet, 93–94, 103

Flush (Woolf), 121

A Fly in Amber (Mirrlees), 65, 73–76

Forbidden Fires, 95, 108

Forbidden Fires (Anderson), 95, 108

Forster, E. M., 115–16, 144n18

For Sylvia: An Honest Account (Ackland), 41–42

Frances Farmer Is My Sister (blog), 134

Francis, Elizabeth, 96

Freeman, Elizabeth, 20, 34, 37, 114, 125

Freud, Sigmund, 51, 71, 118

Freytag-Loringhoven, Elsa, Baroness von: archival collection of, 10;

autobiographical efforts of, 57; Barnes as biographer of, 16, 50, 52; as collector, 54–55; Dadaism and artistic reputation of, 53–55, 156n23; death of, 52; as inspiration for Barnes's *Nightwood*, 58; obituary for, 52–53, 57; as poet, 52, 53, 55, 57

Friedman, Alice T., 92–93

friendship between women, 1–5; Faderman's "romantic friendships," 23; as lateral bond, 143n6; and mentorship or advocacy, 55; Ruth and Naomi as scriptural example, 24; *schwärmerei* and Mirrlees characterization of, 63, 70–72; as sexualized, 5. *See also specific individuals*

Fry, Roger, 74, 121

Fun Home (Bechdel), 26

future orientation: Ackland and, 42; Anderson and, 101, 109; archival failures and, 50; and archive as "tin box" for posterity, 32–34, 46, 49; Barnes and, 56; of biography, 7, 9–10, 15–16, 40, 115; and curation of future experience, 48–49; Freeman's "queer future tense," 37; Hall and, 25–26, 30; and imagined readers, 17, 25, 46; and optimism, 12, 32, 51, 52, 135, 152n58; passion projects and imagined future audience, 15, 17; and preservation of archives, 9–10, 16, 20–21; queer futurity, 37, 46, 50–51; queer optimism and, 52, 155n4; reproductive futurity, 92, 114; and social responsibility, 20; Troubridge and, 20, 25–27, 29–32; Warner and, 33–34, 36–41, 39, 43–45, 48–49

Gallop, Jane, 34
Gallup, Donald, 89–90
Garber, Marjorie, 97
Garland, Madge, 134–35
Garnett, David, 38, 40–41, 43
Garvey, Ellen Gruber, 85
gender identity: "inversion" and lesbianism, 25–27, 30, 125, 150n28
generic experimentation, 111
genre. *See* biography, as genre
Gish, Nancy, 60–61
grief and mourning: "aloneness" and, 45–46; Beach on, 84; *Book of Mutter* by Zambreno, 132; and correspondence as ongoing relationship, 25, 33; melancholia, 51–52, 72–73; Toklas on life after Stein's death, 45

Gurdjieff, George Ivanovich, 95

Halberstam, Jack, 14, 16, 51, 65, 116
Hall, Margaret Radclyffe "John," 1; and affirmation of lesbianism (inversion), 25–26; archival collection, 10; death of, 27–28; obscenity trial of, 4; personal archives of, 3; posthumous destruction of unpublished books, 28–29; Troubridge as creative partner, 29; will and Troubridge as sole beneficiary, 27–28, 30; writing practices of, 29; *Your John: The Love Letters of Radclyffe Hall*, 30–31. See also *The Well of Loneliness* (Hall)

Halperin, David, 12
Harman, Claire, 33, 37, 43
Harrison, Jane Ellen, 68; death of, 62, 64; institutional archives and collections, 10, 16; Mirrlees, intimacy with, 16, 61–64, 70; Mirrlees and unfinished biography of, 50–51, 60–61; Mirrlees as curator of papers, 10, 65–66, 70, 75; Mirrlees on "amber" in life of, 74; Mirrlees on "pattern" in life of, 67, 75; Stewart as biographer of, 66–70; as teacher and mentor, 62–63

Harry Ransom Center, University of Texas at Austin, 10

Hawkes, Ellen, 119

Heap, Jane, 77–79, 99, 102–4; Anderson and literary reputation of, 108; archives at Wisconsin, 99; as editor of *Little Review*, 77–79; on Freytag-Loringhoven, 53; intimacy with Anderson, 102, 103; pictured, *104*, *105*

Heilbrun, Carolyn G., 35, 67
Hemingway, Ernest, 77, 82, 84–85, 87, 101, 156n23
The Heroine Collective (online resource), 138–39
Heroines (Zambreno), 133–34
Herring, Scott, 13–14, 58–59, 147n51
historical opacity, 12, 50, 133
Hoberman, Ruth, 119
Holroyd, Michael, 40
Holtby, Winifred, 5, 22–23, 67
Howard, Michael, 38

I'll Stand By You (Pinney), 44
In Gratitude (Diski), 137
inheritance: biography as literary enactment of, 128; gender and legal disinheritance, 127–28; *Orlando* as demonstration of queer, 128; queer relationships as legally ambiguous, 90–91; Sackville-West's lost, 127–28; Souline as disinherited, 27–28; Stein's provisions for Toklas, 27; Toklas as disinherited, 27, 88–94, 91, 136; in Woolf's *Orlando*, 127–28, 129. *See also* legacy, literary
Internet archives, 138–39
intimacy: public discomfort with intimacy between women, 23–24; use of term, 10–11
intimate archives, 16; as accidental, 50; as biography, 12; emotional labor and creation of, 9–10; and institutional preservation, 12, 13; as "passion projects," 81; preservation as future-oriented act, 9–10, 16; and public as audience, 46; as semiprivate space, 46; as "unfinished," 9–10; use of term, 10–12, 20
"intimate publics" (Berlant), 46
The Invention of Jane Harrison (Beard), 63
"inversion," 21, 26, 29

James, Henry, 6, 70
Jane Ellen Harrison: A Portrait from Letters (Stewart), 68
Jolas, Eugene, 82
Joyce, James, 4, 7, 8, 77, 79

Kahan, Benjamin, 4, 147n45
Kahan, Laura, 4
Kazanjian, David, 70, 108, 160n81
Kazin, Alfred, 96–97
Kenner, Hugh, 7
Knole and the Sackvilles (Sackville-West), 124, 127–28
Kraus, Chris, 138
Krissdottir, Morine, 49

Ladies Almanack (Barnes), 21, 57
Laing, Olivia, 138
lateness: and genre, 35; Mirrlees's "cult of the past" and, 61–62; and queer temporality, 15, 33–34; and style, 34–35
Latham, Sean, 7, 81
Laughlin, James, 85
Leblanc, Georgette, 102, 103
Lee, Hermione, 127
Lee, Sidney, 115
legacy, literary: Barnes and defense of the Baroness', 56–57; and desire for publication, 59; and future orientation, 56; Hall's, 21, 25, 30–31; omission of biographical detail and protection of, 39, 66; posthumous publication of work and, 90–91, 95, 110; Stein's provision for preservation of her, 90; Zambreno and defense of Barnes', 133–34. *See also* posthumous publication of work
Léger, Nathalie, 17, 139, 140, *vii*
Leonardo da Vinci and a Memory of His Childhood (Freud), 118
lesbian, use of term, 11–12
lesbianism: contrasted with feminism as frame for, 4–5; "crystallization" in wake of Hall obscenity trial, 4; cultural visibility of, 4–5, 103; open depictions of lesbian sexuality, 44–45; social acceptability of, 63; as threat to feminism, 21–22, 149n14; Warner's intimate archive as effort to preserve and transmit culture, 46–47
Lessing, Doris, 137
letters. *See* correspondence
Lewis, Wyndham, 4
The Life and Death of Radclyffe Hall (Troubridge): Brittain's critique of, 22–24, 25, 28–31; and erasure of Souline's role, 29–30; and Hall's literary reputation, 28–29; and intimacy as shared creativity, 28–29; publication of, 24–25, 30–31; as unfinished work, 24–25
Life's Adventure (fictional book in Woolf's *A Room*), 1–3
life writing. *See* biographical acts; biography, as genre
Little Review, 53, 54, 77–80, 95, 97–100, 102, 108, 162n1
"Lives of the Obscure" (Woolf), 18–19
Lockwood, J. Samaine, 11
Love, Heather, 12, 19, 65

MacColl, D. S., 69
Madeleine: One of Love's Jansenists (Mirrlees), 63
"mansplaining," 101–2
Marcus, Sharon, 2, 15
Marek, Jayne E., 80
marginalization: archival projects as restoration, 18–19; and biographical acts as resistance, 3–4, 8–9, 82; biographical conventions and, 114; colonialism and, 136–37; and failure as part of queer life, 51; heteronormativity and marginalization of queer lives, 114; and intimate archives as historical record, 12–13; of women as biographical subjects, 118–19; of women in histories of modernism, 3, 82, 95, 129–30, 140
marriage: and conventional biographical narratives, 110–11, 116; Warner and Ackland as committed couple, 44; and women's friendships, 23; in Woolf's *Orlando*, 110–12, 125, 126
Maxwell, William, 32–34, 37–39, 44–46, 49
McFeely, William S., 8
melancholia, 51–52, 72–73. *See also* grief and mourning
memoirs, 85–86; Anderson and, 95–98; biography, 3–4, 16–17, 55, 81–82 (*see also specific writers*); and friendship as lateral bond, 143n6; midcentury modernism and demand for, 16–17, 81–82, 98, 100–101; Toklas and resistance to, 89, 91
Men Explain Things to Me (Solnit), 101–2
Miller, Nancy K., 2, 143n6
Millet, Kate, 81
Mirrlees, Hope, 3–4, 10; and archival control, 16; as Cotton's biographer, 60, 65, 73–76; destruction of documents, 63, 66; and "failed" biographical acts, 16, 50–51; institutional archives and collections, 10; intimacy with Harrison, 16, 61–64, 67, 159n56; literary career and reputation, 60–62, 64; and "normalization," 70–71; and "queer duality" (temporality), 75; religion and, 64–65; on responsibilities of biography, 74–75; and reticence, 51–52, 65, 68–70; and "*schwärmerei*," 63, 70–72; as "subject" of Harrison's biography, 66, 68; and "the cult of the past," 61–62
modernism: 1922 as pivotal year for, 4; 1928 as pivotal year for, 4–5; as masculine movement, 23, 95–96, 106–8, 139, 165n67; and revision as authorship, 58–59; women as marginalized or excluded from, 3, 82, 95, 129–30, 140 (*see also* as masculine movement *under this heading*)
Modernism: Evolution of an Idea (Latham and Rogers), 7
modernist studies, as discipline, 6–8; and biography, 8, 144n42; and feminism, 1, 131–32; and queer theory, 12
Modersohn-Becker, Paula, 132–33
Monnier, Adrienne, 83–84, 86, 87
Moods and Tensions (Mirrlees), 65
Morra, Linda, 13
mourning. *See* grief and mourning
"Mourning and Melancholia" (Freud), 51–52
Mr. Fortune's Maggot (Warner), 35
Mulford, Wendy, 43
Muñoz, José Esteban, 20, 46
Murphy, Esther, 134–35
My Thirty Years' War (Anderson), 53, 81, 95, 96, 98, 108, 113

Nabokov, Vladimir, 8
"Narrative 8" (Warner), 45
"The New Biography" (Woolf), 120
New Criticism, 8, 139
Newman, Sally, 10
Newnham College, Cambridge, 10, 73, 119, 121
Nicolson, Harold, 4–5, 115, 120, 121
Nicolson, Nigel, 113, 128
Nightwood (Barnes), 50, 57–58

objectivity, 22, 23, 115, 123
obscenity trials: Hall's *Well of Loneliness*, 1, 4, 21; Joyce's *Ulysses*, 79; and Woolf's *Orlando* as fiction, 125
obscurity, 18–19, 69
Ohi, Kevin, 13, 92–93
Olsen, Tillie, 13–14
O'Neal, Hank, 59
optimism: and biographical acts, 139; and future orientation, 12, 32, 51, 52, 135,

optimism (*continued*)
 152n58; Snediker's "queer optimism," 52, 155n4
The Orlando Project (Cambridge, online resource), 138
Orlando (Woolf): and archival sensibility, 111–12; as "biography," 117–18, 128–29; death in, 128–29; as encoded love story, 113; as experimental narrative, 110–14, 116–18, 128–29; as feminist critique, 110–11, 126–28; and generic hybridity, 121–22; as gift, 111–12, 121; and identity, 128; imagined audiences for, 111; inheritance law in, 127–28; publication contexts, 21, 117–18; public reception of, 117–18; Sackville-West's reception of, 124; and same-sex desire, 124–26; temporality of, 111–12; and "unfinishedness," 110–12
overreading, 108, 147n45, 160n81

"Paris" (Mirrlees), 50, 60, 63
Paris Review (journal), 132
Parmar, Sandeep, 60–61
passion projects: aging and, 34–35; as biographical genre, 3, 15; and collaboration, 138–39; contemporary forms of, 134–35; defined and described, 14–15; and ethics of recovery, 116, 132–33, 139–40; ethos of, 14–15; and imagined future audience, 15, 17; and paralysis, 59–60; and unfinishedness, 13–15, 59–60
pedagogy: biography and, 20, 115, 129; queer, 7, 13, 46, 92–93
Peers, Roger, 49
pessimism, 52
Phillips, Adam, 9
Pinney, Susanna, 33–34, 43–44
Poe, Edgar Allan, 164n50, 164n53
Poems (Mirrlees), 65
posterity. *See* future orientation; queer posterity
posthumous publication of work: Anderson and, 95; literary legacy and, 25; Stein's provisions for, 91; Warner and, 25–26; Woolf and, 110
Pound, Ezra, 4, 7, 23, 80, 96, 102, 166n95
Powell, Anthony, 61
Pratt, Geraldine, 10–11

Prescott, Joseph, 86
privacy: biographical acts as intended to be private, 24–25; and coded language, 46, 113; intimacy and, 10–11; and omission of personal details from biography, 67–69; sexuality as intimate and private, 36–37
Prosser, Jay, 125
publication: biographical acts as intentionally private, 25; and control of narrative, 28–29; as deferred or delayed, 25, 28–29, 30, 59; and inside jokes, 112; posthumous, 59, 90–91, 110

queer: use of term, 10–12
"Queer and Now" (Sedgwick), 11
queer archives, 12–13
queer feminism: as Sisyphean project, 131, 138
queer futurity, 46, 50–51; Warner's biography of White and, 36–41
"Queering Archives" *Radical History Review* (2014), 12–13
queer pedagogy, 20; and responsibility, 26–27
queer politics: marriage rights, 44
queer posterity, 13; Ackland and, 41–42, 41–44; Anderson and, 37; passion projects and, 15; queer pedagogy and, 7, 13, 46, 92–93; Troubridge and, 30; Warner and, 39–40, 43–44; Warner's "two tenses" and, 37
queer temporality: biography and, 12; and "lateness," 15, 33–35; modernists and, 12; passion projects and, 15; and unfinishedness, 17; and Woolf's *Orlando*, 17, 113–14
queer theory, 11
Quest for Corvo (Symons), 116

Rainey, Lawrence, 5–6
Raitt, Suzanne, 123–24, 126
recovery, literary or historical, 2–4, 17, 139–40; archives and, 116; biographical acts and, 80–81; and curation of future experience, 48–49; and erasure of failure, 65; and fatigue, 131–32; and feminist publishing, 143n9; and future orientation of biographical acts, 17, 42; as impossible, 133, 136; and intimate

archives as biographical acts, 9, 19–20, 48; Kazanjian's "scenes of speculation," 70, 160n81; and marginalized figures, 12; *The Orlando Project* and, 138; of passion projects, 15, 17, 116; and personal creativity, 133; as queer feminist act, 88, 113, 116, 131–32, 139–40; and relationship with the past, 19–20, 42, 61; and repetition, 131; as Sisyphean project, 131–32, 138; and the unrecoverable, 133; Zambreno and "modernist memory project," 80

"The Religion of Women" (Mirrlees), 61–62

Reminiscences of a Student's Life (Harrison), 68

repetition, 131, 139, 171n5

reproductive futurism, 92, 114

reputation: Barnes on Baroness Elsa's, 56–58; of biographers and biography as genre, 8; biographical acts and dilemmas of, 25, 39–40; and public acknowledgment of sexuality, 25–26, 29, 102, 124–25. *See also* legacy, literary; queer posterity

Rich, Adrienne, 12

Richardson, Dorothy, 78

Roger Fry (Woolf), 121

Rogers, Gayle, 7, 8, 81

Rohy, Valerie, 11–12

"romantic friendships" (Faderman), 23

Rosner, Victoria, 10–11

Ryder (Barnes), 57

Sackville-West, Vita, 17, 110–13; as biographer, 124; as biographical subject, 112–13, 122–30; inheritance law and loss of Knole, 127–28; *Orlando* as experimental biography of, 110, 111

Said, Edward, 34–35

Sapphism, 4, 63–64, 71, 72, 169–70n60

schwärmerei, 62–63, 70–72, 71–72, 160n85

scrapbooks, 85, 106–7; Anderson's "Collection" as collage, 103–6

Sedgwick, Eve Kosofsky, 11

The Seductions of Biography (McFeely), 8

sexuality: friendship between women as sexualized, 5; and "honest" biography, 39–40; "inversion," 25–26; open depictions of lesbian, 44–45; and privacy in biographies, 40–41; social justice and, 131–32. *See also* lesbianism

Shakespeare and Company (Beach), 81, 83, 85, 87–88, 113; as curation, 85; as experimental form, 85

Shakespeare and Company bookstore, 82, 87

silence: and absences in history, 51–52; editorial reticence and audience, 39; elision or omission in biographies, 64, 66; failed biographical projects and, 52, 65; gender and, 101–2; and lack of documentation, 60–61; and marginalization, 51–52; Mirrlees and, 51–52, 60–61, 65, 68–70; and unfinishedness, 52, 67

The Sixth Beatitude (Hall), 31

"A Sketch of the Past" (Woolf), 119

Snedicker, Michael, 52, 155n4

Solnit, Rebecca, 101–2

Some People (Nicolson), 120, 121

Souline, Evguenia: and archival collection, 20, 30–32, 138; death of, 28, 30; as Hall's biographer, 16, 20; as Hall's creative partner, 31–32, 151n50; intimacy with Hall, 16, 20, 25–28, 26–27; letters of, 31–32; Troubridge and erasure of, 26, 28–30, 31–32; Troubridge's antipathy toward, 25–28, 138

Spoilamag.com, 80

Stanwick, Michael, 60–61

Stein, Gertrude, 80–81; archives of, 10; and biography as autobiography, 6; on Harrison and Mirrlees, 63; institutional archives and collections, 10; intimacy with Toklas, 80, 92; literary legacy of, 89–90, 110; posthumous publication of works, 90–91, 94; as Toklas's biographer, 88–89; Van Vechten as literary executor of, 90; and will provisions for Toklas, 27, 90–94; and Yale Collection archives, 89–90

Stephen, Leslie, 119

Stevens, Wallace, 102, 106, 166–67n101

Stewart, Jessie, 66–67, 68, 69–70

Strachey, Lytton, 4–5, 8, 40, 63, 159n56

The Strange Necessity, 95

The Strange Necessity (Anderson), 95

Sullivan, Hannah, 57–58

Sylvia Townsend Warner: A Biography (Harman), 43
Symons, A. J. A., 116, 117, 122

T. H. White (Warner), 32, 36, 38, 41, 45, 49, 73
temporality, 15; and aging, 61; archiving and anachronistic mode of thinking, 45–46; chronological organization of biographies, 85, 100, 114–17; Dinshaw's "touching across time," 12, 18, 20, 114, 116; "lateness," 61–62; Mirrlees on women's sensitivity to time, 61–62; Mirrlees' "queer duality," 75; Mirrlees's "cult of the past," 61–62; in *Orlando*, 111–14, 116–17; and "queer duality," 75; "reproductive time" and the biographical form, 114–15. *See also* future orientation; queer temporality
Testament of Friendship: The Story of Winifred Holtby (Brittain), 22–24
Testament of Youth (Brittain), 21
This Narrow Place (Mulford), 43
Three Generations of English Women (Ross), 119
Three Lives (film, 1971), 81
Three Lives (Stein), 81
time. *See* temporality
Toklas, Alice B., 4, 16–17, 80–81; *The Alice B. Toklas Cookbook*, 89; archives of, 10; as archivist for Stein, 89–90; *Aromas and Flavors of Past and Present*, 89; as curator and archivist, 89–90, 89–91; institutional archives and collections, 10; intimacy with Stein, 84, 89–91, 92; and literary recovery projects, 88–89; literary reputation of, 81; queer disinheritance of, 89–94, 136, 138; and resistance to memoir, 89, 91; and Stein's death, 45, 84; and Stein's literary legacy, 89, 109, 110; *What Is Remembered*, 81, 89, 113
To the Lighthouse (Woolf), 112, 117
transition, 52, 57
Troubridge, Una, Lady: and affirmation of lesbianism (inversion), 25–26; and archival control, 28–30, 138; Brittain's critiques of *Testament of Friendship*, 22–23; Day Books of, 26, 30; and epistolary archive, 10, 20, 25, 27–28, 31–32; future orientation of, 20, 25–27, 29–32; as Hall's creative partner, 30; Hall's heir, 27; and Hall's relationship with Souline, 25–28, 138; as literary executor, 25, 31. *See also The Life and Death of Radclyffe Hall* (Troubridge)
The True Heart (Warner), 35
Truong, Monique, 4, 17, 136–37
"The Twenties: American Writers and Their Friends in Paris" (museum exhibit), 86
"Two Letters" (Williams), 106

Ulysses in Paris (Beach), 86
Ulysses (Joyce), 4; Beach and publication of, 80, 82–84, 82–85; Margaret Anderson as editor of, 79, 82–84; obscenity trial for, 79
unfinishedness: archival projects and, 9–10, 52, 88, 108–9; and avoidance of conventional narrative conclusions, 17; Beach and, 83; and biographical acts, 13; and creative paralysis, 59–60; death and, 84, 89, 110; and defiance of generic conventions, 111; delay as legal tactic, 89; and feminist narratives, 110–11; Herring on incompletion and creativity, 13–14; Herring's "ethos of incompletion," 13–14; and historical archives as incomplete, 135–36; and Internet archives, 139; and lack of conventional conclusion, 113; melancholia and, 51–52, 72–73; Mirrlees and biographical failure, 16; modernism and, 88, 135; motherhood and, 132–33; and *Orlando* as ongoing narrative, 111–12; and passion projects, 13–15, 59–60; posthumous destruction of unpublished work, 28–29, 66, 76; and queerness, 13; and queer temporality, 17; and reticence about personal relationships, 67; *Shakespeare and Company* as "incomplete," 84; as subversive feminist act, 11–111, 110–11; suicide and impression of, 110; as symptom of absence, 12–13, 84; and trauma, 51; Woolf's ongoing evolution and, 130; of Woolf's

Orlando, 13, 17, 110–13. *See also* failure, failed biographical projects
The Unknowable Gurdjieff (Anderson), 95

Van Vechtan, Carl, 90
Vaux, Marc, 52
Vicinus, Martha, 20
Vickery, Ann, 10
Virago Press, 35, 143n9
"Virginia Woolf in Her Fifties" (Heilbrun), 35

Wallen, James Ramsey, 14
Warner, Michael, 11
Warner, Sylvia Townsend, 33; aging as influence on, 34–36; "The American Museum," 47–48; and archival collection, 3, 10, 20, 32–33, 36, 45–46; and archives as "tin box" for posterity, 32–34, 46, 49; and archiving as compositional process, 46; as biographer of T. H. White, 32, 36, 38, 41, 45, 49, 73; biographical consciousness of, 73; and control of narrative, 49; and cooperative archival project with Ackland, 42; and curation of future experience, 48–49; and future orientation, 32–34, 36–41, 43–45, 48–49; and imagined audience, 41–42; intimacy with Ackland, 32–33, 36, 44–45, 81; and "lateness," 34–35; and "life in two tenses," 32–33, 37, 40–41, 46, 49; literary legacy of, 35–36; Maxwell and, 32–34, 37–39, 44–46, 49; *Mr. Fortune's Maggot*, 35; on museums and curation, 47–48; "Narrative 8," 45; and protection of biographical subjects, 16, 39; publishing history of, 35–36; and queer temporality, 33–35; *T. H. White*, 32, 36, 38, 41, 45, 49, 73; *The True Heart*, 35
Weaver, Harriet Shaw, 85, 86, 88
The Well of Loneliness (Hall), 1, 24–26; as "antifeminist," 149n14; critical and popular reception of, 21; and crystallization of lesbian identity and culture, 4; and future orientation, 25–26, 30; and "inversion," 21–22, 25–27, 30; obscenity trial of, 4; publication of, 28–29; as testament of lesbian life, 25–26
Westhoff, Clara, 133
What Is Remembered (Toklas), 81, 89, 113
White, Elizabeth Wade, 42, 44–45
White, T. H.: Warner as biographer of, 32, 36, 38, 41, 45, 49, 73
Wilde, Oscar, 4
Williams, William Carlos, 9, 54, 77, 101, 106
wills. *See* inheritance
Wilson, Edmund, 95
"witnessing" as archival mode, 36–37
Women Editing Modernism: "Little" Magazines & Literary History (Marek), 80
Woolf, Leonard, 63, 69, 110
Woolf, Virginia, 61; and archival recovery, 18–19; "The Art of Biography," 121; *Between the Acts*, 110; and biography as experimental genre, 3, 111, 113, 117–19, 128–29; and biography as genre of choice, 121; as central figure in modernist canon, 129–30; on creativity and subjectivity of biographers, 120–21; and depiction of female friendships, 1–2; on fact and biography, 120–21; fears regarding critical reception of works, 4–5; and intimacy with Vita Sackville-West, 111–13, 124–26; *To the Lighthouse*, 112; "Lives of the Obscure," 18–19; on Mirrlees and Harrison, 63–64, 159n56; on modernism as pivotal point in history, 4; "The New Biography," 120; *Orlando* (see *Orlando* [Woolf]); and posthumous publication, 110; publication-day pranks, 112; *Roger Fry*, 121; *A Room of One's Own*, 1–2, 4–5, 135; "A Sketch of the Past," 119; and unfinishedness, 13, 17, 110–12; on women as subjects of biography, 118–20

Yale Collection of American Literature, 81, 89–90, 91
Yonnondio: From the Thirties (Olsen), 13–14
Your John: The Love Letters of Radclyffe Hall (Hall), 30–31

Zambreno, Kate, 4, 17, 80–81, 132–34, 138

A NOTE ON THE TYPE

THIS BOOK has been composed in Miller, a Scotch Roman typeface designed by Matthew Carter and first released by Font Bureau in 1997. It resembles Monticello, the typeface developed for The Papers of Thomas Jefferson in the 1940s by C. H. Griffith and P. J. Conkwright and reinterpreted in digital form by Carter in 2003.

Pleasant Jefferson ("P. J.") Conkwright (1905–1986) was Typographer at Princeton University Press from 1939 to 1970. He was an acclaimed book designer and AIGA Medalist.

The ornament used throughout this book was designed by Pierre Simon Fournier (1712–1768) and was a favorite of Conkwright's, used in his design of the *Princeton University Library Chronicle*.

GPSR Authorized Representative: Easy Access System Europe - Mustamäe tee 50, 10621 Tallinn, Estonia, gpsr.requests@easproject.com